010 - 50

NLL

A Study of Ten Poets

Understanding African Poetry

K. L. GOODWIN
Professor, Department of English
University of Queensland

LONDON
HEINEMANN
IBADAN   NAIROBI

Heinemann Educational Books Ltd
22 Bedford Square, London WC1B 3HH
PMB 5205, Ibadan · PO Box 45314, Nairobi

EDINBURGH   MELBOURNE   AUCKLAND
HONG KONG   SINGAPORE   KUALA LUMPUR
NEW DELHI   KINGSTON   PORT OF SPAIN

Heinemann Educational Books Inc.
4 Front Street, Exeter, New Hampshire 03833, USA

ISBN 0 435 91325 5 (cased)
0 435 91326 3 (paper)

Set in 10 pt Plantin
Printed in Great Britain by
Butler & Tanner Ltd, Frome and London

Contents

Acknowledgements

My thanks are due to the University of Queensland, which provided the opportunity for me to undertake the research and writing of this book, and to a number of London libraries, chiefly the British Library and those at the School of Oriental and African Studies, the Institute of Commonwealth Studies, Senate House of the University of London, the Commonwealth Institute, the Arts Council, and London House.

Introduction

▼▼▼▼▼▼▼▼▼▼▼▼▼▼▼▼▼▼▼▼▼▼▼▼▼▼▼▼▼▼▼▼▼▼

So thoroughly have revolutionary changes established themselves in recent African literature that is is now difficult to recall that twenty-five years ago 'African poetry in English' meant, in the main, poetry by white South Africans. It is true that many black Africans had written poetry in English for publication in newspapers and magazines, both in Africa and, less often, in England or the United States. Over twenty volumes of poetry had, indeed, been published from the time of Phillis Wheatley's *An Elegiac Poem, on the Death of . . . the Reverend and Learned George Whitefield* (Boston, 1770) to Dennis Chukude Osadebay's *Africa Sings* (Ilfracombe: Stockwell, 1952).[1] Their quality is, however, very variable. Several are slight chapbooks or market pamphlets of only a few pages, others were published at the author's or a friend's expense. For the most part they are derived from English models and are naïve, sometimes even pathetic, in their acceptance, or partial acceptance, of the white man's values. Even when they look forward to national independence, as they often do, it is independence seen largely in terms to be set by the colonial powers. Much of this poetry is based on such models as eighteenth- or nineteenth-century English hymns, the stanzaic poems of the English and American Romantics and their successors, or early twentieth-century English and American free verse. African names provide little more than exotic colour in a way hardly more authentic than their use in the white American poet Vachel Lindsay's factitious mélange, *The Congo* (1914).

The last twenty-five years have, however, seen 'African poetry in English' come to mean poetry by black writers, whether in countries that have gained independence from their colonial rulers or in unliberated South Africa. The literary change has been as revolutionary as the political events. An astonishing amount of good poetry has been published in this period, though it is of a kind that may not be repeated in the future. These twenty-five years have seen African poetry undergo the processes first of modernization and then of radicalization and indigenization. It has been a transitional period in which the emphasis has shifted from the English nature of the medium to the African nature of the content.

Dennis Chukude Osadebay's *Africa Sings* (1952) was published shortly before the modern revolution in African poetry. It represented poetry written over a period of some twenty years, much of it having appeared in Nigerian papers and magazines. It is a useful bench-mark against which later developments may be measured. Osadebay's 'Ode to the Palm Tree' (p. 30) begins:

O stately palm,
Thou symbol of a bounteous land,
  A land that flows with milk and honey
  Whose bosom is filled with hidden money,
To thee I raise a greeting hand
And sing a psalm.

This stanzaic ode, its form based on Tennyson's *In Memoriam* stanza
with short prelude and postlude lines, is in language that any hymn-
writing contemporary of Tennyson's might have used: 'stately', 'bounteous', 'bosom', and 'psalm', together with the 'thou' and 'thee' of the
second-person singular and the biblical phrase about a land flowing
'with milk and honey', abundantly create the period flavour. Missionary
hymns and even perhaps Kipling's 'Recessional' (with its line about
'dominion over palm and pine') seem to have provided both language
and, to some extent, sentiment. 'Hidden money' filling the bosom and
'a greeting hand' raised while engaged in singing a psalm may seem a
little untoward, but they are obviously dictated by the necessities of
rhyme rather than consistent thought.

By contrast, the opening poem of Wole Soyinka's *Idanre and Other
Poems* (London: Methuen, 1967), though also describing a palm, seems
more than a century away:

Breaking earth upon
A spring-haired elbow, lone
A palm beyond head-grains, spikes
A guard of prim fronds, piercing
High hairs of the wind   ('Dawn', p. 9)

Nothing in the tradition of English literature can provide an appropriate
background for this poem. Soyinka's diction is original, the result of
close observation and wide-ranging command of the resources of language. In place of the stately formality of Osadebay, he introduces a
vulgar hint of 'breaking . . . wind' (the first and last words of the stanza)
and a pulsating hint of barely repressed sexuality in the 'spikes' that
provide 'a guard of prim fronds'. Yet the poem is a 'celebration of the
rites of dawn', a more ritualistic or religious poem than Osadebay's
solemn ode. It manages, however, to make ritual tense and exciting
rather than pompous and solemn. Its versification, in three- and four-
beat lines, is dictated by dramatic and visual demands. It is an original
kind of free verse, prepared to end lines on such unlikely words as the
preposition 'upon' or the adjective 'lone'.

Osadebay sees his country through the filter of the English poetry
encountered during his formative years. The most descriptive stanzas
of his poem 'Lagos' (p. 54) are a mélange of travel-guide language,
literary clichés, and colonial subservience:

O Lagos, capital of Nigeria,
Protégé of sons of Britain
O Port of Buildings tall and fair
O Place of Beauties rich and rare.

O Lagos, land that calls with luring voice,
O town of slums and seat of deafening noise;
A Pot of boiling Politics,
O Circe full of smiles and tricks.

By contrast, John Pepper Clark's well-known 'Ibadan Dawn'[2] is
a more carefully observed description of a city, though it is self-
consciously expressed in the diction of another English poet, Gerard
Manley Hopkins. To that extent it can be seen as belonging to an early
stage in the modernization of African poetry in English, before the move
to indigenize had become a strong force. It is modernistic because its
British model has shifted from the general tradition of nineteenth-
century poetry to an innovative poet whose work, though written in the
nineteenth century, did not become well known until the 1930s and
whose major influence was not exerted on British poetry until the 1940s
and 1950s. In British and American poetry, the movement away from
the drowsy melodiousness of nineteenth-century models such as
Tennyson and Swinburne began at the end of the nineteenth century.
The most vociferous of the modernizers was the American poet, Ezra
Pound, who persuaded W. B. Yeats to 'modernize himself' and who
was respected as an innovator by such poets as T. S. Eliot, William
Carlos Williams, and, later, Charles Olson. In general, modernization
was a movement towards 'verse as speech', dynamic rhythms growing
organically from the material, the primacy of the line rather than the
stanza, absolute precision of description, the use of hard, clear images
either by themselves or in associated clusters to give the exact nuance
intended, concentration rather than discursiveness, the avoidance of
direct avowals of emotion or thought in favour of their representation
through what Eliot called an 'objective correlative' (that is, a cognate
scene or image), and a belief that poetry was not confined to beautiful
materials but could equally well deal with anything, even the sordid.
That at any rate was the gist of many manifestos issued by Pound,
Williams, Olson, and others, and the programme had a profound effect
on British poetry in the first four decades of the century and on
American poetry up to the 1960s.

Soyinka's 'Dawn' is in these terms a 'modern' poem—or perhaps a
post-mortem one, for its ritualistic identification with its thoroughly
African subject could never be mistaken for the work of a British or
American poet. John Pepper Clark's 'Ibadan Dawn' is by the same
standards an imitative modern poem, closely based on Hopkins's
'Pied Beauty'. His more unassuming poem, 'Ibadan',[3] without being

derivative in diction, also follows modernistic principles: it is spare and concentrated, and relies on images to carry its significance:

> Ibadan,
>   running splash of rust
> and gold—flung and scattered
> among seven hills like broken
> china in the sun.

One image, 'rust and gold', is laid on another, 'broken china' (itself broken from one line to the next), in something like the manner of the Chinese *haiku*—a form that Ezra Pound much admired.

A third instructive example from Osadebay is of philosophical or religious poetry, 'Thoughts at the Victoria Beach, Lagos' (p. 83). The observer's ideas wobble about as he surveys the sky, the sea, and the beach. His conclusion, a belief in an intelligent creator, is clearly suggested in the middle stanza, but the last stanza offers first a profession of nihilism before returning to its conclusion:

> At those wonders I gazed once more,
>   I came to one conclusion as I went;
> All matter comes from glorious Nothing
>   And into glorious Nothing its course is bent.
> All is illusion, naught is real,
>   And life is but a flick'ring light and a dream;
> But there must be some Ruling Cause
>   That plans and guides the Universal Scheme.

The same setting raised thoughts of the meaning of life also in Gabriel Okara, as he watched members of the Aladura sect bathing and praying. His poem, 'One Night at Victoria Beach',[4] is much more specific in the details of the scene, and he is more involved in the scene itself rather than treating it as the text for a sermon or the material for an object-lesson. The movement of his thought seems dictated by the scene, not imposed on it, and his conclusion, a retreat from commitment, is the opposite of Osadebay's. The poem ends with contrasting images of the perseverance of the Aladuras and his own half-hearted, instinctive, but unfulfilled gesture:

> Still, they pray the Aladuras pray
> to what only hearts can see behind
> the curling waves and the sea, the stars
> and the subduing unanimity of the sky
> and their white bones beneath the sand.
> And standing dead on dead sands,
> I felt my knees touch living sands—
> but the rushing wind killed the budding words.

Okara was, with Davidson Nicol of Sierra Leone and Dennis Brutus of South Africa, probably the earliest writer of modernized poetry, and he had to form his style without the mutual advice and criticism that younger poets like Soyinka, Clark, and Okigbo had available during their university careers.

The first significant stage in the formation of contemporary African poetry in English was, then, emancipation from nineteenth-century cultural imperialism and the voluntary adoption of a foreign, but international, twentieth-century style. It was a style comparable in many ways with that of the African francophone poets, for French poetry had 'modernized' itself earlier than English, and both Eliot and Pound worked to some extent from nineteenth-century metropolitan French models. The francophone poets had never faced the problem of choice between older and newer styles or popular and educated ones. The adoption by anglophone African poets of an international style was due in large measure to their tertiary education. Soyinka, Okigbo, and Clark in Nigeria were among the first generation to have the opportunity of attending a national university. The curriculum at University College, Ibadan, like that at other African institutions established by British colonial governments in the 1940s and 1950s, made, at least in the early years, few concessions to indigenous culture, interests, needs or aspirations. The courses and the degrees were those of the University of London, which had a 'special relationship' with the colleges at Ibadan, Accra, Makerere, Khartoum, and Salisbury. A 'liberal education' meant a British education; what passed for universal educational syllabuses were in fact often chauvinistic and even sometimes quite parochial. The narrowly British content of English literature syllabuses was to a large extent offset, however, by young enthusiastic staff-members whose interest in literature extended not only to British writers more contemporary than the curriculum allowed, but also American and European writers. Some encouraged their students to write poetry, making arrangements, for instance, for the duplication of departmental literary magazines. The students themselves, however, took most of the initiative, producing a stream of lively, if short-lived magazines in which verse, serious or light-hearted, could find a place. Yeats, Eliot, Hopkins, and Pound seem to have recommended themselves as appropriate models to aspiring poets; sometimes Dylan Thomas, Robert Graves, or W. H. Auden might be added to the list.

With this background, it is not surprising that Mazisi Kunene (the product of a similarly British-influenced atmosphere at the University of Natal) could say in 1967, 'In fact neo-African literature seems to be rooted more in European literary models than in African ones.'[5] Five years later Kofi Awoonor, a graduate of the University of Ghana, acknowledging his own admiration for Hopkins, Yeats and James Joyce, said, 'The time has come to recognise that we are not outside the mainstream of English writing.'[6]

In a sense this is true. The tradition of world writing in English has been significantly affected by the writing of Africans, and it is not unlikely that Soyinka, at least, has already influenced younger writers outside Africa. But to many African readers it will seem an irrelevance. 'Modernization' in the international sense has been succeeded by strong movements towards political radicalism and indigenization. Writers have urged each other to turn away from international models and materials to local, national, or Pan-African ones and to politicize their writing so that it bears on contemporary social and political problems. While 'art for art's sake' has always been derided in statements made by African writers at conferences, and they have asserted that African poetry has, by the nature of the society from which it springs, an essential communality or functionalism, their own work has not always run parallel to the manifestos they have espoused. The last dozen or so years, however, have seen the detached non-political stance in the early poetry of, say, Clark or Lenrie Peters, replaced by an attitude of political commitment, sometimes negative protest against abuses either in their own country or in South Africa, sometimes more in the nature of a positive political programme. Over the same period, the political poetry of Soyinka, Dennis Brutus and Mazisi Kunene has become less tangential, more direct and bitter in its approach, and even Taban lo Liyong, whose literary, social, and political views tend to be out of step with those of other writers, has adopted a shriller, more assertive tone.

Politicization has raised again in live form some of the questions that were in danger of seeming the soporific space-fillers of writers' conferences: questions about what readership the African writer should seek, how that readership might be effectively reached, what style was appropriate, how publication should be organized, and what language should be used. In the 'sixties, at least in the early 'sixties, most of the writers considered here had their eye fixed mainly on an international market and on securing a place in an international literary tradition. Their focus was wide and long: they could shrug off small, indifferent, or hostile indigenous readerships by contenting themselves with the prospect of being acclaimed by succeeding generations. Since then the focus has narrowed and shortened. The notion of the poet as visionary, diviner, oracle, prophet, and social conscience has come to seem much more immediate. Wole Soyinka's statement at Dar es Salaam in 1971 seems in one sense acceptable today, but in another sense less urgent than either Soyinka or other writers would now think appropriate. He said:

> The writer is the visionary of his people, he recognises past and present not for the purpose of enshrinement but for the logical creative glimpse and statement of the ideal future. He anticipates and he warns.[7]

But his opening statement seemed much less assured about the immediacy of the writer's effect:

> Coming from a people (the Yoruba) whose love of language for its own sake, for its very manoeuvrability is probably unmatched on the continent and maybe even in the world, I testify to this

capacity of the tool to, literally, possess the user. A wise society listens to the seeming incoherence of this medium in possession. Some day perhaps, even a tenth of it will prove visionary. (p. 1)

It is significant, though, that Soyinka uses Yoruba as his example. If the listeners to the message are to be not only the élite who read poetry in English then the form must be made more popular and—the conclusion is inescapable—made available in indigenous African languages. Soyinka himself would go further now and, as a Pan-Africanist, say that it should be available in a Pan-African indigenous language, the obvious one being kiSwahili.

More and more, the place of English as the language of original composition will be questioned. Whether or not kiSwahili becomes a continental *lingua franca* (and the history of attempts to impose second languages suggests that its progress will be slow) it seems likely that, in order to achieve an immediacy of social and political effect, poets and other writers will choose the major language of their initial intended readership or audience. The English version, if it exists at all, may be the work of a professional translator rather than of the author himself.

That is still, however, something in the future. What one can be certain of is that in the last dozen or so years many poets have accompanied the radicalization of their content with a simplification of their English style. Writers sometimes do this anyway as they get older, and if it were a less widespread phenomenon, there might be the temptation to account for it in literary or biographical terms; to say, for instance, that writers were moving on from the early twentieth-century 'modernists' to use as models the freer, more oratorical American styles of the Whitman-E. A. Robinson-Sandburg tradition, or the Black Mountain tradition of Charles Olson and his associates, or the Beat Generation tradition of Allen Ginsberg and others. Though Whitman and Ginsberg are occasionally quoted by African poets, such an explanation would be perverse. The simplest way of accounting for this widespread simplification of style is in terms of the writers' intention in regard to their audience: they want their comments on political and social matters to be influential, so, while continuing to use English as a medium, they eschew the more recondite, identifiably 'poetic' forms of the language.

This move to simplicity as part of a political radicalization has brought poetry in English closer to both indigenous African poetry intended for oral recital and some francophone poetry (itself influenced by indigenous oral traditions). In many African languages the formal distinction between prose and poetry is less marked than between English prose and, say, the poetry of Tennyson or Swinburne. It is, to use a rough analogy, more like the difference between English prose and English blank verse. The move to simplicity, particularly when it is accompanied by a concern for effectiveness in oral declamation, can produce verse in English that is indistinguishable from oratorical prose. It has become poetry so minimal as to lose all indicators of its intended genre: concentration, a recognizable degree of rhythmical repetition, vividness of language or imagery, and shapeliness. Taban lo Liyong and Dennis Brutus can occasionally produce work of this kind. At the other extreme of simplicity is verse that retains a strong rhythm and shape and relies heavily on repetition, but provides minimal content. It is verse written for performance, which, like much traditional poetry, lies flat and cold on the page bereft of its accompaniments of gesture, facial expression, and musical performance. Joe de Graft, Atukwai Okai, Jared Angira, and Oswald Mtshali, for instance, have to be considered as poet-performers rather than merely as literary poets.

Politically radical poems are a form of occasional poem, and like other occasional literature they retain at least some of their interest as litera-ture after the political circumstances that brought them into being have passed. Their value is not just for the occasion, like that of a political speech or pamphlet. To give them this lasting quality, a poet may write simultaneously about a political matter and a personal one. Several African poets, following the lead of some of the francophone Négritude poets, write of Africa as a beloved woman. Their poems are, then, simultaneously Pan-African (or sometimes specifically national) in pol-itics and on the personal level love poems (even erotic ones) addressed to an actual or imaginary mistress. Brutus, Okigbo, Peters, and Awoonor all use this dual significance, Brutus in dozens of poems from quite early in his career, Okigbo towards the end of 'Distances' and in later poems, Peters in Négritude-inspired poems such as 'Your eyes are two faces', and Awoonor in some of his major post-prison poems such as 'The Wayfarer Comes Home'.

In so far as the process of politicization has a common content, it can only be expressed in very general terms. It is vaguely socialist, fairly warmly Pan-African, and vehemently in favour of some kind of revo-lution in South Africa. The range of political doctrine is a broad one, from the Marxism of Atukwai Okai to the sceptical attitude to all European 'isms' of Okot p'Bitek (who once said that 'African socialism may be defined as the government of the people by the educated for the educated'[8]; and was shortly afterwards removed from his post as Direc-tor of Uganda's National Cultural Centre). The range of doctrine about Pan-Africanism is much smaller, the difference being mainly a matter of the vehemence with which it is espoused and the importance placed on it as an immediately practical working concept. Soyinka is the most committed to the concept, Taban lo Liyong the most dubious. In regard to South Africa, the sentiment is almost unanimous, as the many refer-ences to the shootings at Sharpeville and Soweto testify.

The politicizing of content and the radicalizing of the opinions ex-pressed represent a change of belief in the function of poetry by the authors and an increasing personal disillusion about the honesty and effectiveness of African governments and about the lack of progress in South Africa. The heart-swelling paeans to national independence writ-ten by poets like Michael Dei-Anang, though not by any of the poets studied in this volume, seemed hollow from the start. Perceptive writers quickly recognized the continuation of economic and cultural imperialism and the venality of many politicians. The temptation to become the literary equivalent of the traditional praise-singer-at-court (Chinua Achebe's phrase) was resisted for the most part, except perhaps during the time of the Nigerian civil war. Poets, like other writers, have often been in opposition to their own national governments, though there has been some collective pressure at conferences for them to unite in statements of opposition to less immediate objects of political and moral opprobrium such as colonialism or the government in South Africa. This pressure has perhaps played a part in turning some poets to the writing of political poems expressing a radical stance, for there is no more certain way of winning applause at a conference or poetry reading than by reciting a stirring anti-colonialist or anti-apartheid work.

For a poet committed to poetry as a political instrument, literary quality may seem of little importance: an irrelevance or even a subversive hindrance. It is not surprising, then, that the politicization of African poetry in English has been accompanied by a decline in literary quality. I do not mean to suggest that no fine political poems have been written; I do suggest, however, that the need to make a political statement has often directed a poet's attention away from poetic quality.

A second cause for decline is, I think, that many of the poets, in growing older, have become so absorbed in their profession or in administration that they have found less and less time for poetry. As a general rule it is their first or second volume of poetry that contains the best work. After that the quality is more dilute. Poets now in their late forties were among the first university graduates in many countries; they were members of a small educated élite on whom undue burdens were often placed. Many are now university professors: the only major poets who have not been teachers of literature at some time are in fact Lenrie Peters and Gabriel Okara. None have ever had more than a year or two at a time to be full-time writers.

The argument that politicization, radicalization, and increasing professional commitments have reduced the quality of poetry over the period covered in this study might seem like the sounding of a death-knell for African poetry in English. It is true, in any case, that there are indications of a turning away from English towards indigenous African languages. But the impulse behind this movement might also, if paradoxically and even illogically, suggest the future direction for poetry in English. While retaining an originally alien language, poets might thoroughly indigenize or Africanize the materials used in poetry. This is a process that has been proceeding alongside politicization and radicalization. It is not unrelated to the fact that many of the poets have been able to combine the pull of familial or clan affection with the scholarly research interests forming part of their professional academic work. Wole Soyinka has always been a devotee of Ogun and more recently has also used material from the Akan and other traditions; Christopher

Okigbo (an academic librarian rather than a scholar) was drawn back towards the end of his life to the Idoto cult of his family; Okot p'Bitek founded the Gulu Festival in Acholiland in 1965, organized the Kisumu Arts Festival in 1968, and collected and translated Acholi poetry; Taban lo Liyong undertook research in the oral literature of the Masai and Luo; Gabriel Okara has used Ijaw material and John Pepper Clark has collected, translated and edited it in a scholarly fashion; Kofi Awoonor undertook research in the oral literature and history of the Ewe; and Mazisi Kunene is both scholar and poet in Zulu.

The individual motivation in this scholarly commitment varies. It is at one extreme mainly academic, at the other mainly political. The political implication is inescapable at times. One could, for instance, hardly deal with the history of the Ewe, the Acholi, or the Zulu without considering whether the present political boundaries or rights express the interests of the people. Not surprisingly, then, some poet-scholars view their scholarly activity as having major political or social implications. They would agree with Wole Soyinka's definition of the ideal: 'A black scholar is a historicized machine for chewing up the carcass of knowledge to regurgitate mortar for social reconstruction.'[9]

Whatever the motive or the effectiveness, where personal experience or scholarly knowledge of the beliefs, customs and myths of African peoples have found their way into African poetry in English the result has never been less than interesting and has often been expressed in the finest poetry. Although Okara and Kunene were using such material in poetry in the 1950s and Soyinka and Clark by the end of that decade, it took some time to be accepted as a staple for poetry in English. Whereas the African novel in English was an alien form that naturally absorbed African communities as its appropriate material, the first generation of university graduates tended to be a little sceptical of the African material in Négritude francophone poetry, in the 'pioneer' or 'colonial' anglophone poets such as Osadebay or Dei-Anang, and even in the original poetry and translations of the noted Yoruba scholar, Adeboye Babalola. While they were happy to refer to the customs or myths of their people, they did so in the context of a personal voice that remained aware of its international orientation. As Mabel Segun said:

> Here we stand
> infants overblown
> poised between two civilisations,
> finding the balance irksome . . .[10]

Okigbo, Soyinka, and Peters are, at least in the early stages of their work, consciously eclectic, constructing their poems as a vortex of images from all parts of their experience. Peters writes few poems where the setting is clearly Africa, and Soyinka can begin even 'Idanre', his major poem about Ogun, with a personal perception of alien horsemen in the clouds of Ogun's thunder. Even Clark, many of whose earliest poems are set entirely in the villages of the Niger Delta, can intrude his awareness of Gerard Manley Hopkins in 'The Year's First Rain'.

There was, I think, a problem about how far traditional material might affect the content and texture of verse in English. There were perhaps inhibitions derived from familiarity with British and American models. Poetry as a reflection of the individual alert intelligence—the main tradition in English poetry since the late eighteenth century—was at odds with the indigenous African concept of poetry as the distillation and clarification of a community's thought and feeling. Poets trained in the British and American tradition did not want to surrender the individual voice favoured by that tradition, but they wanted to assimilate African material and, in some instances, African rhythms and forms of poetry. With the passing of time, for most poets the pull of African substance and form has increased while the conventions of the British and American tradition have faded. Okot p'Bitek's refusal to concede to the previously accepted norms of poetry in English seemed exotic at first, if thoroughly self-vindicating. *Song of Lawino* never let the reader forget for long that it was the English version of an Acholi poem. But it was so engaging as a poem in English that it substantially affected conventional notions of what was possible in English verse. Soyinka's *Ogun Abibimañ* is, in a sense, the Pan-African extension of a poet's commitment to African materials, though it preserves a good many traces of Soyinka's volatile personality. Its snatches of Akan and Zulu can seem a rather factitious attempt to secure authenticity. The major works in this stream, making fewer concessions than Okot to the existence of an English-speaking reader, and eschewing the superficial credentials of *Ogun Abibimañ*, are the translated modern epics of Mazisi Kunene, *Emperor Shaka the Great* and *Anthem of the Decades*. Kunene uses material from the indigenous oral tradition, and by writing in Zulu avoids almost all influence from the English literary tradition. That is not sufficient, of course, to guarantee that his work will constitute English poetry when translated. In fact, however, Kunene is a highly skilled writer in English. In translating his own work he is prepared to rethink (but not distort) it into English verse. He does not attempt to imitate many of the poetic devices of the Zulu version, but finds other devices to convey the nuances of meaning. The concessions to British or international conventions of English versification are thus minimal, and his success as a poet so great that I have no doubt his method is likely to be at least as much imitated as Okot's was. It will not, of course, exclude other ways of writing poetry—inspiration and genius are too individual for that—but it is likely to provide a major stream in African poetry in English.

Where the African tradition of oral poetry has strongly influenced poetry in English the result can be sharp breaks in tone or sudden switches in material, so that in extreme cases the lines may seem almost atomic, as they flick rapidly from one voice or one symbol to another. This is a notable feature of the work of Kunene, and frequently of

Soyinka, Okigbo, Okot p'Bitek, and Awoonor. As it happens, it is also a feature (though to a less extreme degree) of twentieth-century 'modernism' in the British/American tradition, where it is used for the same purpose: to provide multiple approaches to the theme in order to define it exactly. What is, however, uniquely African is the condensed, oracular, proverbial nature of many successions of lines, especially in Kunene. His 'Triumph of Thought', for instance, is almost entirely made up of such lines:

> So I put thoughts on the palm of your hand
> And let the pleiades race in the sky;
> Winter will try again to overwhelm us
> But we shall be ready with the warmth of blood.
> And you, in the company of twins, will shelter us.
> Then she, the widowed leopard, will retreat into the hill . . .[11]

The palm of a hand gives way to a cosmic image in the second line; then we have an image of seasonal death juxtaposed with an image of human life; the fecundity of this last image is continued in the image of twins, a symbol of cosmic creativity to the Zulus, and the winter image is metamorphosed into a retreating 'widowed leopard'. What may at first seem disjunct is, in fact, a coherent set of images directed by a concept of balance between the human and the cosmic, the bodily and the spiritual, the destructive and the sustaining.

Kunene in his epics has found great subjects. Some of the other poets, however, seem to be groping their way through a succession of trivial subjects, seeking a topic worthy of their talent. Okigbo found his in the journey and return to and union with a multiple goddess who combined qualities of erotic love, poetic inspiration, and, to some extent, communal brotherhood. Soyinka very early found his in the god Ogun, through devotion to whom he explores the philosophical problem of the one and the many. Okot p'Bitek found his, again very early, in dramatic monologues that explore the social problems of newly independent citizens. Gabriel Okara and, at least in his early poems, John Pepper Clark, found theirs in the social life of the Ijaw people. Kofi Awoonor may have found his in the combination of Ewe history and his own imprisonment. Dennis Brutus tried to find his in the romantic self-portrait of the poet as troubadour, lover, and patriot. Taban lo Liyong similarly concentrated on personal individualization, though as a Nietzschean malcontent and prophet without honour. Lenrie Peters, another self-portraitist, presented himself as doctor, liberal, intellectual, and social conscience. Brutus, Taban, Peters, and to some extent Clark and Awoonor have been poets in search of a subject. Brutus's fugitive and persecuted life seemed a ready-made subject, but he was chary of writing naked political poetry and had to struggle hard to give himself the appropriate aesthetic distance from his own experiences. Taban and Peters have both had trouble in finding an appropriate poetic form for their ideas and opinions, which sometimes seem as if they might better be expressed in prose. Clark and Awoonor have never quite laid hold on material great enough to captivate them for more than a few short poems.

My argument has been that such material is likely to be found in indigenous African traditions, deep mines of almost inexhaustible riches. These traditions must be seen, of course, as very different from each other, for it is hardly possible today to subscribe to the superficial cultural Pan-Africanism of Janheinz Jahn's *Muntu*. Perhaps the most ironic result of the dissimilarities of African cultures is that the commonest image in African poetry of the last twenty-five years is not the yam, the palm-tree, the cooking-pot, the sacrifice at dawn, or the Ancestors, but the Christian cross, an alien symbol introduced by the colonial powers. Of the authors considered in this book, only Kunene does not make multiple references to Christianity. Among the other poets, none of the references are entirely favourable, and some are openly hostile, but the prevalence of Christian symbols, particularly of the cross, Easter, and the mass testifies to the efficacy of colonial acculturation if not to the irreversibility of personal Christian faith. There is also a good deal of biblical language in Taban lo Liyong (where one might not expect to find it), Soyinka, Brutus, Peters and Awoonor. The only other subject common to the major poets is Pan-Africanism, the notion of Africa as more than a continent or a European geographer's term, but as a group of countries having, partly through a common colonial experience, the need and potential for social and political solidarity. Pan-Africanism is an important aspiration, though it rarely by itself forms the staple of a successful poem. It tends to be incorporated into a complex of political, cultural, and individual aspirations in the pervasive images of unity and homecoming. In their various ways all the poets considered here express a longing for or an achievement of unity of being as the result of an often long and difficult journey of homecoming. They see themselves as having been subverted by European values, as having drawn away spiritually and often physically from their homeland. They experience the need to return, and they express the culmination of their homeward journey in images of sacrifice, sexual union, feasting, singing, and dancing.

In some respects I have been begging the question by talking about 'major' poets, as if they were co-extensive with the ten poets chosen for this study. The ten were chosen because they seemed to me the best African poets writing in English in the last twenty-five years, and I have drawn the generalizations of this Introduction largely from their work. Those generalizations can, however, be substantiated from the work of other African poets, including several whose work I should like to have considered in detail, such as Joe de Graft, Mbella Sonne Dipoko, Syl Cheney-Coker, Kwesi Brew, Atukwai Okai, Jared Angira, Richard C. Ntiru, and Keorapetse Kgositsile.

It is interesting that there is a marked dearth of good women poets, an imbalance by no means so evident in the short story or the novel. In some countries, it is true, women have been less encouraged than men to seek higher education and proficiency in a foreign language. But one literary difficulty in the way of a woman poet is the prevalence in both anglophone and francophone poetry of a myth that presents the land of Africa as a woman. She was in the past raped and pillaged by foreign invaders. Now, however, she is in the process of returning to natural subjectivity to (rather than partnership with) her indigenous lover. She has become his adornment and joy again. Whether found in Senghor or in Okara, Peters, Brutus or Soyinka, the hints of such a myth are patently unsuitable for use by a woman poet. A woman wanting to write on political subjects might have to establish an entirely new symbolism. In a way it is simply a more extreme instance of the difficulty all African poets face: how to find and express in English a myth that embodies what they believe to be true about matters of the gravest importance. The ensuing chapters direct attention to those who have succeeded, or nearly succeeded.

The ten poets have been grouped in such a way as to show the trend to Africanization in the poetry of the period. All were 'modern' poets from the start, or rapidly became so. Most experienced in their careers a gradual political radicalization. All felt the pressure to 'Africanize' their material and style, to emancipate themselves from European ways of thought and expression. But some, here called the 'Internationalists', remained largely captive to the European, and particularly the British, tradition of poetry. Some, such as Taban, Awoonor and Soyinka, synthesized indigenous African traditions and the European tradition. And three, Okara, Okot p'Bitek and Kunene, were able to write as Africans with only minimal influence from Europe.

Notes to Introduction

1. Apart from Phillis Wheatley's other volumes, notably her *Poems on Various Subjects, Religious and Moral* (London, 1773), they include:

    E. H. Appah, *An Ode to Africa and Other Verse* (London: Stockwell, 1939);

    J. Benibengor Blay, *Immortal Deeds: A Book of Verse* (London: Stockwell, 1940), *Memoirs of the War* (Ilfracombe: Stockwell, 1946), *King of the Human Frame: A Tale in Verse* (Ilfracombe: Stockwell, 1947);

    Herbert I. E. Dhlomo, *Valley of a Thousand Hills: A Poem* (Durban: Knox, 1941);

    Kweku B. Awooner-Renner, *This Africa* (London: Central Books, 1943);

    Michael F. Dei-Anang, *Wayward Lines from Africa* (London: United Society for Christian Literature, 1946);

    R. Tombekai Dempster, Bai Tamia Moore and Harmon Carey Thomas, *Echoes from the Valley* (Cape Mount: Douglas Muir Press, 1947);

    Gladys M. Casely Hayford, *Take um so* (Freetown: New Era Press, 1948);

    R. E. G. Armattoe, *Between the Forest and the Sea: Collected Poems* (Londonderry: Lomeshie Research Centre, 1950);

Godwin Azubuike Ibekwe, *In the Course of Life* (Bukuru: Aut, 1950); Daniel Ekpenyong Ekpiken, *Kano Cinema Tragedy, and The Catechism of Man and Woman* (Kano: Aut, 1951); Crispin George, *Precious Gems Unearthed by an African* (Ilfracombe: Stockwell, 1952); Anthony Kemno Obiyo, *June for All Junes* (Owerri: Aut, 1952).

2. *Poems* (Ibadan: Mbari Publications, 1962), p. 27; *A Reed in the Tide* (London: Longman, 1965), p. 13.

3. *Poems*, p. 31; *A Reed in the Tide*, p. 12.

4. In his *The Fisherman's Invocation* (London: Heinemann Educational Books, 1978), pp. 28-9.

5. 'Portrait of Magolwane—the Great Zulu Poet', *Cultural Events in Africa* (London: The Transcription Centre) No. 32 (July 1967), Supplement I.

6. 'Kofi Awoonor: An Interview with John Goldblatt', *Transition* 41 (1972), 43.

7. 'The Choice and Use of Language', a paper delivered at the Unesco 'Meeting of Experts' on 'The Influence of Colonialism on the Artist, his Milieu and his Public in Developing Countries', Dar es Salaam, 5-10 July 1971, in *Cultural Events in Africa* No. 75 (1971), 2-6 (p. 5).

8. 'Indigenous Ills', *Transition* 32 (August/September 1967), 47.

9. 'The Scholar in African Society', in *Second World Black and African Festival of Arts and Culture: Colloquium on Black Civilization and Education: Colloquium Proceedings*, vol. i (Federal Military Government of Nigeria, 1977), pp. 44-53 (p. 46).

10. 'Conflict', in *Reflections: Nigerian Prose & Verse*, edited by Frances Ademola (Lagos: African Universities Press, 1962), p. 65.

11. *Zulu Poems* (London: André Deutsch, 1970), p. 37.

1 Dennis Brutus

▼▼▼▼▼▼▼▼▼▼▼▼▼▼▼▼▼▼▼▼▼▼▼▼▼▼

Of the major poets writing in English, the one who is least 'Africanized' and most alienated from the indigenous traditions of his homeland is Dennis Brutus. His style and tone, though they have shifted somewhat over his career, always draw on European rather than African models. His subjects, on the other hand, are largely drawn from experiences in South Africa, though they are seen as exemplifications of problems common to all humanity.

The reconciliation of local material with a wider humanitarian intention is something that he struggled with in a revealing interview of 1970.[1] He affirmed his belief that we live in 'one world' and should seek to be citizens of the world rather than conventional, sentimental patriots of a single country; but he also asserted that his own 'greatest commitment—personal as well as poetic—is still to South Africa'. What justified the narrowed, local perspective, he said, should not be emotional attachment to a country or landscape or the desire to create a locally related persona for a poet in exile. It could legitimately, however, be the need to do what one can, to write about what one knows best, to see broader problems in terms of the particular human beings one understands—in terms, that is, of 'the South African predicament' as he calls it earlier in the interview (p. 54).

Brutus's finely-tuned nervous sensitivity to criticism, real or potential, is typical of his whole attitude. He often seems to be a poet on the defensive. The explanation is to be found in his condition of exile. Banned from writing, confined to one district of South Africa, arrested on charges of breaking these restrictions, shot when trying to escape, sentenced to eighteen months' imprisonment, most of it spent on the notorious Robben Island, and living in exile since 1966, Brutus is understandably brooding and self-questioning about his relation to the land where he grew up and worked.

As a South African by upbringing, whether in exile or not, he is something of an anomaly: the inhabitant of a country ruled for hundreds of years by a white minority, where the black majority seemed until recently to be defeatist or quiescent about their condition. The point is made by another exiled South African, Ezekiel (now Es'kia) Mphahlele, in a review of one of Brutus's volumes of poetry:

> Among Africans who are busy asserting their identity, brandishing Pan-African rhetoric while barricading themselves more and more as national entities—among these the South African finds himself an outsider. And yet the South African Black national

anthem, the oldest in Black Africa outside Ethiopia, is Pan-African—it speaks of *Africa*. So it isn't that the South African is incapable of sharing Pan-African sentiments. It is that at the national level, he is welcome in only a small fraction of the continent. Even the well-meaning host who gives him asylum, such as it is, is dismally ignorant of the essence and goals of the South African struggle. He simply cannot, or does not want to try, to project himself into the agony of southern Africa.[2]

Another reviewer in the same journal made the further point that Brutus is alienated not only by being a *South African* black but by being a member of the minority group of 'Coloureds', smaller even than the white population, and by having received an education markedly different from that of most of his black and coloured compatriots. The point is put bluntly, brutally, and exaggeratedly:

> Brutus is worlds apart from the changing environments of black Africa. Though 'non-white' by legal definition, he is essentially the product of English colonial civilization and culture.[3]

Mphahlele's assertion of the cultural and social homelessness of the South African exile could hardly be more adequately demonstrated. As Brutus himself says in one poem, 'I am alien in Africa and everywhere' (*A Simple Lust*, p. 121). His situation has, indeed, been even more alienated than that of other South Africans of mixed ethnic origin, for having been born in the former Southern Rhodesia (now Zimbabwe) he has never held even minimal rights in South Africa.

Almost every theoretically plausible criticism has been made of black South African writers: that they are self-pitying, obsessed with apartheid, raucous, rhetorical, timid, politically naïve, or too narrow in outlook. Brutus has sustained vehement attacks from John Pepper Clark, Pol Ndu, and Bahadur Tejani, for instance. Clark complained of the raw, wounded quality of his material:

> Something of the troubadour that he proclaims himself to be, Brutus cuts a tough figure of great bravura, with quite a brutal Elizabethan hold on words, and a strong smell for all the right sentiments to stir the would-be crusader safe in his liberal seat somewhere in Europe and America. Reading the work of Dennis Brutus, much of it re-modelled rhetoric, one comes back to that old excuse by Mphahlele that certain situations like those in South Africa really are too paralysing for words. Perhaps—for what does one do to a dog holding up a mauled paw? A child in a fit of convulsion? Dennis Brutus in his book is a man battering his head against the bars of a cage in which he and his kind are undoubtedly held down by a devilish gaoler. The sight is terrible enough, but one gets the feeling sometimes, a wicked one no doubt, that a little less shouting and more silence and mime might not only make for manly dignity but also command attempts at rescue and action.[4]

Self-pity is the only charge made by both Clark and Pol Ndu. Where Clark attacked the distortion of poetic values by political ones and discovered a swashbuckling quality, Ndu complains of timidity verging on cowardice, misplaced charitableness, and the displacement of action by intellectuality:

> He apparently wants to fight. But his fight must not be bitter. It is not a fight of life and death—for him. It is the mercenary soldier's fight: gradual, curious but most cautious.
>
> .   .   .   .   .
>
> Much as Brutus' anti-Marxist theory of universal bent to greed might sound intellectual, the practical realities of the South African situation needs [*sic*] a realistic and grim facing up, a combat. The anti-apartheid fighter could lose the battle in the short run, even lose his life, but at the moment of death, he should realize a special expiation and satisfaction, a traumatic canonization. It is this final leap into sainthood which Brutus severally refuses or fears . . .[5]

Bahadur Tejani's generally unfavourable treatment of *Letters to Martha*[6] is a much more reasoned piece of literary criticism, though like Ndu he refers to Brutus's political naïvety. This expression when used by Brutus's critics generally refers to his tendency to see political problems in moral terms (somewhat like Lenrie Peters), his universalism (to be contrasted with chauvinism or Pan-Africanism), or his charitableness to his opponents. The mingling of vehemence and tenderness is, indeed, one of the characteristics of his work, and if he is politically naïve he is not morally naïve. Searching self-examination of his own motives and of the probable consequences and by-products of his actions runs through his work. He often has a feeling that whatever he does will not be the best possible action and will be open to criticism. In one poem he reaches the point where he asks of his professed supporters:

> What do they expect from me?
> and what do they expect me to do?
>
> (*Stubborn Hope*, p. 11)

When Brutus began writing poetry at the age of fourteen or fifteen it was against a background of Romantic literature largely acquired from his mother. Gray, Wordsworth and Tennyson (including the *Idylls of the King*) were among her favourites. At high school he went on to Browning and at Fort Hare College read widely in the Elizabethans and Victorians prescribed by the English literature syllabus. In the few years immediately after taking his B.A., when he was school-teaching in Port Elizabeth, he came to admire Donne, Hopkins, Yeats and Eliot. His earliest extant poem is the last poem in *Sirens, Knuckles, Boots*, his first collection. It was one of some fifty to a hundred poems he wrote to a girl called Dulcy whom he met when she was a student at St Thomas Aquinas high school in Port Elizabeth and he was a teacher there. 'So

for the moment, Sweet, is peace"[7] plays on her name, in the transmu-
tation Dulcy/*Dulce* (Latin)/Sweet. Brutus says that:

> The Dulce poem, as far as I remember, took thirty versions—at
> least thirty. Others perhaps a dozen, maybe twenty. The more
> clotted they were, the more hard work there was, but normally
> some of it would come to your mind whole. An entire sentence or
> phrase would come straight-away, and this would establish the
> idiom for you. Then the rest would be pruning of a multiplicity of
> ideas, to make them function simultaneously. (*Benin Review*, p. 49)

'So for the moment, Sweet, is peace' was written about 1950. The
next extant poems are from about 1961, some written to the woman
who sent the manuscript of *Sirens, Knuckles, Boots* for publication to
Mbari, one at least, 'Nightsong: City' (*A Simple Lust*, p. 18), to a white
woman with whom he had a love affair in the early 'sixties. This poem
he regards as the first in which he

> achieved magically the simultaneous writing for South Africa and
> a particular woman.... It was in the process of writing it that I
> discovered one could do the simultaneous statement, which I've
> done ever since. (*Benin Review*, p. 49)

As Brutus himself notes in this interview, his style had hardly altered
between 1950 and 1961. He recognizes in fact (something not always
perceived by critics of his later poetry) that he has always had several
styles available: a simple lyrical style of direct statement in strict metre
and often in rhyme, somewhat like Wordsworth; a complex, knotty
style based on Donne, Browning and Hopkins; a relaxed conversational
Yeatsian style; and what he called in another interview 'terribly loose,
very bad free verse'.[8]

Sirens, Knuckles, Boots was a more-or-less haphazard collection of
poems written between 1950 and late 1961 or early 1962, assembled in
part by one of the women to whom some poems were written and sent
to Ulli Beier for publication by Mbari. Brutus at the time was working
in Johannesburg and studying Law at the University of Witwatersrand
on a scholarship. He had been banned from teaching in schools, even
private ones, and issued with an order preventing him from writing or
publishing and another preventing him from leaving Johannesburg
(though his wife and family were living some 700 miles away in Port
Elizabeth). His wife co-operated with him by sending telegrams from
time to time purportedly relating to some family emergency so that he
could have the confinement order set aside for twenty-four or forty-
eight hours and travel about on underground political activities. This
clandestine roving is what brought the Don Quixote-troubadour image
to the forefront of his mind.[9] The danger involved also caused him to
realize, as he states in a note published in *Sirens, Knuckles, Boots* (p. 22):
'Time may be running out at this end: house arrest looms, and it is
never sure how much rope(!) one has. It may be more difficult for me to

keep in touch in future.' In fact, the volume appeared late in 1963 when he was imprisoned following an unsuccessful attempt to leave southern Africa and an escape from police custody in which he was seriously wounded by a bullet.

The first poem of *Sirens, Knuckles, Boots*, 'A troubadour, I tráverse all my land', concerns the adventurous clandestine life he led before his arrest, defying banning orders, evading the Saracen scout cars used by the police, giving the African National Congress sign of the upraised thumb. It is a poem that, like 'Nightsong City', combines the political and the sexual: he is for instance, in the first quatrain, exploring and investigating both the land and the body of his mistress, or in the sestet being pulled away from his 'service' of her by 'the captor's hand'. The troubadour image works well at the beginning, for medieval trouba-dours commonly engaged in illicit love affairs, spiced with the ever-present danger of discovery and punishment. Such an interruption to freedom and pleasure was, however, unlikely to be at the hands of the Saracens. The lord of the castle was the one likely to be captured by Saracens while he was away fighting in the Crusades; the troubadour was a minstrel who took advantage of the lord's absence at the wars to woo the castle ladies. To this extent, then, the troubadour image was suggestive of a life of pleasure during a state of war, of irresponsibility and fecklessness. This may be one reason why Brutus did not develop it fully: it held too many contradictions and unwanted overtones. In this poem, however, he ignores the problem and ends up with the troubadour snapped off like a frayed end (with 'strand', as he suggests in the *Palaver* interview, also functioning as an anticipation of the desolate shore of Robben Island), wearing no lady's favour but only prison uniform branded with an arrow.

The Petrarchan sonnet form seems appropriate, by association, for a troubadour song, though Brutus has moved the form of the poem even further from the spontaneity of sung work by limiting the rhymes to only two over the whole fourteen lines. No other extant poem is in such a tightly limited virtuoso form.

Several of the other poems anticipate shades of the prison-house. Mostly they express the general menace of the police state. In 'Some-how we survive' (*A Simple Lust*, p. 4), 'boots club the peeling door'; in 'The Sibyl' (p. 6) there is the pathetic fallacy of 'autumn's austere nemesis'; and in the poem from which the title of *Sirens, Knuckles, Boots* is taken, 'The sounds begin again' (p. 19), there is little but a succession of brutal images. Sometimes, however, Brutus feels that his own imprisonment in particular is inevitable.

> I eggdance with nimble wariness
> —stave off my fated splintering

he says in 'More terrible than any beast' (p. 7); and autumn for him has an air of death in 'Autumn comes here with ostentation' (p. 13). His reaction to imminent brutality is sometimes retributive violence, some-

times resort to inner stores of tenderness, sometimes personal retreat
into the comfort of understanding female companionship and sex.
'Time—ordinary time' (p. 10) looks forward to a successful revolution
sweeping

> these papered clerks and all
> into a messy bloody waste.

'Waiting (South African Style): "Non-Whites Only" ', 2 (p. 11) ends in
murderous thoughts typified by the American murder-mystery play,
Arsenic and Old Lace; 'Off the Campus: Wits' (p. 12) has several images
of preparation for guerilla warfare; and 'A common hate' (p. 22) speaks
of hatred bringing two underground political activists into deeper love
though it is not entirely clear that it is their hatred of apartheid rather
than the hatred directed against them by the ruling system that is held
in common. Brutus is never particularly well-disposed to retribution as
a response. He seems to recognize it as natural and inevitable, but also
as something needing examination. In 'This sun on this rubble after
rain' (p. 9), for instance, he suggests that it is likely to be an immediate
product of ill-treatment, particularly imprisonment ('sun-stripped'),
rather than a rationally argued response. The second response is tenderness, one of the most familiar words in Brutus's poetry. Faced with
brutality, the individual, generally in company with a woman, takes
courage from a self-generated, positive tenderness that seems to keep at
bay the political situation. This is the way of 'Somehow we survive'
(p. 4) and 'Between the time of falling for the flowers' (p. 5). The third
response, comfort in companionship and sex, is, however, by far the
commonest. Often it is represented as a necessary respite from the
political struggle, though the recipients of Brutus's love are never
treated merely as convenient ports of call. The struggle is always,
however, represented as primary, most directly in 'It is the constant
image of your face' (p. 24), where he tells a woman that:

> ... you, you know, can claim no loyalty—
> my land takes precedence of all my loves.

Sexual love can even seem, in so far as it requires a temporary respite
from the political struggle, like treachery to the land he loves, or his
sexual love can be so acute that it seduces him from his primary love, as
he confesses in the second half of this poem.

In 'This sun on this rubble after rain' (p. 9), he seeks to justify such
respite, even if it results in psychological hurt:

> Bruised though we must be
> some easement we require
> unarguably, though we argue against desire.

He argues against desire almost boorishly in 'Gaily teetering on the
bath's edge' (p. 25), where he uses ascetic theological arguments to

justify his morose refusal to respond to the woman's invitation. In an
echo of Auden's 'Lay your sleeping head my love',[10] he disdains

> this emphasis on sheer carnality
> re-iteration of mortality
> and [sees] all immediate joys ephemeral

That is as ungallant as he gets. In 'No Banyan, Only' (p. 14), on the
other hand, he expresses deep affection that eschews sex as something
almost sordid or at any rate demeaning as a representation of this
particular relationship. 'Carnality'—the puritanical language of 'Gaily
teetering on the bath's edge' is in use again—can obstruct the view of
time and peace; certainly it is alien to 'The quiet wisdom of the body's
peace'. Instead of bodies lying side by side (as in, say, a poem by
Donne), it is their minds that are attached. This is companionship,
affection, and understanding through and through, with no consuming,
supplanting kernel of sex at the centre. This is not one of the passion-
less sexual pastimes, 'making a little winter-love in a dark corner' that
Ben Jonson speaks of as one of the kinds of 'cold business' that a person
may 'mis-spend the better part of life in'.[11] Their 'golden bodies' are
indifferent to the 'dross' of sexuality, the technicolor of Gauguin's false
island paradise. But what the woman offers him is something as transcendent as the Platonic love of two souls that the metaphysicals write
about. Like some of the metaphysicals, Brutus expresses the point in
contemporary scientific imagery, drawn in this instance from Hershey's[12] discovery that the double-helixed DNA was the genetic
material of cells. The implication is that their souls are twined in a
double helix; the plain statement is that the woman has provided him
with psychological salvation, 'Content', and 'heartsease balm'. In the
final stanza this gift is, in a metaphysical conceit for which he has to
beg the pardon of St Francis of Assisi, compared to the steady,
gentle 'ecstasy' (a favourite word with Donne) of animals. St Francis
is referred to as 'Poverello', the poor man or beggar, for he was
often called 'il poverello d'Assisi'; Assisi is however in the province of
Perugia, so that 'Perugian' rather than 'Paduan' may be the correct
reading.

This most Donne-like of all Brutus's poems stands among a set of
poems in which female comfort does not exclude a sexual relationship.
'It is the constant image of your face' (p. 24) is one. 'Let not this plunder
be misconstrued' (p. 28) presents harsh imagery of sexual possession in
combination with the assertion of a need for tenderness achieved
through pain. 'Kneeling before you in a gesture' (p. 30) avoids this
ambiguity by contrasting the warm, safe, maternal enfolding with the
harshness of the police state. 'So, for the moment, Sweet, is peace'
(p. 33), though written well before Brutus was in any danger from the
police, also speaks of the sexual relationship as bringing refuge and
relief from pain. He is cradled by Dulcy as if in the sunlit trough of a
wave in stanza one, or in an earth depression ('delf' being an old word

for ditch) that is cracked by a 'fissure' in stanza three. The fissure is of
his own making, caused by his own restless heart, as he explains in the
middle stanza. Their love cannot feed on itself, like the pelican of
medieval beast lore feeding its young from the blood pecked from its
own breast; pain cannot be shaken off at will; nor can the self free itself
like a mollusc from the convuluted shell it has inhabited in the past, for
then it would be entirely unprotected. Continuing the imagery begun
with 'trough', he prays to be kept 'in quiet's acquiescent curve'.[13] This
is a poem clearly written under the influence of Gerard Manley Hopkins, as the daring compounds and the concentration on the pain of the
individual soul make evident.

Though many of these early poems contain exegetical difficulties
none are, I think, intransigent. Like the metaphysical poets (but unlike
his other ostensible model, Browning), Brutus generally makes the
scene abundantly clear in the first line. 'A troubadour', 'the time of
falling for the flowers', 'Her seer's eyes', 'This sun on this rubble after
rain', 'Time—ordinary time', 'At the counter an ordinary girl', 'Autumn comes here with ostentation', 'Sleep well, my love', 'It is your
flesh that I remember best', 'A common hate enriched our love and us',
'Gaily teetering on the bath's edge', 'How delicately the blossoms fall',
'Kneeling before you'; all these definitive and often highly pictorial
expressions are from the first lines of Brutus's poems. One can be in
little doubt, then, of what he is talking about, even if some of the details
remain unclear. The other factor that makes even the most difficult of
his poems easier to explicate than some of Donne or Browning is that
his syntax remains clear and simple. Despite the frequently demanding
verse forms, there is an absence of grammatical inversion, convolution,
complexity, or unidiomatic usage. When it is pointed out by some
critics, then, that Brutus's second volume contains much 'simpler' poetry one has to recognize both that a simple approach is found in some
of *Sirens, Knuckles, Boots* (for example, in 'Nightsong: City', 'The
sounds begin again', and 'Gaily teetering on the bath's edge') and that
even the most difficult of the early poems have straightforward syntax.

One reason why Brutus likes to state the subject at the beginning is
that he often thinks of his poems in terms of a musical analogy, particularly the exposition, development, and recapitulation of sonata form.
In the *Benin Review* interview he points out that 'This sun on this
rubble after rain' is a poem of this kind. 'Somehow we survive', 'Nightsong: City', 'The sounds begin again', 'A common hate enriched our
love and us', 'Gaily teetering on the bath's edge', and 'For Bernice'
(p. 29) would have been equally appropriate examples.

The remaining early poems appended to the first section of *A Simple
Lust* fall into the same categories as the poems of *Sirens, Knuckles,
Boots*. There is a plangent elegy, 'For a Dead African' (p. 34), more
meditative than the somewhat brassy 'At a Funeral' (p. 17), and opening
with the memorable line 'We have no heroes and no wars'. The date of
'Lutuli: 10 December 1961' (p. 35) is the day Chief Albert Luthuli, or

former Chief as the South African government would have it, was due to receive the Nobel Peace Prize in Oslo, after grave doubts that he would be permitted to leave South Africa. (He was, in fact, not permitted to visit either Sweden or the United States, where he had been invited, and the investiture ceremony in Oslo actually took place a day late.) Its imagery of the masterful African lion roaring might be compared with the autumn imagery of 'Autumn comes here with ostentation'. All but one of the other poems combine individual love with love for the country. The sense of love (both for a woman and for the land) easing his pain of loneliness and desperate, restless seeking is poignantly expressed here. In 'I might be a better lover I believe' (p. 40) he yearns for a secure, lasting relationship, replacing the present situation where neither woman nor land can be Brutus's or the rightful owner's. In 'When last I ranged and revelled all your length' (p. 42), he admits, though 'wryly', that he is now 'the slave of an habituated love', irrespective of present appearances or conditions. Brutus's characteristic blue or green imagery for love continues to operate in these additional early poems.

One poem, 'The springs of the flesh flow slack' (p. 38), seems incapable of a plausible political interpretation. It appears to be a naked self-confession of deep-seated melancholy that is only temporarily assuaged by sex.

The last four of the early poems included in the first section of *A Simple Lust* were reprinted from a small volume called *Thoughts Abroad*, published by Bernth Lindfors in Texas with Brutus's identity (barely) concealed under the pseudonym, 'John Bruin',[14] so that it could circulate in South Africa. The remaining poems of this volume are mostly to be found scattered through *A Simple Lust*, according to their date of composition. Three were omitted entirely, including 'I have a sense' (*Thoughts Abroad*, p. 21), which was rather too optimistic, in a Martin Luther King style, about the outcome of Brutus's campaign, and 'The copper-beeches resume' (p. 23), which was rather too despondent about his own future usefulness.

Sirens, Knuckles, Boots was published while Brutus was awaiting sentence. Most of the eighteen months' sentence was spent on Robben Island and it was while in solitary confinement there that he re-examined his attitude to poetry. He came to despise what he had written, even asking his wife (in one of the six-monthly letters he was allowed) to destroy it all. He adopted a new policy for the future:

> The first thing I decided about my future poetry was that there must be no ornament, absolutely none. And the second thing I decided was you oughtn't to write for poets; you oughtn't even to write for people who read poetry, not even students. You ought to write for the ordinary person: for the man who drives a bus, or the man who carries the baggage at the airport, and the woman who cleans ashtrays in the restaurant. If you can write poetry which

makes sense to those people, then there is some justification for writing poetry. Otherwise you have no business writing. (*Palaver*, p. 29)

In the circumstances, it is not surprising that Brutus over-dramatized the change. As I have suggested, he had written poems in a direct, simple style before, and even his ornate poems are not opaque. It is true, however, that the poems written in the few years immediately after his release are colloquial and straightforward.

He was released in 1965, but was still subject to restrictions on travel and a complete prohibition on writing or publication. After some six or eight months, he decided to circumvent the prohibition in the only way legally available, by writing letters. 'Letters to Martha', written over the next four to six months, were addressed to his brother's wife, but intended for later publication. His brother was now on Robben Island and in the poems Brutus sought to explain something of a prisoner's feelings. The poems, he said,

> tend not to capture immediately an experience ... And as the experience moved further away from me or I moved further away from it in time and it became less intense, it became more manageable. I could at first only write about it from the outside, but later on I could live inside it, to some extent ... the sharper ones were written further and further away. (*Palaver*, p. 32)

The original publication of *Letters to Martha* (London: Heinemann Educational Books, 1968) included some early poems and some poems written after 'Letters to Martha', without any clear indication of which were which. Several reviewers found the sequence confusing, with the result that the poems were rearranged in four more-or-less chronological groups in *A Simple Lust*. The first group, 'Early Poems', ranges from the mid-fifties to the first half of 1963, before he was imprisoned. In style they range from the clotted polysyllables of 'Longing' (p. 46) to the simple vignette of 'Train Journey' (p. 49). Brutus speaks of personal loneliness in 'No, I do not brim with sorrow' (p. 45) and 'Longing' (p. 46), and expresses the familiar need for comfort in 'Nightsong: Country' (p. 47) and 'The Mob' (p. 48). 'The Mob', though occasioned by an attack by whites on a group of people demonstrating against the Sabotage Bill, is much more general in implication than the description 'occasional' poem would suggest. Brutus has in fact said 'I try to avoid "occasional poetry", because I have a guilt about it' (*Benin Review* interview, p. 53). The text of 'The Mob' mourns his countrymen (in language drawn from biblical laments), and sketches the outline of a hostile mob of 'faceless horrors', but it hardly alludes to the circumstances and not at all to the reason for protest and reaction. (The bill in fact defined sabotage in the widest terms, imposed heavy sentences of from five years' imprisonment to death, and gave the Minister of Justice, the future Prime Minister and President, Mr B. J. Vorster, power to issue orders confining a person to his house. At the end of July 1962 the government issued a list of 102 people, including Brutus, whose words past, present or future, might not be reproduced in any way. Later Brutus, with others, was placed under house arrest.)

The most complex of these poems is 'Longing', one that Brutus himself thinks highly of. It sustains the image of a ballistic missile with an atomic warhead, but 'desire's trajectory' is such a confused arc that it ends at 'My heart', from which it presumably originated. The poet, then, destroys himself (which is plausible as the outcome of unsatisfied love), but seemingly because his longing is directed towards himself (which is presumably not what Brutus meant).

The second section of the rearranged *Letters to Martha*, 'Poems about Prison', begins with a poem written after 'Letters to Martha', but on a chronologically prior subject, his own thousand-mile journey in custody from Johannesburg to Robben Island. Colesberg was the half-way stop, where porridge was issued. The poem begins with soft-edged images ('clammy', 'sucks', 'rheumy', 'pap') and ends with hard-edged ones ('steel', 'shoot', 'frosty glitter', 'chains', 'awkwardly'), suggesting a psychological movement from the despondency of arrest, trial, sentencing, and early imprisonment to the rigours and resolution of life in a maximum-security prison. Both stars and manacles 'glitter', providing a suggestion that, although seemingly distant and unhelpful, the heavens are in sympathy with the prisoners.

'Letters to Martha' (written 'for your consolation' as Poem 9 says) discuss the feelings of a prisoner, the experiences of prison, the impotence and anger of relatives. Despite the conversational tone of voice ('of course', 'perhaps', 'you know', 'simply prisoners', 'I remember'), these poems are neither artless nor relaxed. It is doubtful whether some of the diction would be readily intelligible to 'the man who drives a bus'. Words like 'proximity', 'coprophilism', 'doppelgänger', 'montage', 'compeers', 'aphorisms', 'demagogic' and 'extrapolation' are not likely to be immediately accessible to all readers. Nor do these poems lack ornamentation. Poem 3, for instance, has

> notions cobweb around your head,
> tendrils sprout from your guts in a hundred directions ... (p. 55)

Poem 5 begins with a complex image:

> In the greyness of isolated time
> which shafts down into the echoing mind,
> wraiths appear, and whispers of horrors
> that people the labyrinth of self (p. 56)

and continues with the wraith or ghost image to the end. Poem 13 (p. 63), which deals with scraps of remembered quotation used as a defence mechanism, ends with a quotation (not quite accurate) from Ariel's song, 'Full fathom five', in *The Tempest*. Poem 15, to take one of many possible examples, ends with a strophe where the assonance

of the accented syllables in 'destiny' and 'potential' and the alliteration
of 'destiny', 'diabolic', and 'divinity' strengthen the poet's assertion
—here a theological assertion.

These poems are not, then, unpremeditated outpourings or naked
statements. They are carefully contrived rhetorical and poetic artefacts.
Rhetorical repetition is in almost constant use to reinforce mood or
message. Poem 1 ends with two lines each containing 'endure'; Poem 3
ends with a strophe patterned on 'lust ... love ... love ... human
hunger'. Poem 4 has a middle strophe (the only one with four lines in
this carefully balanced work) based on 'currency ... purchase ... procure', the 'procure' here having both a general meaning and a specifically sexual one in this context. Poem 9 has a structure throughout its
entire length of 'not-knowing ... not knowing ... thought ... remembered ... knowledge ... knowledge'. The rhetoric is expertly handled;
while the intention and the effects may not always be subtle, the means
certainly are.

But there is one feature of these poems that above all indicates that
they are not the simple statements of direct feeling that Brutus's own
announced programme would have them or that most commentators
have taken them to be. It is a feature that indicates, too, Brutus's lack
of composure, his continuing restlessness, his difficulty in thinking
himself back into 'the status of prisoner'. It must, after all, be impossible
to write quite unaffectedly to a sister-in-law (or, indeed, anyone) in
these circumstances. The feature that betrays Brutus's unease is the
extraordinarily frequent use of the impersonal 'one'. This is not a
colloquial usage in English: it almost always indicates some artificiality
or embarrassment. In the eighteen poems there are eighteen uses of the
impersonal 'one', 'oneself' or 'one's'. 'One' learns about prison weapons
and 'one' is chilled in Poem 2; 'one' welcomes the companionship of
fellow prisoners in Poem 10 (a particularly ill-at-ease poem, with its
formal, reserved language of 'closer contact', 'compeers', 'honest toil',
and 'redeeming hours'); and 'one comes to a callousness' (another
unidiomatic expression signifying some forcing of the personality) in
Poem 11.

In pointing out these qualities, I am in no sense suggesting that they
are faults. It is true that in Poem 14 Brutus uses 'rhetoric' as a pejorative
term, to be put into the same category as something 'falsified', or as
'heroic posturing' or 'demagogic bloodthirstiness'. My own usage is,
however, as a descriptive stylistic term; and my purpose in making
these observations is to demonstrate the degree of artfulness and con-
trivance in these poems that Brutus wanted to be simple, straightforward, and without ornament.

There is not, in fact, a sharp contrast in style between his pre-prison
and his post-prison poems. All he has come to eschew is the richly
ornamented metaphysical style of his most complex poems such as 'A
troubadour' and 'Longing'. He could not suddenly cut himself off from
the continuity of his poetic experience and practice, despite the trauma

of Robben Island. Indeed, in choosing to relive, in part, that trauma in 'Letters to Martha' he made it almost inevitable that he would fall back into his poetic armament. His fastidious pain and distaste for many things in prison life—enforced homosexuality (and perhaps unenforced homosexuality as well), brutality, duplicity, victimization and deprivation—can be expressed only in language that is chosen and not spontaneous, artificial rather than natural. Despite the sense of camaraderie in Poems 10, 12 and 14, the dominant mood is one of alienation and loneliness even in the company of other prisoners. The poems that mention the companionship of other prisoners do so almost with astonishment, or at least a sense of rarity:

> It is not all terror
> and deprivation
> you know ... (Poem 10, p. 60)

though, he seems to be saying, it is not far from it. In other poems, such as Nos 2, 3, 5, 6, 7 and 8, he obviously shrinks from the brutality of other prisoners.

In a lecture given at the University of Wisconsin, Brutus provided some of the horrific background to Robben Island. In 1964 when he arrived there were 1,100 political prisoners and 200 criminal prisoners. The criminal prisoners were placed in charge of the political prisoners, with responsiblity for feeding them, taking them to work, overseeing the work (breaking stones or working in the lime quarry) and disciplining them. At the instigation of the warders (all of them white), they used sexual assault to break an individual's morale and self-esteem, and were themselves rewarded with marijuana. Prisoners were starved into submission, beaten if necessary, then when on the point of consent to homosexuality left alone without food or water, though with an occasional beating. Most then found themselves begging for sexual assault in order to get food and water.[15] This is the background to Poem 7, one of the more general, least particularized of the poems, presumably either because it was written early in the sequence or because Brutus found the subject, even after the lapse of considerable time, still very unnerving.

The poems grouped as 'Postscripts' and 'On the Island' are similar in kind to 'Letters to Martha'. 'On the Island' consists of four generalized vignettes, but the use of the impersonal 'one' indicates that Brutus still suffers at the memories. 'Postscripts' are more personal in their relationship to Martha. The first is a kind of postscript to 'Letters to Martha' 9: now he speaks of 'picking the jagged bits embedded' in his mind to send her, where he had earlier spoken of sending 'these fragments, random pebbles'. There are now, however, two additional purposes acknowledged, apart from consolation for his sister-in-law: 'some ease for my own mind' and 'that some world sometime may know'. 'Postscript' 2 is an appendage to 'Letters' 1, 3 and 15, searching for 'the stubborn will the grim assertion of some sense of worth' beneath the horror, ugliness and brutality of prison life. 'Postscript' 3 takes up the bird imagery of 'Letter' 17, though this time not as a symbol of freedom, grace and communion with those outside but as a representative of the 'raucous greed and bickering' within the prison. In both poems, Brutus is aware of himself as poet, deciding whether to use an image and for what purpose. Whereas Wole Soyinka in 'Vault Centre' accepts and elaborates without self-consciousness the natural associations of birds with freedom and grace, Brutus is hesitant: in 'Letter' 17 he draws attention to the fact that birds as a symbol of freedom are 'clichés'; in 'Postscript' 3 he considers the possibility of using them as a symbol of 'grace' (a word he always uses with theological overtones), but rejects it as untrue to the observable facts. In 'Postscript' 3 it seems as if the birds have participated in the fall of man; they too are victims of original sin.[16] This sombre theological mood is continued in 'Postscript' 4, with its biblical language ('The wind bloweth where it listeth') and its language of lachrymose devotion ('this vale of tears'); it looks back to 'Letter' 4 and forward to 'Postscript' 5. There is a strong sense in both these 'Postscripts' of the finality, the unpredictability, almost the arbitrariness of eternal damnation, 'damned' being a word used in both. It is a strain perhaps derived from St Thomas Aquinas, a strain that John Calvin found very congenial. One of the popular Thomist hymns found in most Catholic hymn books is 'Lauda, Sion, Salvatorem', one stanza of which refers to both good and guilty sharing in the sacrament to their own grace or damnation. In J. D. Aylward's translation it reads:

> The good, the guilty share therein,
> With sure increase of grace or sin,
>   The ghostly life, or ghostly death:
> Death to the guilty; to the good
> Immortal life. See how one food
>   Man's joy or woe accomplisheth.

It is this kind of theology that explains lines like the end of 'Postscript' 5, where Brutus, 'desolate', meditates on 'how easily I might be damned'. Whether he meant damned eternally, damned by losing his stoic humanity and self-respect, damned by succumbing to the pressures and temptations of the prison, or all of these damnations (the possibilities range from the most cosmic to the most temporal) it is impossible to tell. Brutus always prefers to leave the detailed application of his poems open to more than one interpretation. In this instance, though, the possibilities intended by him are to some extent defined by a consideration of the almost contemporary poem, 'Our aims our dreams our destinations' (pp. 82–6).

It is one of the poems written between Brutus's release from prison and his exile from South Africa, the poems grouped as 'Under House Arrest'. It has echoes of Milton (notably in the argument of I, ending in the Satanic manifesto, ' "Evil be thou my Good" ') and Gerard

Manley Hopkins (in the exclamatory nature of the almost physical intellectual suffering). The temptation to curse God, to despair, or to lapse into agnosticism seems always under control. The testing of God against the standards of human companionship and fortitude (standards that Brutus always reverts to in his poetry) is never likely to result in condemnation. The ending brings divine and human standards together. 'Suffering humanity' may, Brutus suggests, share suffering with Christ, and thus share in the redemption of the world and in transfiguration into the divine. The final lines draw together two New Testament gospel images of humanity linked with the godhead: Jesus transfigured in the presence of his disciples (St Luke, ch. 9) and Pilate's words about the suffering Jesus (St John 19:5) emphasizing his humanity and, because he was dressed in a purple robe and a crown of thorns, his divinity.

The first of the poems in this section, 'On a Saturday afternoon in summer' (p. 73), presents another theological and psychological struggle, this time for 'repose'. Brutus distinguishes clearly between 'repose', a harmony of massive tensions, and 'rest', a negative absence of tension. It is a distinction reminiscent of the Thomist phrase used in 'A troubadour': 'motion sweeter far than rest'. And it carries over both into 'For Bernice' (p. 76), where Bernice is described, in a curious mixed metaphor, as 'the still oasis in a whirling vortex', and into 'Equipoise' (p. 81).

The fundamental belief in humanity also emerges strongly from these poems, in particular from 'Our aims our dreams our destinies' (p. 87), 'It is a way of establishing one is real' (p. 80), and 'The companionships of bluegum trees' (p. 92). Alongside it, however, is a fierce and bitter understanding of the evil man can do. Two poems interpret the annual Afrikaner commemoration of 'Blood River Day', 16 December 1838, when the Zulu army of King Dingane was decisively defeated and the Voortrekkers were able to make their settlement at Natal secure and to establish Pietermaritzburg. In the *Palaver* interview, Brutus calls it 'a once-a-year tribal ritual when whites celebrate their historic victory over the blacks in a battle which raged until the river [formerly the Ncome] ran with blood' (p. 33). Both of Brutus's poems, 'Blood River Day' (p. 77) and 'Their Behaviour' (p. 79), ameliorate the scene of blood-lust and ferocity, one by ending with the earth as a symbol of universality, the other (like several of Lenrie Peters's poems) by refusing to be self-righteous or sanctimonious. In 'Their Behaviour' he compares the magnification of the individual human predicament in apartheid to the way in which individual sexual passion can be magnified and corrupted in orgies, the sexual fastidiousness being typical of both Brutus and of Lenrie Peters.

Meditation on human evil brings Brutus to despair and near-despair in some of these poems. 'One wishes for death' (p. 87) expresses a desire for death in the face of unhappiness and disgust at 'the boundless opprobrium of life'. The following poem, 'Steeling oneself to face the day' (p. 88), with some weariness but much more determination, speaks of the daily continuance of a bitter struggle. The next poem, 'Let me say it' (pp. 89–91), written a month before he left South Africa, is the bitterest of all. It is a self-congratulatory piece stating and taking satisfaction in what Brutus had achieved in the struggle against racialism. He had been the President of the South African Non-Racial Olympic Games Committee (SANROC), which had successfully campaigned to have South Africa excluded from the Olympic Games and, using the threat of non-participation in the Games as a lever, had persuaded Britain and New Zealand to break off Rugby competition with South Africa. The isolation of the country from international sport was a bitterly resented manœuvre, a heartfelt deprivation, as Brutus says, for those 'who are artists in deprivation'. The poem (a personal reassurance which Brutus, in the *Palaver* interview, said he regretted seeing reprinted) ends with a statement of determination to 'flog fresh lashes across these thieves'.

To do that, he had to leave South Africa and continue the campaign from London, where he became also the Director of the World Campaign for the Release of South African Political Prisoners. Part III of *A Simple Lust* contains the poems of his London-based years, July 1966 to September 1970 (and part of 1971), a period when he did a great deal of travelling throughout the world in generating support for the campaign against apartheid. Some of these poems were first published in *Thoughts Abroad*, three are reprinted from *Poems from Algiers*,[17] and another three from an anthology, *Seven South African Poets*, edited by Cosmo Pieterse (London: Heinemann Educational Books, 1971). A number of poems also date from the first year or so of Brutus's residence in the United States, for in September 1970 he took up the first of his academic appointments as a professor of English there.

Apart from the travel poems, the largest group of poems in 'After Exile' is those where Brutus contrasts South Africa and England, using 'grey' as a symbol for South Africa (particularly the Robben Island prison) and silver and flaming or 'burning' roses for England. He laments his exile, complains of the seductive comfortableness of England, worries about those still on Robben Island, examines his soul for any evidence of dereliction from the cause, and thinks about the future. He had always praised the difficult virtue of patience, in 'It is your flesh that I remember best' (p. 20) and 'Events have a fresh dimension' (p. 61), for instance. Now he fears that patience may lapse into inertia, that he will succumb to the English atmosphere of tranquillity. He has to keep reminding himself of the South African condition in this 'green placid earth' populated by 'efficient unhostile people' (p. 112). He has to struggle to 'recover some stubborn will'.

The effects of his meditating on the two countries vary considerably, as can be seen in the three consecutive poems, 'Nearby in the park' (p. 166), 'Country and continent' (p. 167), and 'Does the heart survive the death of love' (p. 169). The first concentrates on knowledge of the self, capturing, like a Wordsworthian epiphany, a rare moment of self-understanding and content. The second complains of the succubus-like possession that South Africa and the whole of Africa have upon him. The bright, clear self-depiction of 'Nearby in the park' has given way to uncertainty, a sense of 'ageing', and a vision of unending agonized desire for his country. 'Does the heart survive the death of love' suggests that love may be faltering as one ages, but it leaves open the question of whether it is individual love for South Africa or for England, or some institutional affection for or involvement with South Africa.

The sense of ageing fires is carried over into some of the large group of poems concerned with international political campaigning.

> I must lug my battered body
> garbage-littered
> across the frontiers of the world,
> recite my wear-shined clichés
> for nameless firesides (p. 130)

he writes in Sydney, Australia. In Teheran he feels lonely, and oppressed by 'the labours waiting for me' (p. 125). Flying to Algiers he feels that 'I am alien in Africa and everywhere' (p. 121); flying from Algiers, 'I am driftwood' (p. 141). In another poem he reverts to the troubadour image for which he had been criticized:

> I *am* the exile
> am the wanderer
> the troubadour
> (whatever they say) (p. 137)

But the sense of purpose and achievement remains. In 'Shakespeare winged this way using other powers' he prays that he may be

> armed with such passion, dedication, voice
> that every cobblestone would rear in wrath
> and batter down a prison's wall
> and wrench them from the island where they rot. (p. 127)

In 'And I am driftwood', an otherwise melancholy poem bordering on self-pity, he ends with a humble sense of achievement, discerning

> traceries of patterns like wisps of spume
> where I have gone
> and snailtrails in seasands on a hundred shores
> where I have dragged my sad unresting loins
> —tracks on a lunar landscape that suggest some sense (p. 143)

There is no false self-congratulation in all this. He knows that 'Fry's still sell chocolate' (p. 116) the manufacture of which depends on black sweated labour.

Poems of exile, travel and political activism do not constitute the whole of the 'London' poems. There is also, for instance, a group of personal poems. ' "Bury the great duke" ' (p. 108) is a reminiscence of trying to recite Tennyson's 'Ode on the Death of the Duke of Wellington' to his schoolmaster father, and finding himself disappointed that his father was disappointed at his inability to continue. 'Finding this rubbish, this debris, of mine' (p. 138) is a mildly jocular speculation on having his papers sorted after he is dead by 'curious strangers' hands'.

The sequence of four love poems beginning with 'I will lie with you' (p. 148) develops from simple eroticism to increasingly impenetrable obscurity. 'I will lie with you', with its patina of 'l' sounds, is an account of love-making that rises to a climax and then fades into night: there are no 'l's in the last line. 'The sand wet and cool' (pp. 149–50), with its Hopkinsesque diction of 'warmgold folds', 'silkchill skeins' and 'unfolding upflowering', seems for the first half as if it is going to be a similar poem. It turns out, however, that the 'perfection of sensuality' described is 'an untrue innocent idyll', an attempt at slander (or perhaps, if it were in South Africa, an attempt at a criminal charge). But the fiction becomes for the would-be lovers the reality, and they delight in

> the stolen sensuous carnal delight
> the spray-bright, spume-chill, bladed air (p. 150)

There is much in this poem to remind one of the metaphysical wit of Brutus's earlier poems. The sinuous, darting intelligence, the strength of fabulation, the image-making, the linguistic delight and the wit all come together in the final lines, where 'bladed' refers to many things: the increasing chill of the air; the cutting, slanderous rumours that are blown about; the imaginary sexual thrust; and the sharp 'shell-blades' in the sand where they lay.

'The archer circles' (pp. 151–2) has a phallic symbol, the arrow (Sagitta) of the centaur-archer yearning to unite with 'soft flesh', as its central image. The double setting for the pageant is an heraldic jousting field peopled by centaurs and other fabled beasts and also the heavenly procession of the astrological houses. It seems to be a very complex self-image of the poet: as centaur, arrow, admirer of female beauty, plaything of fate, jouster, trader and bull, but above all (for he returns to this image at the end) the arrow of desire and action and the half-man, half-beast centaur. It was a brilliantly inventive idea to have the centaur both in the heavens (as Sagittarius) and on the jousting field, representing both the centaur's own dual nature as man and beast and man's dual nature as earthly activist manipulated by the heavens. This is the basis of the image, but many subsidiary images are drawn in with wit and deftness. Taurus as an astrological house, representing one aspect of the poet and his destiny, is not directly mentioned: instead the star (Aldebaran) forming the bull's-eye in the constellation, Taurus, is used. In this way, a link is made with the arrow, one of whose natural targets is the bull's-eye. The use of Taurus, a constellation visible over most of Africa, perhaps suggests an African setting, and there may even be a hidden reference to the 'bull's-eye' as a name for the small reddish-centred cloud said to portend a storm in the Cape of Good Hope region. It is also worthy of note that Taurus as a constellation also includes the Pleiades, traditionally associated with poetry. In these ways, then, a poem apparently about sexual love can be seen to have both a political significance (with South Africa as the female and the rest of Africa, as centaur armed with an arrow, yearning to possess her) and a poetical significance.

The poem progresses by alternating pageant-like scenes with shorter commentaries or choruses. The first scene presents the archer and his arrow; the second the panoplied willing object; the third the two crea-tures in love:

> Two persons disport themselves
> are arrayed
> for this fortuitous deployment—
> a perennial balletic jousting
> in the panoply of being,
> the accretions of circumstance,
> and traffic among the bales of time
> in the strange barter of dross and glass (p. 152)

The last two lines bring us once more to Africa, with their oblique reference to the standard bartering counters of the white conquerors: 'dross and glass'. This time, however, Brutus opens out any narrow African political significance in the image by taking it as a symbol for the whole of life and love, whether in Africa or elsewhere.

This is a poem more complex, metaphysical and intellectual than the early poems, 'A troubadour' or 'So for the moment, Sweet, is peace'. Brutus is now able to write this kind of poem with complete command of his poetic resources. There are no loose ends, no slips in the logic. The influence is still from Donne and Yeats, with, in this instance perhaps, something of Edwin Muir's heraldic world.

The last in this group of love poems is 'Sequence' (p. 153). It presents a fragmentary story of the speaker in love with and in awe of a beautiful but bellicose woman poet. He sees her first on a stage, 'Under spot-lights', presumably reading from her work or making a speech. As we learn from section V, she is a spectacular, if rather over-pitched per-former, one who is capable of 'tearing a passion to tatters'. He imagines her as a vindictive Greco-Roman goddess in section VI, destroying a landscape in pique. It is presumably her espousal of thoroughgoing anarchistic violence as a political solution (perhaps to the South African problem, perhaps to the wider problem of international capitalistic repression) that engenders this image in him.

The protagonist has alternative political views (which perhaps, as another speaker in the same seminar or rally, he enunciates from the same stage, or possibly puts to her privately). These she treats with crushing scorn. Her 'invincible disbelief' of the speaker's point of view wounds his intellectual and sexual pride. His sexual attraction is dissipated by the haughty disdain with which she treats him and his ideas, 'wronging' him (perhaps by misrepresentation, by refusing to take his ideas seriously, or by wounding disrespect for him as a person).

This opposition between sexual urges and intellectual opinion displays a reinforcement of many of Brutus's familiar attitudes, particularly his wariness of young hotheads (like those who adopted 'heroic posturing' and 'demagogic bloodthirstiness' in 'Letters to Martha' 14) and his cautious self-examination. The third parenthesis of section I is the best example of his wariness. Having persuaded himself that it is not wrong to admire this goddess sexually, he allows himself to dream that she might be the actualization of his sexual ideal, a person in whom his 'bat-frenzy' might 'come to fruit-perfect rest'. The image of his restless self as a frenzied bat reminds him of the food of bats, fruit, and fruit sets his mind off on the classical tales of the golden apples with which Atalanta was won, of Midas whose food turned to gold, and of Paris who gave the golden apple to Aphrodite in return for her promise that he should marry the most beautiful woman in the world. The outcome of this cluster of references is delight and fear when faced with stunning beauty: early in the poem, then, we are presented with the central complex of moods. Brutus's characteristic caution, his 'world-knowledge-saddened' nature, leads him to 'forbear' from hoping to gain her: he is too introspective, too wary of romantic illusion, too experienced, to believe that the realization of the dream is possible.

The poems in this section of *A Simple Lust* also include two elegies, one for Arthur Nortje (pp. 163–5), one for Chief Albert Luthuli (pp. 170–5). The elegy for Nortje, like Auden's elegy for Yeats, uses winter imagery as a setting. But Brutus rejects the conventional association of winter with death and sees the promise of future growth in the holly berries of Christmas, a symbol of the continuance of poetry and of Nortje's memory and reputation. In a prose tribute on Nortje's death Brutus said 'As a poet he was perhaps the best South African poet of our time';[18] the poem, however, in accordance with Brutus's dislike of poetic propaganda, makes no such judgement.

'For Chief' is a more public, less personal tribute. Running through its stately measure are most of the terms that define Brutus's values: grace, humanity, calm, freedom, pain, will, patience, endurance, courage, resolve, fire; most of them used more than once. There is also a sense of enormous moral forces gathering to bring justice not immediately but at least within imaginable time; in that sense the poem is a product of the relative optimism of Brutus's middle years in London. This poem and the one in memory of Nortje are rare examples of occasional poetry in Brutus's work, but they show how, like all successful elegists, he could move beyond the personal occasion to the wider cause.

Brutus's range of styles is evident throughout the twenty years of poetry-writing collected in *A Simple Lust*. From the earliest years he displayed an ability to write both very tightly packed metaphysical poetry and loose, unadorned, colloquial poetry, with many stages in between. What he dropped from his repertoire was not complexity and wit but highly formal imposed structures like the sonnet form of 'A troubadour' or the quatrains of 'Erosion: Transkei'. His prison experience concentrated his mind on poetry of direct statement, but his practice, even in the year following his release, was not always in accord with his intentions. His London years certainly produced, alongside poems of naked statement, a substantial number of poems elaborately conceived and executed. The variety of his verse, like most things about himself and his work, is recognized by Brutus himself. In 'Sometimes a mesh of ideas' (p. 136) he speaks of three kinds of poetic inspiration: the complex of ideas in a complex of images that delights the 'mental eye'; the 'musical clangour' of 'the thrust and clash of forged and metalled words'; and 'a nude and simple word' that rouses human sympathy. 'The archer circles' (p. 151) is an example of the first kind; 'a simple lust' (p. 176) an example of the third kind. The second kind can be seen not so much in whole poems as in portions of poems, often towards the end, where frequently the sound, particularly alliteration, seems to seize the language, and drive it through rhetorically to a climax. 'Shakespeare winged this way' (p. 127) is an example. The last strophe gains a good deal of its energy from the repeated patterns of sound: 'hewed . . . hacking . . . hardness' and 'rock . . . wrath . . . wrench . . . rot' are reinforced by the assonance of the last syllable of each of the last seven lines, all containing a back vowel, and by the final near-rhyme of 'rock . . . rot'.

Brutus's feeling that the unadorned style had displaced an earlier complex style is clearly stated in the poem 'When will I return'.[19] In it he speculates on when he will return to 'the tightly organised complexly structured image and expression' with its richness of association. In another poem, 'When will my heart' (*Stubborn Hope*, p. 12), he even speculates on whether 'the lyric impulse', the desire 'to fashion something beautiful', will ever return to him. Both poems were written before he left South Africa. It is clear that his fears were groundless, for both in South Africa and during the years in England he wrote a number of complex and lyrical poems.

The 1970s, the years Brutus spent in the United States, were regrettably not so fruitful. He continued to write poetry, but much of it is little more than prosaic counsel, aphoristic advice, or simple rhetorical statement and exhortation suitable for reading to audiences with only a low threshold tolerance for poetry. Some poems are very brief, consisting of two images: this is a style that culminated in *China Poems*.

Stubborn Hope, the volume that incorporates most of the work of this period, is, then, a disappointing volume. Even the poems that it includes from the 1950s and 1960s, poems which were unavailable when the earlier volumes were compiled, are largely appendages to other groups of poems; they can nearly all be related to works in *A Simple Lust* on grounds of association in subject, attitude or style. *Stubborn Hope* is a carelessly arranged collection, which even repeats one poem ('You have your private griefs', pp. 48–9) from *A Simple Lust* (p. 159).

It begins with an early poem, 'Words for Farewell' (p. 1), in 'In Memoriam' stanza form and, to some extent, diction. It introduces a large group of poems about personal love scattered through the volume, many of them concerned with the ending of affairs. The most complicated is another from the South African period, 'Love; the Struggle' (pp. 56–7). It attempts to use the protracted imagery of a soldier arming for battle as a metaphor for the lover putting aside the delights of love for the quotidian concerns of the day. The imagery of modern warfare is, however, infiltrated by the vaguely medieval imagery that Brutus always has ready to hand. 'Time's battery rocks and salvoes' in one stanza are followed by 'fairplay', 'arduous strife', 'Seas confront with seethe and trouble', and 'I gird' in the next. This conflation of different periods of warfare makes for some difficulty in the interpretation of the refrain, which moves from 'Ah Love, unshoulder now my arms!' to 'Unshoulder, Love, unshoulder all my arms!' A modern soldier is unlikely to have 'shouldered' more than a single personal weapon; on the other hand, in a medieval arming song the plea to 'unshoulder' arms would be nonsensical, as it would suggest taking a suit of armour off the shoulders rather than putting it on for battle. This, then, is a complex poem that has gone out of control.

Many of the love poems combine a woman and a country as the object of affection. 'I have not, out of love, cursed you yet' (p. 5) has in its first line a concise ambiguity: 'out of love' may, in this context, mean 'as a result of love' or 'when I have fallen out of love with you' and both meanings make good sense. 'You tested my love for my real true love' (p. 6) expresses, briefly, one of the points made in 'It is the constant image of your face' (*A Simple Lust*, p. 24), that love for a woman can almost, but not quite, rival the poet's love for the land. 'I must speak' (p. 24) refers to the gradualness with which a loved one, either person or land, may be convinced of the need to assert 'the truth in blood, or action or belief'. All three poems were written before Brutus left South Africa.

The later poems about South Africa and the campaign on which he is engaged tend to be more prosaic, oratorical and bare of imagery. 'There are no people left in my country' (p. 41), for instance, is a finely constructed and passionate statement of how he cannot afford to think of the people whose freedom he fights for as individuals, but it achieves its effect using largely prosaic, unmetaphorical language. Many of the other political poems of these years are the kind of propaganda poem that Brutus often expresses distaste for. 'Sharpeville' has several strophes of chopped-up prose, including

> Because it epitomized oppression
> and the nature of society

more clearly than anything else;
it was the classic event (p. 89)

'I am a rebel and freedom is my cause' (p. 95) has similarly prosaic lines
such as

Many of you have fought similar struggles
therefore you must join my cause[20]

These are crude poems obviously designed, probably in spite of Brutus's fastidious revulsion, for political rallies. *Stubborn Hope* does, however, contain some political poems that avoid this crassness by using
the familiar identification of beloved woman and country: 'Having fled,
I display a fugitive's jealousy' (p. 65), from Brutus's London period, is
an example.

The experience of prison generally provides a concentration of the
mind. *Stubborn Hope* has poems from the years immediately before his
imprisonment until well into the 1970s. 'When they deprive me of the
evenings' (p. 8) looks forward with apprehension to his inevitable
imprisonment. 'I remembered in the tranquil Sunday afternoon' (p. 9)
refers to his imprisonment while awaiting trial. He thinks of Federico
García Lorca, the Spanish poet arrested and assassinated in 1936 who
also liked to think of himself as a troubadour. The poem is suffused
with typical García Lorca images: plaza, church, bullring, tropic light,
salt sea, wild orange, frangipani. It must have been written at a time
when Christopher Okigbo was also finding García Lorca a fruitful
influence.

'On torn ragged feet' (p. 29), 'For a while I was the tattooed lady of
the prison' (p. 29), 'Nothing in my life' (p. 58), 'Robben Island
Sequence' (pp. 58–60) and 'At Night' (p. 83) are all set in Robben
Island. The earliest are 'Nothing in my life' and 'Robben Island
Sequence', written in the year after his release. Both are full of images
of brightness, to which 'Robben Island Sequence' adds images of sharpness and laceration. The naked horror of these poems is on the whole
more effective than the horror accompanied by commentary of the later
ones or the horror accompanied by overt moral outrage and a call to
action in 'Swatches of brassy music' (pp. 44–6), a poem that juxtaposes
the gaiety of a nightclub with the remembered bleakness of the prison.

The sharp, lacerating beach-front of Robben Island seems to have
suggested an image for life in 'Sherds' (pp. 30–1) and 'It was a sherded
world I entered' (p. 31). In a way it is a more concentrated image than
the image of garbage used earlier for the fragmentary worthless quality
of life in 'I must lug my battered body' (*A Simple Lust*, p. 130) and
'Finding this rubbish, this debris, of mine' (*A Simple Lust*, p. 138). All
are poems developed on the resonance of a single word, as is very clear
in both the 'sherd' poems from their self-conscious reference to the
poetic use of this 'image' and its meaning for the poet. A trace of the
same image can be found also in one of the earlier, South African

poems, 'Dear wonderful woman' (p. 15), a tribute to his mother including commendation for her 'courageous grasping of our jagged life'.

Another of the more overtly biographical poems is Brutus's self-justification to his children, 'For My Sons & Daughters' (p. 4). He struggles to communicate his concern for them by piercing through their natural response to all his 'derelictions'. The justification, not 'mitigation', he is careful to point out, is

> my loneliness; my failures; my amalgam wish to serve:
> my continental sense of sorrow drove me to work
> and at times I hoped to shape your better world.

That melancholy self-image needs to be set alongside the self-confident jauntiness of an almost contemporary poem, 'I will be the world's troubadour' (pp. 22–3). In it he speaks not of being burdened with the task, but of gaily 'Knight-erranting' and 'jousting' and being a 'cavalier' who produces 'a world-wide scatter of foes'. A somewhat later poem, from the London years, 'I come and go' (p. 25), combines both images of himself. He is 'a pilgrim grubbily unkempt', one who can say 'I plod or shuffle or amble'; but he is also 'stubbornly cheerful defiantly whistling hope'.

Many of the poems continue subjects used earlier. There are travel poems (one of the best being 'Crossing Kabul to Samerkand', p. 34) and poems about London. The London poems include '—and the air is filled with' (p. 35) which, like 'Crossing the English coast' (*A Simple Lust*, p. 100), uses material remembered from 'the paper thrillers of those perennial English wars' that he read as an adolescent. 'In England's green and pleasant land' (p. 39) parodies Blake in order to develop the theme of 'mouldering English humbug' that he had referred to in 'I am alien in Africa and everywhere' (*A Simple Lust*, p. 121).

'The New York Times reports they say they are hurt' (p. 42) takes up the theme and the last line of 'Let me say it' (*A Simple Lust*, pp. 89–91). In that poem, written just before leaving South Africa, he celebrated the increasing sporting isolation of the country and vowed to 'flog fresh lashes across these thieves'. Now in 1971, with isolation in Rugby and cricket achieved, he can say 'Indeed I flog fresh lashes across these thieves! and they bleed . . .'

Another theme continued in *Stubborn Hope* is that of elegies on the death of friends and admired leaders. The earliest in the volume is 'I remember the simple practicality of your reminiscences' (pp. 63–4), from the London years. It celebrates the life of Che Guevara, the freedom fighter in Cuba and South America. He was one of the 82 who, in November 1956, under Fidel Castro's leadership, sailed on the barely seaworthy yacht *Granma* to begin the Cuban revolution. Discovered by Batista's soldiers before they landed, only a remnant of the force remained to struggle to safety in the mountain chain of the Sierra Maestra. Though wounded in the landing, Guevara was one of only 12 survivors who reached the mountains and helped to set up the nucleus of a guerilla army. His death in Bolivia in 1967 was greeted with dismay by radicals, especially youthful ones, throughout the world, and, as Brutus notes at the beginning, it produced some very emotive poetry in stark contrast to the 'simple practicality' of Guevara's *Reminiscences of the Cuban Revolutionary War* (1963, English translation 1968). Brutus, always sceptical of claims to heroism, especially his own, characteristically speculates on whether this book is as 'meretricious and falsified' as T. E. Lawrence's *Seven Pillars of Wisdom,* but decides that the un-doubted sufferings of Guevara authenticate his account.

'In Memoriam: I.A.H.' (pp. 68–9) and 'For Frank Teruggi' (p. 89) celebrate South African freedom fighters. The first makes a number of intellectual points about Haroun's death, the first half negative ('it does not matter . . . he chose not to speak . . . it does not matter . . . they can touch him not'), the second half concentrating on his positive contri-bution. The last strophe takes the bleak and dishonest official version 'dead of natural causes' and wittily turns its last word into an affirmation of 'our cause'. 'For Frank Teruggi' is an entirely different poem, with-out intellectualization: it offers a stark imagistic scene followed by a simple generalization of the meaning of his death.

Two poems celebrate poets who defied repressive authority. 'No matter for history' (p. 90) is an elegy for Pablo Neruda, the Chilean Marxist poet who died on 23 September 1973, less than a fortnight after President Allende, also a Marxist, had died in a right-wing military coup. 'They hanged him, I said dismissively' (p. 41) may be an appen-dage to the earlier elegy on Arthur Nortje, though he is not named here; his death in 1970 from an overdose of sleeping tablets was attributed by his friends to the South African Government's refusal to renew his passport or to give him any assurance of being able, if he returned home, ever again to leave the country. (Brutus also refers to him as 'KAN', from the initials of his full name, Kenneth Arthur Nortje, in 'Our allies are exiles', pp. 84–5.)

So far I have referred to poems of the 1970s that continue earlier themes and styles. There was, however, one stylistic development in these years that brought an earlier strain to an extreme. It was the miniaturist poetry represented in the South African years by poems such as

> Strelitzias
> phoenixes
>
> in the late level afternoon light
> take flight,
> exquisitely. (p. 3)

These poems consist generally of two superimposed images (here a flower and a bird) in the manner of imagist poems or Japanese *haiku.* Brutus took this miniature style to an extreme as a result of visiting the People's Republic of China in 1973 for an international table-tennis

tournament. Before going, he came across a new translation of the
poetry of Mao Tse-Tung by Willis Barnstone and Ko Ching-Po.[21] Its
extreme economy, particularly in the *chueh chu* form, greatly impressed
him, and while he was on his visit he wrote some poetry in English
roughly based on the same models. They were published, with the text
in his own calligraphy and a Chinese translation by Ko Ching-Po, as
China Poems. About half are reproduced in *Stubborn Hope*.

According to Brutus:

> The trick is to say little (the nearer to nothing, the better) and to
> suggest much, as much as possible. The weight of meaning hovers
> around the words (which should be as flat as possible) or is brought
> by the reader/hearer. (*China Poems*, p. 35)

One of the examples he goes on to give seems to be another poem about
Nortje:

> Exile:
> schizophrenia:
> suicide (p. 35)

But to limit the meaning in this way is not what Brutus intended and
not what the form makes possible. In leaving the multitude of possible
meanings to be imported by the reader, Brutus was merely putting into
practice an idea he espoused in the *Palaver* interview, that

> all people are poets. Some are just ashamed to let it be known, and
> some are shy to try, and some write but don't have the guts to show
> it to others. But we are all poets because we all have the same kind
> of response to beauty. (p. 29)

Minimalist poetry is, in effect, an attempt to force the reader to be a
poet.

Some of Brutus's China poems are nothing but a phrase (not even a
sentence) of description. 'Beyond the trees' (p. 75) is a very simple
example, with only two elements: trees and horizon. Some add a sentiment, as in the two 'Poplar' poems (p. 76). In the *China Poems* publication, the second of them was accompanied by a note referring to one
of Mao's poems:

> (In his tribute to his first wife, who was beheaded by a warlord
> because she refused to divorce him, Mao refers to his wife in the
> poem as a poplar.) (p. 15)

This explanation was dropped from *Stubborn Hope* presumably because
it might limit the reader's interpretation. Some add further elements of
description, like 'Earthworks covered with moss' (p. 77), the result
being a surrealist collage or, more exactly, a collage like the Fenollosa/
Pound interpretation of the primitive Chinese written character: that
is, the elements, though disparate, have one aspect in common, as rose,

iron rust, cherry and flamingo have redness in common.[22] Some have an element of wit in them, like 'China' (p. 78), or of witty political irony like 'On the roofs' (p. 75); some offer condensed paradox, almost oxymoron, like 'At the Long Wall' (p. 77), with its Vietnam-War cliché; several have an element of directly stated moral precept.

Poetry like this is harder than it looks, as some of the early Imagists knew very well. Brutus has only variable success, but he may be more concerned with success in stimulating the reader or listener into poetry than with strictly literary achievement. In any case, the minimalist poems represent only a fraction of his work in the 1970s.

Since the publication of *Stubborn Hope*, his published poetry has followed no new lines. There are, for instance, travel poems like 'Berlin Notes' or 'Crossing the Atlantic' and elegies like 'In Memoriam: Solomon Mahlangu'.[23] Over the last thirty years, Brutus's poetry has in fact changed little. He began with a wide range of available styles and his career has concentrated at various times on one or another of them. His earliest poems are bejewelled metaphysical artefacts in imposed forms. His poems in the year after his release from Robben Island mostly adopt a rhetorically shaped simple style. And in 1973 he went to the extreme of minimalism. But he has always been able to write in various styles and his precepts have remained constant: determination, unremitting struggle, fortitude, patience, hope (both political and spiritual), tenderness, passion, vulnerability and sceptical self-examination.

Notes to Chapter 1

1. Bernth Lindfors, '"Somehow Tenderness Survives": Dennis Brutus Talks about His Life and Poetry', *The Benin Review* 1 (1974), 44–55. The quotations in this sentence are from p. 55.
2. 'Debris, Driftwood and Purpose' [a review of, *inter alia*, Brutus's *Poems from Algiers*], *Africa Today* 18, No. 2 (April 1971), 67–71 (p. 70). The Zulu song, 'Nkosi Sikekela' ('O Lord, guide the destiny of our land'), adopted by blacks as a national anthem in South Africa, is referred to in a poem written by Brutus on 26 June 1967, South African Freedom Day, 'Today in prison', *A Simple Lust*, p. 109.
3. Robert M. Wren, 'Human Adaptation in African "Tales", Novels and Poems' [a review of, *inter alia*, Brutus's *Letters to Martha*], *Africa Today* 18, No. 3 (July 1971), 73–6 (p. 75).
4. John Pepper Clark, 'Themes of African Poetry of English Expression' (1964) in his *The Example of Shakespeare* (London: Longman, 1970), pp. 39–60 (p. 50). Clark is discussing Brutus's first volume, *Sirens, Knuckles, Boots*.
5. Pol Ndu, 'Passion and Poetry in the Works of Dennis Brutus', in *Modern Black Literature*, ed. S. Okechukwu Mezu (Buffalo, N.Y.: Black Academy Press, [1971]; special issue of *Black Academy Review* 2, Nos. 1 & 2, Spring-Summer 1971), pp. 41–54 (pp. 46, 47).
6. 'The Prison Poems of Dennis Brutus', in *Standpoints on African Literature*, ed. Chris L. Wanjala (Nairobi: East African Literature Bureau, 1973), pp. 323–43.

7. *A Simple Lust* (London: Heinemann Educational Books, 1973), p. 33. This volume incorporates all the poems of Brutus's *Sirens, Knuckles, Boots* (Ibadan: Mbari Publications, 1963), correcting the layout of some pairs of poems originally consolidated into one. The biographical information in this paragraph comes from Dennis Brutus, 'Childhood Reminiscences', in *The Writer in Modern Africa*, ed. Per Wästberg (Uppsala: The Scandinavian Institute of African Studies, 1968), pp. 92–8; Bernth Lindfors, ' "Somehow Tenderness Survives": Dennis Brutus Talks about his Life and Poetry'; and another interview in *Palaver: Interviews with Five African Writers in Texas*, ed. Bernth Lindfors et al. (Austin: African and Afro-American Research Institute, University of Texas at Austin, 1972), pp. 25–36.

8. *Palaver* interview, p. 27. In this interview Brutus also discusses 'So for the moment, Sweet, is peace', giving a slightly different account of its genesis and inclusion in *Sirens, Knuckles, Boots* from the account in *The Benin Review* interview. In an earlier interview with Cosmo Pieterse (1966), Brutus says that he himself sent the manuscript of *Sirens, Knuckles, Boots* to Ulli Beier at Mbari: see *African Writers Talking: A Collection of Interviews*, ed. Dennis Duerden and Cosmo Pieterse (London: Heinemann Educational Books, 1972), pp. 53–61 (p. 57).

9. See *Palaver* interview, p. 27.

10. The same poem also lies behind 'Nightsong: City' (p. 18), as he points out in the *Benin Review* interview, p. 49.

11. Ben Jonson, *Explorata or Discoveries*, 11 ('Jactura vitae').

12. All texts have 'Hersey' but this must be a misprint; there seems little doubt that the American geneticist Alfred Day Hershey is meant.

13. Brutus discusses this poem in the *Palaver* interview, pp. 35–6. He is wrong to take 'trough' as meaning the crest of a wave and 'shadeless' as colourless. He relates 'delf' to the older (and more accurate) term for 'Delft ware', the glazed domestic earthenware (often blue in pattern) from Delft in Holland, and the 'fissure' is then a crack in one of the pieces. The alternative reading I have offered seems to make the poem more consistent.

    The pelican image, he says, came to him from one of the hymns attributed to St Thomas Aquinas—a source from which several phrases in the early poems come. The hymn used here was 'Adoro te devote, latens deitas', presumably encountered in one of the popular Catholic translations by E. Caswell or J. D. Aylward.

14. 'John Bruin', *Thoughts Abroad* (Del Valle, Texas: Troubadour Press, 1970). The 1975 reprint (from Austin, Texas) has Brutus's name added. Bernth Lindfors's 'John Bruin: South African Enigma in Del Valle, Texas', *Africa Today* 18, No. 4 (October 1971), 72–7, is in part a jocular piece of mock-astonishment and obfuscation, concealing his own part in the publication, in part of piece of serious literary criticism.

15. See Dennis Brutus, 'Poetry of Suffering: The Black Experience', *Ba Shiru* 4, No. 2 (Spring 1973), 1–10.

16. See the *Palaver* interview, p. 31, for evidence that the Christian theological doctrine of grace is important for Brutus. In the interview he discusses the 'Colesberg' poem (pp. 52–3) in these terms.

17. A volume of nine poems and a commentary, reproduced from Brutus's elegant and dashing italic calligraphy. They were written in 1969 while attending the first Pan-African Cultural Festival in Algiers and published

by The African and Afro-American Research Institute, The University of Texas at Austin, 1970.

18. 'In Memoriam Arthur Nortje, 1942–1970', *Research in African Literatures* 2, No. 1 (Spring 1971), 26–7 (p. 27).

19. *Stubborn Hope* (London: Heinemann Educational Books, 1978), p. 13. This volume includes material earlier printed in *China Poems* (Austin, Texas: Occasional Publication of the African and Afro-American Studies and Research Center, University of Texas, 1975), *Strains* (Austin: Troubadour Press, 1975), and *South African Voices*, ed. Bernth Lindfors (Austin: African and Afro-American Studies and Research Center, University of Texas, 1975).

20. A note on this poem at its first publication in *South African Voices* (p. 33) states that the poem was 'based on speech of Yassir Arafat to General Assembly of the United Nations'.

21. *The Poems of Mao Tse-Tung* (Toronto, New York, London: Bantam Books, 1972).

22. See Ezra Pound, *ABC of Reading* (London, 1934, 1951, etc.), ch. 1.

23. See, respectively, *West Africa* 27 August 1979, pp. 1559–60; *Ufahamu* 9, No. 1 (1979), 56; *Okike* 15 (1979), 3–7.

2 Christopher Okigbo

▼▼▼▼▼▼▼▼▼▼▼▼▼▼▼▼▼▼▼▼▼▼▼▼▼▼▼▼▼▼▼▼▼▼

Despite his use of translations from, references to, and rhythmical imitations of West African poems in the oral tradition, Christopher Okigbo's poetic milieu is basically European. He constructs poems on the analogy of European musical compositions, in a sequence of movements with themes, developments, variations, repeats, and reminiscences. As an undergraduate, reading for a Classics degree at University College, Ibadan, he was well-known as a jazz player on clarinet and piano, and as a jazz composer. Having graduated in 1956 and been appointed Private Secretary to the Federal Ministry of Research and Information in Lagos, he turned from the composition of music to apply himself seriously to writing poetry.[1] It is obvious both from the substantially varying published versions of his poems and from the testimony of friends such as Sunday O. Anozie[2] that he was a writer who very carefully revised his work, not only before publication but often afterwards as well. He seems to have been diffident about committing himself to print and never satisfied with what he had done. The earliest of his adult poems to be preserved seems to be 'Song of the Forest', one of 'Poems: Four Canzones (1957-1961)' published in *Black Orpheus* in 1962.[3] It was not, however, the earliest to be published: that was the second of the 'Four Canzones', 'Debtors' Lane', which appeared in 1959 in *The Horn*, the journal published under the editorship of J. P. Clark (a close friend of Okigbo's at this time) by the students of the English Department at Ibadan.[4] Okigbo chose not to include these early poems in his collected volume, *Labyrinths*. They are suffused with barely concealed source material, Virgil's Eclogues in 'Song of the Forest' and 'Lament of the Flutes'; T. S. Eliot's *The Waste Land* in 'Debtors' Lane'. They are apprentice works, of which fragments were to be used again elsewhere.

The same cannot be said for two poems written some years later that also found no place in *Labyrinths*. They are 'Dance of the Painted Maidens' and 'Lament of the Masks: For W. B. Yeats: 1865-1939'. Both were published in 1965, having been commissioned for occasional publications. Their influences are Nigerian rather than European, 'Lament of the Masks' in particular having a close affinity with several Yoruba *oriki*.[5] They appear to have been omitted from *Labyrinths* solely because they could not be fitted into the thematic pattern. Nor could they find a place in 'Path of Thunder', the collection published with *Labyrinths* that Okigbo left unfinished at his death.

One of the reasons why Okigbo revised his poems so much was that they gradually shaped themselves into a sequence and required modification or even substantial re-writing to take their due place in it. Another reason was that in construction they are heavily influenced by musical analogues. Okigbo told Lewis Nkosi that when working on 'Heavensgate', the first part of *Labyrinths*, 'I was working under the spell of the impressionist composers Debussy, Caesar Franck, Ravel, and I think that, as in the music of these composers who write of a watery, shadowy, nebulous world, with the semitones of dream and the nuances of the rainbow, there isn't any clearly defined outline in my work . . .'[6] This is modestly and accurately said.

However much Okigbo might use lines from Yoruba, Igbo, or Ewe praise-songs or Ashanti drum invocations, the mood and to some extent the shaping of his poems is Middle Eastern, Mediterranean, and European. Their strongest affinities in tone and texture are with late nineteenth-century European music and poetry, with Debussy, Mallarmé and other French Symbolists, the poets of the 1890s and their twentieth-century heirs such as Eliot and Ezra Pound. It is soft-edged poetry, the scenes filmy, insubstantial, and dissolving into one another. The order is not that of narrative, drama, or logic, but that of a dream or vision, held together by repeated fragmentary motifs and by a gradually emerging theme. It has a sense of impending revelation, not unmixed with danger, towards which the poet strives or is borne along. The poet is initiated into rites and mysteries that are arcane and troubling, and involve imagery of sexuality and sacrifice. The poetry makes use of correspondences between the world of the senses and the unseen spiritual world, in Okigbo's case notably using geometrical symbols (as is true also of W. B. Yeats) and architectural ones. It draws on material from wherever it is available, no matter how recondite or inaccessible to the ordinary reader, for it is concerned with mystery, and mystery is not susceptible to demotic exposition.

The mystery is the mystery of life and death, individual identity, relation with one's society or relation with the unseen world, and the creative act of composition. The work of art expressing this tends to work towards a moment of revelation by or union with the divine, though it may be only a transitory moment, for such works tend to be concerned more with process, the continuing act of becoming, than with result, the state of being.

The mystery religions of the Ancient Near East, up to and including the Greek Eleusinian mysteries; the tradition of Neo-Platonism as expressed by Plotinus, Porphyry, or Swedenborg; New England Transcendentalism; and even the superficial eclecticism of such sentimental para-religions as theosophy may all provide material for writers of this cast of mind. In the Introduction to *Labyrinths*, Okigbo indicates some of his own sources and also conveys the wistful dreamy anguish of the whole undertaking. He refers to the Babylonian hymn, the 'Lament of the Flutes for Tammuz', that was sung in Syria at the secret rites for Adonis (identified with Tammuz, the Sumerian, Babylonian, and Assyrian god who suffered death and resurrection every year). A note to

'Fragments out of the Deluge' X, refers to the twin-god of Irkalla, a symbol of sexual and social unity and harmony in Sumerian myth. The Introduction mentions Palinurus, helmsman to Aeneas, who fell overboard, was murdered when he made landfall, and was left without burial. According to Virgil, Aeneas on his visit to the underworld (a mysterious descent) reassured Palinurus about his being remembered and honoured while he waited to cross the Stygian lake.[7] In many of these myths, water, rivers, or the sea are prominent. In the Introduction, Okigbo refers to the sirens who tempt mariners to destruction, using as his source Debussy's third orchestral *Nocturne*, 'Sirènes', which has a part for female chorus. In the same sentence he includes as a 'dissonant dream' (for the women here are sufferers not tempters) the five Franciscan nuns whose death by drowning is commemorated in Gerard Manley Hopkins's poem, 'The Wreck of the Deutschland'. The sirens' temptation to spiritually enervating sensual delight and the nuns' sacrifice of themselves in the cause of the suffering Christ are 'associated', says Okigbo, 'in the dominant motif "NO in thunder"'. Here, then, is an example of the association of disparate materials in both a superficial motif, the sea, and a thematic one, the mysterious 'NO in thunder'. To understand this puzzling quotation and its probable meaning for Okigbo, one has to go back to the source, a letter from Herman Melville to Nathaniel Hawthorne after receiving a copy of Hawthorne's novel, *The House of the Seven Gables*. Melville identifies and characterizes Hawthorne's religious outlook, a courageous reliance on the god within and a refusal to be terrified by the threats of external religions, whether ostensibly devoted to God or to the Devil. The whole idea (derived in part from Carlyle's chapters on 'The Everlasting No' and 'The Everlasting Yea' in Book II of *Sartor Resartus*) must have appealed to someone like Okigbo, who saw no contradiction between Christianity and animism. Melville wrote:

> There is a certain tragic phase of humanity which, in our opinion, was never more powerfully embodied than by Hawthorne. We mean the tragicalness of human thought in its own unbiassed, native, and profounder workings. We think that into no recorded mind has the intense feeling of the visable [*sic*] truth ever entered more deeply than into this man's. By visable truth, we mean the apprehension of the absolute condition of present things as they strike the eye of the man who fears them not, though they do their worst to him,—the man who, like Russia or the British Empire, declares himself a sovereign nature (in himself) amid the powers of heaven, hell, and earth. He may perish; but so long as he exists he insists upon treating with all Powers upon an equal basis. . . .
>
> There is the grand truth about Nathaniel Hawthorne. He says NO! in thunder; but the Devil himself cannot make him say *yes*. For all men who say *yes*, lie; and all men who say *no*,—why, they are in the happy condition of judicious, unincumbered [*sic*]

travellers in Europe; they cross the frontiers into Eternity with nothing but a carpet-bag—that is to say, the Ego. . . . What's the reason, Mr Hawthorne, that in the last stages of metaphysics a fellow always falls to *swearing* so? I could rip an hour. . . . here I have landed in Africa.[8]

The romantic, idealistic, mystical, iconoclastic, eclectic, and indivi-dualistic cast of all this, the emphasis on the search for a personal accommodation with the universe, gets close to the spirit of *Labyrinths*. Shortly before he completed the final form of *Labyrinths*, Okigbo told two interviewers about his family religion. To Marjory Whitelaw he said

I am believed to be a reincarnation of my maternal grandfather, who used to be the priest of the shrine called Ajani, where Idoto, the river goddess, is worshipped. This goddess is the earth mother, and also the mother of the whole family. My grandfather was the priest of this shrine, and when I was born I was believed to be his reincarnation, that is, I should carry on his duties. And although someone else had to perform his functions, this other person was only, as it were, a regent. And in 1958, when I started taking poetry very seriously, it was as though I had felt a sudden call to begin performing my full functions as the chief priest of Idoto.[9]

Talking to Robert Serumaga, he identified the 'regent' as his maternal uncle, and then answered a rather audacious, if diffidently asked, ques-tion about his beliefs:

SERUMAGA Perhaps this is a pertinent question: does your being a Christian, conflict in any way, in your own mind, with your other duties in this other . . .
OKIGBO Oh no, I think it is just a way of going to the same place by two different routes.[10]

That journey is spoken of variously in the Introduction to *Labyrinths* as 'a ceremony of innocence', 'something like a mass', 'an attempt to reconcile the universal opposites of life and death in a live-die propo-sition', 'psychic union with the supreme spirit that is both destructive and creative', 'man's perennial quest for fulfilment', and a journey to 'the palace of the White Goddess'. In this journey Okigbo obviously felt a spiritual affinity with some predecessors and contemporaries (Mallarmé, Rabindranath Tagore, Malcolm Cowley, García Lorca and Peter Thomas) or at any rate found in their work useful images and symbols. In the earlier publication of 'Silences: Lament of the Silent Sisters'[11] Okigbo has an epigraph from Mallarmé's dramatic poem *Les Noces d'Hérodiade: Un Mystère*. Both this poem and the eclogue that inspired Debussy, 'L'Après-midi d'un faune', provided a tone and mood, a method of composition by motifs, and an occasional phrase for Okigbo. Tagore, a skilful musician and prolific composer of songs, produced in *Gitanjali* a dialogue or duet between God and the soul. Malcolm Cowley's *Exile's Return: A Literary Odyssey of the 1920's* offered Okigbo the excitement and pity of the lost generation, the American exiles in Paris, and a spirit of literary iconoclasm and inventiveness. García Lorca was an amateur musician of great ability and a poet who sympathized with the condition of black Americans and West Indians. There are, indeed, several resemblances between him and Okigbo, for he also was diffident about the publication of his work; he was considered a mannered, obscure poet; and he died in a civil war at the age of 37 (Okigbo was 35). His poetry, which Okigbo may have encountered in the translation by Stephen Spender and J. L. Gili,[12] contains a number of images used also by Okigbo, including salt water, bells, orange blossom, music, dolphins, mushrooms and the cross. In it, sexuality and death are inextricably linked and pervade almost every poem. Peter Thomas was a lecturer in English literature at the University of Nsukka from 1960 who formed a close friendship with Okigbo when he came as Assistant Librarian. They discussed poetry, poetics, and music, and Thomas conveyed to Okigbo his belief in the White Goddess, the demanding and devouring muse of poetry as expounded by Robert Graves. It was one of Thomas's poems that gave Okigbo the title for 'Heavensgate',[13] and the pervasive image of the orangery in *Labyrinths* may have come from Thomas's poem 'Romney's Mistress'.[14]

The poetry of T. S. Eliot, particularly *Ash Wednesday* and *Four Quartets*, can also be seen as an influence. The fragmentary scenes, the fondness for evanescent sensory imagery, the musical snatches, and the sense of religious ritual often suggest Eliot, as, of course, do images of bird-song and bones, for instance. In method and imagery Ezra Pound's *Cantos* also exerted a considerable influence. J. P. Clark has pointed out the indebtedness of the second movement of 'Watermaid' (p. 11) to *Cantos* IV and CVI;[15] and there are also the motif '& the mortar is not yet dry' in 'Siren Limits' III (from *Canto* VIII), the coral image in 'Lament of the Silent Sisters' V (from *Canto* CVII), and words and phrases such as 'rockdrill' and 'the errors of the rendering'.

Allen Ginsberg's *Howl* provided a few touches, such as 'Rockland' in 'Initiations' (Rockland being the madhouse in *Howl*, III), 'catatonic pingpong' in 'Distances' IV (used more than once in section II of *Howl*), and even perhaps the Moloch reference in 'Lament of the Silent Sisters' II (from *Howl* II). Okigbo was an admirer of Ginsberg and other Beat Generation poets when he was at Nsukka.

The influence from these sources is partly a kind of spiritual affinity (Okigbo's eclecticism ignoring basic differences in his mentors provided they had something significant to say to him), partly the use of remembered or half-remembered phrases, often wrenched out of context and substantially altered in meaning. J. P. Clark pointed out very aptly, for instance, that p. 11 of 'Watermaid' takes over from Pound images like 'The bright aura and dazzle, the armpit, the lioness, the white light, the waves as escort, the crown and moonlight, the transience of the maid like "match-flare in wind's breath", the mirrors and gold crop' (*The Example of Shakespeare*, p. 56) but applies them to a 'downward' movement in place of Pound's upward revelatory movement.

The borrowed images find their own new or renewed meaning in Okigbo's work. What is more pervasive than the images borrowed from a variety of sources is the method of composition by fragments that dissolve into one another as in a dream, a method that he found in Mallarmé, Eliot, and Pound, and in impressionistic composers such as Debussy.

Using this method, he found a large part of his material not in Middle Eastern myth or Western poetry, but in his own village of Ojoto and its cult of the river-goddess, Idoto. This is how 'Heavensgate' begins. If Idoto merges into 'Anna of the panel oblongs', the watermaid-lioness, the 'Queen of the damp half light', the dancer, the Silent Sisters, or Ishtar, then that is the way of dreams and of Okigbo's structural models. But in these dissolving scenes the village and (particularly in the drum passages) West Africa are always close at hand as material. Critics who dismissed Okigbo's work as unAfrican and thoroughly perverted by Western culture had failed to read it closely.

Okigbo's Introduction provides a good commentary on the 'organically related' poems of *Labyrinths*. The note of religious worship and self-discovery is evident from the beginning. The sacrifice to Idoto, the goddess of the village stream, is undertaken by a celebrant who is about to set out on a journey. He is an Odyssean figure, but also 'a prodigal'. While Okigbo is careful in the Introduction to emphasize the mythical character of this figure, comparing him (p. xiv) with Orpheus, Gilgamesh, Aeneas, Ahab in *Moby Dick* (or does he mean Moby Dick himself?), and Eliot's Fisher King, he is also 'a poet-protagonist' whose anguished struggles reflect Okigbo's own spiritual journey. The poet is prodigal not of his poetic resources (for Okigbo is a cautious, even parsimonious, writer, reusing material rather than carelessly tossing it aside) but of life itself. It is not too extreme to say that the sense of shedding parts of himself in an inexorable progress to early death is inherent in Okigbo's work from the beginning. But he is also a prodigal returned 'to his father's house' as the biblical parable of the Prodigal Son puts it; that is, he has returned from a foreign country to his own religion and awaits poetic inspiration to celebrate its mysteries.

'The Passage' is an introit by the celebrant as he comes, stripped of all other concerns, into the presence of the goddess. Unlike Shakespeare's lark at 'heaven's gate', he does not sing. He waits, listening, and crying, in a phrase from the *De Profundis*, Psalm 130, 'out of the depths'. His meditation takes him in the second movement (p. 4) to the 'dark waters' of the primeval beginning of things, before the spirit of creation moved on them. His expectation of revelation is a confident one, for it is just before dawn (a propitious time for an Igbo to sacrifice) and 'the fire that is dreamed of' will shortly rise. (One should remember too that the

oilbean, sacred to Idoto, is a tree of life and of knowledge.) The rainbow/
boa image promises both the fructifying quality of rain (producer of the
natural life so abundantly represented in the next strophe) and the
combat of rain and sun necessary for the physical production of the
rainbow but also indicative of the destruction that can be bound up
with creativity. Nyong J. Udoeyop is perhaps right to see the fusion of
Judaeo-Christian and West African mythology in both parts of the
rainbow/boa image as being then teased out into the Christian image of
the 'tangled-wood-tale' of light in the midst of darkness and the
African image of the mother, whose death, mourned by the sunbird,
represents the atrophy of traditional religion.[16]

The third movement (p. 5) presents shadowy images of a black-clad
Christian procession to the town church. The silence of the worshippers
gives way to organ music. At the console, with its oblong panel of
draw-stops for the various ranks of pipes, is Anna, the name both of the
Virgin Mary's mother and of Okigbo's own mother. To Anna is addressed a litany, 'hear us', corresponding to the petition 'give ear' at the
end of the first movement. The ethereal organ music is fragmentary,
synaesthetically reminiscent of faded orange-leaves pressed between
the pages of a leather-bound book. The protagonist neither enters the
church nor joins the procession; he still listens, now from 'among the
windplayers', the African reed-flute players.

In 'Initiations' the protagonist enters the ritual initiations of religion.
Its three movements are meditations on obscure people who have influenced his life, and hence they require footnotes. Kepkanly (the origin
of the nickname is explained by Anozie, pp. 51–2, as a corruption of the
Igbo words for 'left, right', '*aka-ekpe, aka-nli*') initiated him into Christianity, the initiation represented imaginatively as a cross scarred like
a slave-brand on his chest. The 'pure line' of childhood innocence or
natural religion is used in cross form, thus generating planes and angles
(as in Yeats's geometrical theorizing). Again, the initiation into Christianity is represented by John the Baptist (who baptized Jesus), whose
bowl of water (salt representing sin) symbolizes the mystical washing
away of sin and, according to Okigbo, of life too. The Christian Trinity
seems to be hinted at in the 'orthocenter', the point of intersection of
the verticals drawn from the three apices of a triangle to the opposite
sides. The fourth angle (that is, the fourth right angle, from which a
four-sided figure can now be made) represents the Christian notion
of duty and obligation. Okigbo's satiric presentation of four-square
and rhomboid figures as representing those who accept the moral
duties of Christianity gives way to a further meditation on Kepkanly.
Unlike Anozie, I do not see Kepkanly as a symbol of 'the pagan god or
bleeding Christ', one who miraculously illuminates the connexion
between joy and death. He is, according to Okigbo, a 'half-serious
half-comical' creature who dies when he unexpectedly receives back-
pay. This is the state of the typical espouser of Christianity: he initiates
others into his religion but delights to the point of absurd excess in

riches. 'God's light', true spiritual illumination, shines not from him to the poet but 'between' Kepkanly and Haragin; they do not transmit it, they block it out, but are unsuccessful in preventing it reaching the poet.

Jadum, who puts the lute to his lip, is half-madman (for one does not play a lute with the mouth), half-prophet (for the lute can speak to the willing ear). His advice is prudential, to avoid danger and scandal. The smell of sex from bedrooms in Jadum's imagery is taken up in Upandru's advice to conceal one's sexual proclivities and even to censor them. His advice to the ram-like poet is 'Disarm'; the reply is that this is impossible except by plucking out, that is castration, in the words of the Igbo proverb:

> Except by rooting,
> who could pluck yam tubers from their base? (p. 9)

In between Upandru's two pieces of advice about sex is a brief discussion of poetry as prophecy and as a means to an end (logistics). The suggestion is perhaps that sex is, in the poet's view, also a means to an end, namely poetry.

Throughout these initiations into Christianity, practical behaviour, sex, and poetry there runs the motif 'the errors of the reckoning'. The poet-celebrant-traveller is modestly uncertain of whether he understands these experiences.

The four movements of 'Watermaid' present a single narrative. This is a moment, but only a moment, of illumination, not from a village explainer ('excellent if you are a village; but if not, not', as Gertrude Stein said of Ezra Pound) but from the Idoto-watermaid-lioness figure. It is illumination coming through sexual union ('man with woman'), the combative union of rain and sun again. It is a vision of the White Goddess, sexual union with whom generates poetry (in the theory of Robert Graves, as conveyed to Okigbo by Peter Thomas). But it is fleeting, leaving the poet again solitary and abandoned, though with a song ('a broken monody') to remind him of it.

Lustra (the title of Ezra Pound's 1916 volume of poetry) were in Roman times offerings for the sins of the whole people, but the first movement of Okigbo's 'Lustra' seems a personal ritual of cleansing and preparation. Imagery of the poet going to the heights for inspiration from the fountain of poetry is combined with an African sacrifice of an egg and a hen. The second movement, however, does suggest universal salvation, with its imagery of the bruised and silenced Messiah coming again and of an African sacrifice of vegetables accompanied by 'five fingers of chalk'.

The five is transmuted in the third movement into a personal 'pentagon', the shape of each frond-stem on a palm-tree trunk. In this movement the Christian reference has given way entirely to the African funeral ceremonies accompanied by 'Thundering drums and cannons', ceremonies recognizing the continuity of earthly life with the life of the spirits.

'Newcomer' consists also of three movements, following the pattern of all the previous sections, except the one that is central in position and in illuminating experience, 'Watermaid', which has four movements. We are back at the opening rite of worship, worship that fuses 'remembrance of calvary' and the animistic 'age of innocence'. The humorously coarse petition at the end of the first movement seeks preservation for his indigenous burial mound from the clinging remnants of Christian faith, with perhaps a hint drawn from Ginsberg's *Howl*, where Angel (of Sodomite ancestry) is one of the characters.

The poet is a 'newcomer' returning to the traditional religion, but the second movement introduces another newcomer, the first child of his sister-in-law, Georgette, who was married to his beloved elder brother, Pius. The biblical imagery of the cock crowing 'thrice' at St Peter's denial of his master reflects on Okigbo's similar renunciation; and there is humorous sexual play with cock and 'bulrushes' (again with a biblical reference to the infant Moses' cradle). The new birth acts, then, as a 'bridgehead' of expectancy in the third movement, leading on to 'Limits'.

If expectancy, preparation and silence are the chief motifs of 'Heavensgate', 'Limits' opens with chatter like that of the weaverbird. The tongue of the poet has been unloosed after his ritual cleansing and sexual initiation. He is quite jaunty to the goddess now, the 'Queen of the damp half light'. He impudently refers to the 'nude spear' of Léopold Sédar Senghor's Négritude ideology and to Wole Soyinka's riposte about the tiger and his tigritude (Okigbo was, of course, on Soyinka's side in this famous ideological dispute).

In section II, the poet-narrator seems to be listening to one of the sirens' songs about himself. He is a shrub overshadowed by poplars, diffident and exploratory. He needs to try on masks of the self, the various selves, and to relate them to his soul and his poetry (or voice). Then, if he is successful, soul, selves, and voice will cohere in a shrub that has been metamorphosed into 'A green cloud above the forest'.

The motif of section III is one of unreadiness, '& the mortar is not yet dry', quoted by Ezra Pound from a letter of Sigismondo Malatesta in 1449 to say that the plaster on the walls of his newly-built chapels is not dry and so Piero dei Francheschi cannot paint them. Okigbo seems to be suggesting that the world is not yet ready for his masterwork,

> Then we must sing, tongue-tied,
> Without name or audience,
> Making harmony among the branches.

What the poet may do, however, is go through the 'high-arched gate' and follow the 'little stream' to the lake, in search of 'the big white elephant'. It is an elusive creature, its whiteness akin to that of the 'white light' surrounding the watermaid-lioness and to that of the White Goddess. Like Udoeyop, and unlike Gerald Moore and Sunday Anozie,[17] I do not see it as an emblem of futile endeavour or disappointment.

At worst it is phantasmagoric and chimerical, or, as Okigbo says in the Introduction, p. xi, a 'demonic obsession', in pursuit of which the poet 'becomes disembodied or loses his second self'. Section IV has him anaesthetized by his overpowering memory of the sexuality of the 'Oblong-headed lioness' to which he willingly yields himself up. 'Oblong-headed' indicates, of course, the obsessive fanatical quality of this figure, in accordance with the geometrical imagery of 'Initiations'. She is indeed credited in the note to 'Limits' V with being responsible for the destruction of 'the poet's second self'. 'Second self' is not a term that occurs in the lines of poetry themselves, and perhaps Okigbo's prose notes should not be regarded as definitive or restrictive of the poetic meaning. The second self that gives itself up to unconsciousness at the end of 'Siren Limits' IV is not an *alter ego* so much as the second role that the poet has assumed in *Labyrinths*. He was the supplicant, quietly and expectantly preparing and waiting in 'Heavensgate'. He was the chattering active weaver bird in 'Siren Limits', developing his poetry and coming to a feverish crisis in the pursuit of the white elephant and the encounter with the lioness, two images for the destruction of this role.

'Fragments out of the Deluge' begins with an empty sarcophagus. The hero of the poem is metamorphosed into a branch of fennel, into 'the radiance of a king', into Gilgamesh and his 'second self', Enkidu, and, by implication from sections VI and VII, into the despised, misunderstood, and risen Christ. These are 'the limits of a dream' while the human poet part of the hero lies anaesthetized. Sections VI and VII deal with the life, message and reception of Christ, and their presentation by such devoted, if misguided, disciples as Father Flannagan and the drowned nuns of Hopkins's poem. Christ is presented as offering 'seed wrapped in wonders', that is, the message of salvation expressed through miracles. His hearers interpret it, however, in the jargon of twentieth-century positivist philosophy or sociology as 'a truth-value system'. They ask him to achieve political reform: 'do a rock-drill'. Later, when Christianity becomes a political force, its faith is used for political ends by the 'mongrel breeds' of Europe.

Section VII reverts to the resurrection of Christ, perhaps as viewed through the 'frame of iron' of the doctrinaire Christian creeds. Like a scavenger, Christ eats the lion of death, trampling within its body. There may be overtones here of 'A living dog is better than a dead lion' (*Ecclesiastes* 9:4) and of the traditional 'harrowing of hell' or the triumph over sin and death by Christ. In any case, Okigbo's point is that the details do not matter: the direction of the kite's circling over the burning market is immaterial. Life has triumphed over death: 'lilies' have grown from the 'rosebeds' of death.

The pilgrims who come to the cross come with 'burnt-out tapers', the appropriate symbol for the death of an excommunicate.[18] They have apparently misunderstood the message of salvation, for they seek the 'keyword' in 'stone', an image of hardness of heart or spiritual obduracy, akin to the earlier 'frame' and 'mould' of 'iron'. The message they receive, inevitably a perverted one, is to set fire to the grasses in existence already, to destroy, in other words, existing religion that nourishes the people.

The Christian legions who seek to do this are warned of in section VIII by the sunbird; dwelling among the oilbeans (the spiritual life of African religion) he announces them as 'A fleet of eagles'. In section IX the warning is taken up by the prophetic blind dog and by Emma, the nurse. The coming dawn, a false one no doubt, should not be welcomed:

> Give him no chair, they say,
> The dawn's charioteer . . .

The warnings are, however, in vain. The eagles of Christianity arrive in section X, with a motif drawn from a Scottish folk-rhyme:

> Malisons, malisons mair than ten,
> That herry the Ladie o' Heeven's hen;
> The robin and the wren
> Are God's bird and hen.[19]

But the incantatory rhyme is inefficacious. The eagles kill the sacred African bird, even when he takes refuge at the top of the bombax tree (whose masses of beautiful silky fibres displayed from the bursting seed-pods form another, if barely hinted at, symbol of African religion). They kill the tortoise and the python, twin-gods of the forest, like the twin-god of the Sumerian underworld, Irkalla, who combined the male and the female. Social unity and harmony and proper sexual union between male and female are thus destroyed.

These gods lie without song or long-drum in section XI, gathering mould. Neglected, they 'grow out' of the recollection and observance of the people. But the Sunbird, like Christ earlier in 'Limits', is resurrected, at least in dream or at least as a 'shadow' or spirit. His song now is of another disaster, not the coming of Christianity this time, but civil war. Picasso's *Guernica*, a vision of the Spanish Civil War, does in fact contain a bird singing with upraised head. The slits of his tongue (like the slits of a talking drum) are represented, says Okigbo, by an artist, stilling the song but making it imperishable with his glue. That is the function of the artist: to warn, to depict, to make permanent. In Nigerian terms, the destruction due to Christianity is balanced or cancelled out by the destruction due to civil war. This was first published in 1962; its prophetic warning, however, went unheeded.

'Silences' takes up the question of how the poet is to find the appropriate words for his song. The imagery is of drowning and destruction, and one is tempted to say 'yes' to a settled religious belief, which would act as 'compass or cross' or 'an anchorage'. Or, as it is put in section II of 'Lament of the Silent Sisters', one is tempted, indeed one begins, 'To cry to the mushroom of the sky'. In section III, however, the people who are 'hollow' in lacking religious belief (as in Eliot's *The Hollow*

Men) find that they have with them 'an urn of native earth', providing some comfort at any rate. Okigbo is using phrases from a passage in Malcolm Cowley's *Exile's Return*:

> the country of our childhood survives, if only in our minds, and retains our loyalty even when casting us into exile; we carry its image from city to city as our most essential baggage:
> Wanderers outside the gates, in hollow
> landscapes without memory, we carry
> each of us an urn of native soil,
> of not impalpable dust a double handful
> anciently gathered . . .[20]

In section IV, the responsory between Crier and Chorus becomes more frenetic, as the Silent Sisters hurl single lines back and forth between them, expressing hopeful signs, fear, resolution, and bewilderment in a series of proverbial sayings based on the ever-changing face of the sea. In almost every case, the reply by the Chorus is less hopeful and more cynical than the line by the Crier. This pattern is continued in section V, which, according to Okigbo's Introduction, begins with an almost recognizable tableau of Obafemi Awolowo betrayed by his party deputy and Patrice Lumumba murdered. The surface images indicate little of this, however, except for the image of Judas. There are fragments of gothic window detail: 'Pointed arches', 'Pieces in the form of a pear', and almost overpowering religious music: 'painted harmonies From the mushroom of the sky'. The pressure to conform to religious faith is almost overwhelming: 'And how does one say NO in thunder?' The answer comes in the final strophe, using images from the short story of S. Rajaratnam, 'At Eight-fifteen in the Morning', as Okigbo noted in the original publication in *Transition*. That answer involves suspending one's quest for certainties, dwelling among memories, cultivating the senses and silence.

Just as 'Lament of the Silent Sisters' drew on one common form of African poetry, with its crier and chorus, so 'Lament of the Drums' opens with an invocation drawn from the invocations of Ashanti drummers.[21] As Okigbo points out in the Introduction, the drums are 'the spirits of the ancestors, the dead', and their invocation is to the elements of which they are made: cedar for the body, antelope hide for skins, cane for tendons. There is also a prayer that war, in the images of tanks, iron, and detonators, should not intrude.

Section II is the message of the drums, fearful that their message will be one of blood, fearful that they will be silenced, sent into Babylonish captivity, or martyred like the betrayed Christ. The incense of religious observance and poetic inspiration and the 'high buskin' of Athenian tragedy mingle in 'a web of voices all rent by javelins'. But the call to celebrate Nigeria (symbolized by elephants, used so often as a national emblem) remains, as a mystic sevenfold call.

Section III evokes the death of Palinurus, betrayed and murdered, left unburied, and hence unable to pass across the Stygian lake. The comparison in Okigbo's mind (but only barely in the poetry) is with the betrayed Chief Awolowo and with his son killed in a car accident. Palinurus is 'A half-forgotten name', but worthy of being remembered by the sea and by the fishermen on the water. This middle section of 'Lament of the Drums' is the only one in which drums do not occur. It is instead taken up with a lament for Palinurus in the context of the sea into which he fell and which pervades so much of the whole poem as an image of multifariousness in life and poetry. It has its share of invective against the politicians, the 'Masks and beggar-masks', the 'Broken tin-gods' without vision, who have imprisoned Awolowo. And the last strophe seems to combine a plea for the 'naked' Awolowo grieving over his dead child, and for the unburied Palinurus.

Section IV returns to the drums. They are still fearful of being silenced and of being ineffective: a mere 'rococo Choir of insects'. The expression of ineffectiveness, impotence, or irrelevance to present need takes on yet another image in the poem. But the religious and poetic call that ended sections I and II ends this section also, as the drums lead into another formal lament, this time the Babylonian lament of Ishtar for the cyclically regenerating god Tammuz. It is a lament for the crops, the people, and the Great River (here no doubt to be identified with the Niger and with Nigeria herself).

Since 'Siren Limits' IV, the protagonist of the poem has been in suspense on a horizontal stone sarcophagus, while dreams and laments and a survey of the state of Nigerian politics have ensued. Now at the beginning of 'Distances' he returns to the poem and, rather suddenly, achieves a spiritual home-coming, a return as a 'phantom', not as 'flesh'. By the end of 'Distances', after witnessing the bloody rites of Death and then passing through a curious archway, the protagonist is reunited with the watermaid and enters her bridal chamber. 'Distances' is a rather desperate attempt to pull the poem together by many echoes of the previous parts. It is, however, an attempt that, by the nature of the previous context, can have only limited success. Okigbo has anticipated his conclusion already, and the sequence of tableaux in 'Distances', even union with the watermaid, can hardly alter or give greater emotional expression to the solution he has already adumbrated: a turning inward to the self for sustenance and enlightenment. There is, therefore, something factitious about 'Distances'; many of the details seem contrived and far from inevitable.

In section I a voice calls him from a 'white chamber', with an accompaniment of laughter that in T. S. Eliot would indicate spiritual insecurity. Something of the factitiousness of 'Distances' can be sensed in the desperate description of the 'white chamber' as an 'anti-hill'. In section II, the poet seems not to be 'chief acolyte' but only a re-anaesthetized observer of the horrific rites of the white chamber of Death. He is back in the state of being disembodied, without even any sense of space, time, or memory, a similar condition to the end of 'Siren Limits'

IV. He watches the indiscriminate, off-hand way in which Death murders her own devotees and attendants. Suddenly animate again in section III, he is part of a line of pilgrims representing, it would seem, all the people of Nigeria, bound for destruction at 'Shibboleth', where the biblical Ephraimites were destroyed by a word out of their own mouth. 'From Dan to Beersheba' was a proverbial Judaic expression for 'from the extreme north of the country to the extreme south', or 'from one end of the country to the other'. Here there are 'prophets martyrs lunatics' as well as 'dantini',[22] 'dilettanti', 'vendors princes' and 'negritude Politicians'; there is a clearing, a garden, and a tall wood; a landscape out of Dante or T. S. Eliot.

Section IV introduces a geometrically overlaid archway, encumbered with mystic forms. Beyond it is 'an immense crucifix'. We are in fact going through or by all the symbols of the poem, symbols that have for the most part been discredited. The language remains forced: 'the catatonic pingpong of the evanescent halo' wrenches Ginsberg and vapid ninetyish religiosity together; the strophe on 'form' is like a bad parody of Tagore. Section V continues progress past further re-encountered symbols, some of them now altered however. The stone is now 'molten'; the crucifix scar on the breast is now 'two swords'.

The atmosphere of section VI is even more excited, and the occasional rhyme begun in section III is continued. The poet is called into the cavern of the watermaid, who reveals to him her incorporation of much of the rest of the imagery of the poem: blood (of sacrifice, anguish, and death), branches (of reincarnation and poetry), breath (the individual voice of the poet). It is a 'chaste' instant, but one redolent, as is so much of the whole poem, with sex. The orangery, the stream of Idoto, and the drum are among the final images. But the last line emphasizes the solitary self-reliance that is necessary: 'I am the sole witness of my homecoming'.

One reason why 'Distances' is unsatisfactory, and why, therefore, the whole sequence of *Labyrinths* must remain unsatisfactory, is that it does not resolve the problem of dealing both with the nation and the individual. The individual alone has the final vision, but he has had to pass through the chamber of death and see indiscriminate slaughter from which he himself was immune. The band of pilgrims is 'bound for Shibboleth', but the poet apparently detaches himself from them. What happens to the rest of the pilgrims? They are left scrambling beyond the mystic archway, amid incoherent proverbial fragments.

What has happened, I think, is that in the course of writing the separate sequences that make up *Labyrinths* Okigbo tried, perhaps in response to hostile criticism, of which he encountered a good deal, to turn his poem from a highly personal quest into one that reflected his opinions about the nation. He was, after all, writing in a period when African writers faced highly emotional demands that they should expose and interpret the political meaning of their own countries and of the whole of Africa. Okigbo, having begun his major work, could not, despite massive revisions, make the personal and the national meanings cohere. Nor, indeed, could he quite make the religious and the poetic meanings of his myth cohere.

These constraints did not apply to the poems he wrote after the first Nigerian military coup of January 1966 and the first massacre of Igbos in the following May. These poems, published originally under the title 'Poems Prophesying War: Path of Thunder' in *Black Orpheus* 2 No. 1 (February 1968), 5–11, appeared over twelve months after Okigbo's death in battle. They presumably would have been linked into some kind of sequence if he had lived. They all predate the outbreak of the civil war between Federal Nigeria and Biafra, the last being probably written in May 1966, shortly after the massacre of Igbos.

'Thunder Can Break' welcomes the 15 January coup, which removed Sir Abubakar Tafawa Balewa, the Sardauna of Sokoto, and Chief Akintola, with almost unalloyed delight. The story of what has happened is still unclear to Okigbo. But he is certain that a miracle, made, alas, with iron, but still a miracle, has been wrought, and he would like the 'Faces and hands and feet' behind it to be revealed. 'Obduracy, the disease of elephants', that is, the harsh unyielding attitude of the former political régime, has been broken by the thunder of a military coup.

'Elegy of the Wind' looks beyond the coup to the poet's interpretation of its meaning in his own life and the life of humanity. He prays that he may follow on the wind of song to the gates of the white light of truth and turn them from iron, repelling questers, into the succulent, 'tremulous' leaves of cotyledons. He speaks as a mature, even ageing, man, who observes a new generation with their motorbikes and their disrespect for the 'branch' of their elders. Yet he also retains the fear of the child. The blood-letting is like circumcision; it must be followed by healing. His 'chant', already escaped from him, must inevitably be of the inextricable mingling of good and evil, air and earth, heaven and hell, as symbolized by the feathered serpent.

'Come Thunder' is neither a celebration nor an elegy; it is a direct warning that the coup has not been the last of death-dealing. 'The death sentence lies in ambush along the corridors of power'; an immense volcanic upheaval threatens to erupt over the whole continent: 'The last lighted torch of the century', for it was the last continent to gain political freedom.

'Hurrah for Thunder' is in two parts. The first is a jaunty, impish jig, delighting in the coup and using the sarcastic exaggeration of some of the Yoruba *oriki* to describe the fall of the seemingly impregnable elephant, the archetypal old politician, such as the Sardauna of Sokoto. The second looks beyond the coup, and uses the style of Igbo proverbs to refer to the dangers of seeking spoils from the coup and following in the wake of the discredited politicians by making impossible promises.

'Elegy for Slit-drum' and 'Elegy for Alto' are companion pieces, one in imitation of the chief African instrument, the other in imitation of one of the chief instruments of the jazz orchestra (the alto saxophone).

Both have Okigbo as poet ('mythmaker') and citizen within them. The first is a little more hopeful than the second, which is full of bleak despair. But even in 'Elegy for Slit-drum' the imagery is of melancholy import. 'One tongue full of fire/one tongue full of stone' balances enthusiasm for a new political spirit against the bleak political conservatism of the old order. The 'panther' of the coup has delivered only 'a hare' in the administration of General Aguiyi-Ironsi. A little humour (quite often near the surface of many of Okigbo's poems) intrudes with the cabinet of government revived as a metaphor through its 'timbers'. The 'elephant' of the old order has been supplanted by the 'mortars' of the new military régime, which will presumably be more independent of British imperialism (Sir Abubakar Tafawa Balewa having been a close friend of the British Prime Minister, Harold Wilson). But Okigbo is fearful of reprisals, of old scores that may yet be settled, so the motif throughout is 'Condolences' and he ends with advice to forget the details of the coup and be merciful.

In 'Elegy for Alto', Okigbo is the 'horn' that is said to 'paw the air howling goodbye'; he is the sacrificial ram (no longer a 'he-goat on heat') into which the sword will be plunged. This is, then, an elegy for himself, in advance of his own death. The obsession with his own death that has haunted so much of his poetry is here openly expressed. The political prospects are dismaying: the eagles presage an 'iron dawn'. Still, the poet has a 'glimpse of a dream', but he, the former Sunbird, is in a cave with 'mortally wounded birds'. Ahead lies only a cyclical repetition of national self-destruction, with one new star succeeding another.

These are poems with little to obstruct the reader in the way of recondite imagery. They are directly related in statement, imagery, and lament to the situation of 1966. Many readers found this a refreshing change and hailed his last poems as his best. Even Chinua Achebe thinks that this opinion

> has substantial merit ... there is that undeniable fire in his last poems which was something new. It was as though the goddess he sought in his poetic journey through so many alien landscapes and ultimately found at home had given him this new thunder. Unfortunately when he was killed in 1967 he left us only that little, tantalising hint of the new self he had found.[23]

It is certainly true that he had left behind him the languid *fin-de-siècle* air of his early poetry. He had not, however, emancipated himself from the musical motif as the main constructional element, so that even his last poems tend to lack emotional or intellectual shape. They are, of course, unrevised, and it may be that Okigbo would have wanted to reconstruct them, to remove some of the naïve applause-winning slogans, and to make the changes of tone and mood less arbitrary.

Okigbo achieved notoriety in his own lifetime for his dedication to his art, his intolerance of Négritude and its literary programme, and his obscurity. That reputation was gradually overcome by the effect of his

immense personal influence on younger writers such as Okogbule Won-
odi and Pol Ndu and ultimately by the tragic circumstances of his death
in battle (unburied like Palinurus) and the posthumous publication of
Path of Thunder. But at his death he had not solved either his own
intellectual problems or the problems of poetry-making; though a tragic
figure, he is not necessarily a good model for poetry.

Notes to Chapter 2

1. See 1962 interview with Lewis Nkosi in *African Writers Talking: A
   Collection of Interviews*, ed. Dennis Duerden and Cosmo Pieterse (London: Heinemann Educational Books, 1972), pp. 134–8.
2. Author of the most substantial critical treatment of Okigbo, *Christopher
   Okigbo: Creative Rhetoric* (London: Evans Brothers, 1972). Anozie's discussions of Okigbo's poems are often based on versions earlier than the
   final versions authorized by Okigbo, that is, those in *Labyrinths* (London:
   Heinemann Educational Books, in association with Ibadan: Mbari Publications, 1971). All my discussions are based on these final versions.
3. *Black Orpheus* No. 11 (1962), 5–9. The 'Four Canzones' are 'Song of the
   Forest' (p. 5; dated 'Lagos, 1957'), 'Debtors' Lane' (p. 6; dated 'Fiditi,
   1959'), 'Lament of the Flutes' (p. 7; dated 'Ojoto, 1960'), and 'Lament of
   the Lavender Mist' (pp. 8–9; dated 'Nsukka, 1961').
4. *The Horn* 3, No. 2 (1959), 6–7; *The Horn* also published 'On the New
   Year' in vol. 3, No. 4. See W. H. Stevenson, '*The Horn*: What It Was and
   What It Did', *Research in African Literatures* 6, No. 1 (Spring 1975), 5–
   31; reprinted in *Critical Perspectives on Nigerian Literatures*, ed. Bernth
   Lindfors (London: Heinemann Educational Books, 1979 [Washington,
   D.C.: Three Continents Press, 1976]), pp. 209–35. See also Joseph C.
   Anafulu, 'Christopher Okigbo: 1932–1967: A Bio-Bibliography', *Research
   in African Literatures* 9, No. 1 (Spring 1978), 65–78; the numerals given
   in the details of publication should, however, be treated with caution.
5. 'Dance of the Painted Maidens' deserves republication from its obscurity
   in the souvenir programme for the festival of poetry held at the Royal
   Court Theatre, London, during the Commonwealth Arts Festival 1965:
   Verse and Voice: A Festival of (Commonwealth) Poetry, ed. Douglas Clev-
   erdon (London: The Poetry Book Society, 1965), pp. 63–5. 'Lament of
   the Masks' is more readily available in *W. B. Yeats: 1865–1965: Centenary
   Essays on the Art of W. B. Yeats*, ed. D. E. S. Maxwell and S. B. Bushrui
   (Ibadan: Ibadan University Press, 1965), pp. xiii–xv. On the sources of
   'Lament of the Masks' see also Donatus I. Nwoga, 'Plagiarism and Authentic Creativity in West Africa', *Research in African Literatures* 6, No.
   1 (Spring 1975), 32–39; reprinted in *Critical Perspectives on Nigerian
   Literatures*, pp. 155–63.
6. *African Writers Talking*, p. 138. Okigbo said almost the same thing in his
   response to a questionnaire after A Conference of African Writers of
   English Expression, held at Makerere in 1962. Okigbo's response is
   printed in *Transition* No. 5 (July/August 1962), 12. The word 'watery',
   with its rather unsuitable overtones, also stands at the beginning of
   'Heavensgate.'
7. Anozie, pp. 145–6, points out the resemblances between an earlier form of
   'Lament of the Drums', III, and 'Palinuro insomne' by the Argentinian

poet, Silvina Ocampo. 'Palinuro insomne' is reprinted in a book Okigbo obviously knew well: J. M. Cohen, ed., *The Penguin Book of Spanish Verse* (Harmondsworth: Penguin, 1956), pp. 432–3.

8. ?16 ?April 1851, *The Letters of Herman Melville*, ed. Merrell R. Davis and William H. Gilman (New Haven: Yale University Press, 1960), p. 124.

9. Marjory Whitelaw, 'Interview with Christopher Okigbo, 1965', *Journal of Commonwealth Literature* No. 9 (July 1970), 28–37 (p. 36).

10. *African Writers Talking*, p. 145.

11. *Transition* No. 8 (March 1963), 13–16.

12. First published as F. García Lorca, *Poems*, translated Stephen Spender and J. L. Gili (London: Dolphin Book Co., 1939).

13. See Peter Thomas, 'Great Plenty to Come: A Personal Reminiscence of the First Generation of Nsukka Poets', *The Muse* (Nsukka) No. 4 (May 1972), 5–8; and Hezzy Maduakor, 'Peter Thomas and the Development of Modern Nigerian Poetry', *Research in African Literatures* 11, No. 1 (1980), 84–99. A less influential rôle is accorded to Thomas by Michael Echeruo in an interview recorded in *Dem Say: Interviews with Eight Nigerian Writers*, ed. Bernth Lindfors (Austin: Occasional Publication of the African and Afro-American Studies and Research Center, The University of Texas at Austin, 1974), pp. 5–15. For Thomas's own account of his influence at Nsukka see his 'Shadows of Prophecy', *Journal of Modern African Studies* 11, No. 2 (1973), 339–45.

14. See Peter Thomas, *Poems from Nigeria* (New York: Vantage Press, 1967), pp. 64–5.

15. 'Themes of African Poetry of English Expression', in his *The Example of Shakespeare* (London: Longman, 1970), p. 56.

16. Nyong J. Udoeyop, *Three Nigerian Poets: A Critical Study of the Poetry of Soyinka, Clark and Okigbo* (Ibadan: Ibadan University Press, 1973), pp. 103–4.

17. See Udoeyop, p. 116, n.

18. See Dante, *Purgatorio 3*, 132 for 'a lume spento' (with tapers quenched), the title used by Pound for one of his early volumes of verse. Dante is describing the funeral procession of Manfredi.

19. Robert Dick Duncan, 'Rhymes Relating to Birds', *The Zoologist* 2 (1844), 556–60 (p. 557). A variant of this stanza is given (p. 115) in 'The Laverock's [i.e., skylark's] Song' in William Cadenhead, *Flights of Fancy and Lays of Bon-Accord* (Aberdeen, 1853), pp. 114–16.

20. *Exile's Return: A Literary Odyssey of the 1920's*, 2nd ed. (New York: Viking Press, 1951), p. 14.

21. See Donatus I. Nwoga, 'Plagiarism and Authentic Creativity in West Africa', pp. 32–9 (pp. 155–63). Nwoga refers to the Ashanti texts in R. S. Rattray, *Ashanti* (Oxford: Clarendon Press, 1923; reprinted 1969), pp. 278–80, and J. H. Kwabena Nketia, *Our Drums and Drummers* (Accra: Ghana Publishing Corporation, 1968), p. 42.

22. In Italian, *dantini* would be miniature editions of *The Divine Comedy*. This seems hardly probable as a meaning, in spite of the fact that 'Distances' does bear some resemblance to scenes in Dante's work. Okigbo might just possibly have meant 'dantes', in the Renaissance sense of undefined African beasts.

23. 'Africa and her Writers' in his *Morning Yet on Creation Day: Essays* (London: Heinemann Educational Books, 1975), p. 29.

3 Lenrie Peters

▼▼▼▼▼▼▼▼▼▼▼▼▼▼▼▼▼▼▼▼▼▼▼▼▼▼▼

If Okigbo, despite his occasional obscurity, is basically a musical and instinctive poet rather than an intellectual one, Lenrie Peters is the reverse. His poetry proceeds from and is conducted by the intellect, though on his own evidence it emerges piecemeal rather than fully formed and may even seem to him like a refuge from serious, disciplined, scientifically directed thought. In a self-fascinated way, he writes very frequently of the process of composition. The last of the thirty-two poems in his first volume, for instance, is 'Turning the pages of my diary slowly'.[1] In it he speaks of coming across 'entries of bare folly', 'scattered references', ' "to be developed" signs', 'unwholesome sentences', and 'ill-developed rhymes'. This evidence of sleepless nights, this random jotting preparatory to the formation of a poem, he considers to be instinctual not rational; he says it is the product of

> The many evenings when I could not think
> But sat enjoying my pulse till daybreak.

He even jocularly suggests at the end that it may be evidence of mental regression, as if a 'recessive mutation' were to turn the mammal back into a reptile. It is also an activity that enables him to speculate on the future. If he looks at 'tomorrow's page' it

> Shows the shimmering wrinkles of age
> And the trenched island of horror.

In his latest volume, one of the recent poems, 'On this public day of rest'[2] is also about writing poetry. On a public holiday he sits at his desk

> trying to string words together
> Had I not assumed this burden,
> I might be walking on the cliffs, or reading
> rather than invoke the muse
> who perhaps has deserted me
> like Rosemary and the rest.

But unlike Rosemary (to whom he had dedicated *Poems*) 'and the rest', the muse is inescapable. At inconvenient moments in a busy life

> she throws you the hint of an idea
> which when you are composed, has gone.

The muse's notion of poetry is that it is 'the search for the silvery vein of truth', but the poet admits that he playfully sometimes serves up 'a plateful of deceit'.

Though a medical doctor himself (a specialist surgeon), Peters is wary of the encroachment of science, technology, and management on everyday life and often speaks disparagingly of the scientist, technocrat, entrepreneur, and politician. In 'Lost Friends' (*Satellites* 39) he finds that former companions are now 'imprisoned In dark suits and air-conditioned offices' and 'have no time for dreamers', as he characterizes himself. In 'The room is ten foot square' (*Satellites* 43) the protagonist tells an English committee interviewing candidates for a hospital surgical post that he is 'a writer', causing consternation and embarrassment.

Peters obviously sees the writer's self-imposed but inescapable task as an isolating, even alienating one. In 'On this public day of rest' he speaks of failing to give lifts to schoolchildren in his car because 'All seats are taken by the jealous muse'. He also sees the poet's mission as a very serious pursuit of truth. In the opening poem of *Satellites*, 'Skyflood of locusts' (*Satellites* 1; *Selected Poetry* 1), he depicts the poet as holding the light of truth 'to fight against the night'. That truth is not intellectual truth, but 'Ecstasy and passion', which will beat a way through the 'winged canopy of locusts' that represents the general immoral direction of the world. In an early poem salvaged from *Poems* for his third volume, *Katchikali*, Peters establishes mind and senses as occupying compass directions opposite to each other. The poem opens with the statement

The mind
Is like the desert winds
Ploughing the empty spaces
Listless, fastidiously laying down the dust.[3]

The senses meanwhile are upon 'the ageless shore', where they are 'forever shipwrecked on the tides of passion'. But by themselves they are 'barren'; they need the mind as much as the mind needs them. When the mind arrives it will find that its intellectual quest is satisfied only by 'the sum total of existence', that is, mind and senses united, which in itself provides 'the explanation and the vision'.

Despite this emphasis on the neglected status of the senses, Peters himself is one of the most intellectual of African poets. I do not mean that his senses, his image-making and musical faculties, for instance, do not operate imaginatively in his poetry; I mean that his poetry proceeds by ideas rather than by sensory sequence. The ideas dictate the images and the structure; the images are kept under control rather than creating the outline of the poem. This is not perhaps what we would expect from a poet who states that the mind is too dominant, but it is what we would expect from the *persona* he presents in many poems. In 'We have lived as if in vacuum cylinders' (*Katchikali* 12) the protagonist writes of his own need for intellectually stimulating debate and berates the woman he has lived with 'for more than ten years' for being unwilling or unable to provide it. He wants to talk about and be part of 'Civilization' which, he says, 'is not the Gorgon's head, nor has truth been flogged to rags'. He wants them together to 'discover life in the great commerce of ideas', but the woman is silent or at best sourly refers to their difference in skin colour: 'I don't mind your being black.'

A considerable number of Peters's poems discuss matters that in substance and style bear a marked resemblance to articles in serious weekly periodicals, the *New Statesman* or *The Listener*, for instance, to take British examples. It is a feature of his verse that grew in middle career. *Poems* has only one clear example, 'If I was asked' (p. 38; *Satellites* 23), a discussion of space exploration in terms of the metaphysical and psychological questions it raises. The tone is one of serious concern that drifts into jaunty gestures of levity because the poet is uneasy and troubled at not knowing the real answers: this kind of embarrassed and worried smile is characteristic of Peters. He finds space travel a distasteful irrelevance, incapable of offering any real answers to his 'innate discontent'. He confesses himself a 'non-progressive element' in society in relation to technical marvels, but one fundamentally concerned with the mysterious workings of the world, standing, as he puts it in a surgical metaphor in another poem, 'Mine is the silent face' (*Satellites* 5; *Selected Poetry* 4), 'at the cutting chaotic edge of things'.

Satellites has more examples of this poetic leader-writing. 'Yevtushenko disdains' (26; *Selected Poetry* 19) discusses external pressures on the writer to conform; 'On the Death of Winston S. Churchill' (31) is a memorial elegy; 'The panic of growing older' (32; *Selected Poetry* 22) is a light-hearted meditation on giving in to the world's expectations; 'They dance wildly' (37) comments on youthful hedonism and the search for meaning; 'Remember they say the dead' (41) is a Remembrance Day meditation; and 'On Exploding the Chinese Bomb' (48) discusses the horror and hatred of destructive armaments.

Katchikali has as its second poem a discussion of the Soviet response to the Chinese nuclear bomb, 'Yesterday they signed a document in Moscow'; 'They have stood waiting' (13) is a generalized meditation on waiting; 'Two centuries from now' (14; *Selected Poetry* 36) is another light-hearted look at the serious effects of creeping technology; 'The Spectator' (17) comments on involvement and non-involvement; 'The English summer brooks no delay' (18) finds English behaviour rather shameless and embarrassing; 'Does death so delude us' (20) is one of many meditations on death; 'I hear weeping in my dreams' (35) takes up again the question of 'the savagery of war'; 'Vain clarion youth' (37) reverts to the hedonism of youth and, very significantly in view of Peters's general attitude, rejects as superficial its 'riotous tremor of sense'.

The point of view expressed in 'Vain clarion youth' is not an aberration. At this stage of his career, Peters several times expresses disapproval of the heart uncontrolled by the head. Poem 43 is another of his meditations on ageing and it rejects the dictates of 'desire', the sort of unheeding reckless surrender to sensation that finds 'the bright-eyed

youth in his sports electric chair'. When in the final stanza he says
'Reason can be winged' I take it that the primary meaning is 'shot
down', as a sportsman is said to 'wing' a bird. The commonest assault
on reason comes from love and marriage (a subject on which Peters is
rather disenchanted at this stage):

> love is the worst of all
> heart without head,
> even marriage,
> confound the notion,
> is something of self annihilation

It will be noticed that many of these poems of opinion were rejected
by Peters from his *Selected Poetry*. They represent, in fact, a way of
writing poems that he has largely grown out of. The 'New Poems' in
Selected Poetry bear hardly a trace of this style. In its place there
developed a more monitory and celebratory style for the very large
number of poems concerned with the present state of Africa.

Poems on this subject occur right through Peters's career, many of
them being written in the 'leader-writer' style, but they change as the
circumstances change from immediate post-Independence (The Gambia, Peters's home country, became independent in 1965) to over a
decade later; and they change to a more insistent, more hortatory note
as they come to dominate all other material in *Selected Poetry*. In the
first volume, *Poems*, there is a degree of naïvety in some of the African
poems. The prefatory poem begins with the exhortation:

> Open the gates
> To East and West
> Bring in all
> That's good and best (p. 5; *Satellites* 15)

'We have come home' (pp. 8–9; *Satellites* 16; *Selected Poetry* 13), a
poem about his return to The Gambia after several years of study in
England, opens with penetrating observations about the personal cost
of being away and about what he believes to be appropriate political
attitudes shortly after independence:

> But it is not the time
> To lay wreaths
> For yesterday's crimes.
> Night threatens
> Time dissolves
> And there is no acquaintance
> With tomorrow.

After that, however, it succumbs to the Romanticism of Négritude.
Drums, forest, the dawn, the beaches, and the sea lead up to the stirring
slogan at the end as Peters appeals to

That spirit which asks no favour
of the world
But to have dignity.

'One long jump' (pp. 23–4; *Satellites* 25) is about primal Africa, first
love, and the innocence of youth. All are now irrecoverably in the past,
'lost for good' after 'One long jump' beyond which there is 'no progres-
sion'. It is the finest of the early poems about Africa. 'Where are the
banners now' (p. 42; *Satellites* 50) is a quizzical comment on the
apparent loss of vision after the Independence celebrations have ended.

In *Satellites* two further poems take up the question of Africa's
purpose and destination. 'Messianic conveyances' (22), with a measure
of serious jocularity, suggests that Christ's message would find a response in Africa. Having been rejected by the West, he is 'contemp-
tuously sold' to Africa. Peters suggests that Africa will accept him, 'Not
as an intermediary to God or truth', for 'We do not befriend Mortal or
spiritual Dictators', but for 'the glory of your message', which is summarized as 'Thought before action; others before self'. It is more a
Peters formulation than a Christian one. 'In the beginning' (45) is a
much longer and much more political poem. It reviews the movement
to Independence from Tanzania to The Gambia, the movement for
Pan-African Unity, the OAU, foreign intervention, and UDI by comparison with the reality of Independence. It is a vigorous poem, with
inset dialogue in stripped, demotic language used to represent typical
scenes. Its anger and disillusion are a foretaste of the long sequence of
similar poems in the 1970s.

Katchikali continues the vein of poems about Africa. 'Come let us
listen together' (3; *Selected Poetry* 30) is a celebratory poem about The
Gambia, symbolized by its river. Most of it is descriptive and non-
political, but in the second last stanza Peters refers to the introduction
of slavery and to the country's 'need of help', presumably economic and
technical. At the end he takes up the earlier tourist-brochure strain
with an injunction 'go and see'. (A few years later The Gambia experienced something of a tourist boom after Alex Haley's *Roots* directed
attention to the Manding and their exodus as slaves to America. In
'Some think the past' (*Selected Poetry* 76), Peters is rather sceptical,
even cynical, about Haley's understanding, motive, and achievement;
and in 'Juffure, your years of violence return' (*Selected Poetry* 78) he
sees corruption and extinction for the village from which Kunta Kinte,
Haley's supposed ancestor, came.) 'Come let us listen together' is a
poem in the same mode as 'The city lies bemused' (*Satellites* 10; *Selected
Poetry* 8), another descriptive, celebratory, nostalgic and rather
Négritude-inspired piece. A more original treatment of a Négritude
theme is 'Your eyes are two faces' (5; *Selected Poetry* 32). As he looks
into the eyes of Africa he sees two faces, one of sensuality, one of
indolence (symbolized by driftwood, snails and anemones). Neither, he
thinks, will save the world, and he exhorts Africa to be ready for change.

'There will be time for homecoming' (*Katchikali* 42) and 'Plea to Mobutu' (45) were both dropped from *Selected Poetry*. 'There will be time' looks forward to the complete removal of Western influence. 'Plea to Mobutu' is an occasional poem advising President Mobutu of the Congo Republic (Kinshasa) not to execute Moise Tshombe, the leader of the secessionist revolt in Katanga. It was presumably written in 1967 when it seemed that Tshombe would be extradited from Algeria and the death sentence passed on him *in absentia* carried out.

Two of the most important African poems from this volume are 'You talk to me of "self"' and 'It is time for reckoning Africa' (63 and 64; *Selected Poetry* 54 and 55). They are urgent, irritated, almost exasperated poems in an insistent three-beat four-line stanza. 'You talk to me of "self"' is directed against the glamour of Senghor's Négritude and Nkrumah's doctrine of the 'African personality'. Peters holds up by contrast an image of an African village, using terms such as 'squalor', 'degradation', and 'ignorance'. This harsh language is carried over into the next poem, but here directed against the African metropolis and its government of 'disorder', 'incompetence', venality, dishonesty, and cruelty; and its infrastructure of chieftains ('"Maudors"') and holy men ('Marabus'). Like the previous poem it is addressed directly to Africa as an accusation, but in this poem Peters goes on to question what will happen, and to exhort Africa to remedial action now:

> Africa
> this is the lost time
> and future time . . .

As in other poems, he discounts reliance on outside aid as a solution: the opening of the poem dismisses such escapes: 'never mind New York, America—it's ours'. It is a vehement and patriotically African poem, despite the limp ending about taking

> . . . the straight path
> from world to better world
> branded across the sky.

In the 'New Poems' of *Selected Poetry*, that is, the poems of the 1970s, Peters concentrates heavily on the condition of Africa. If many poems in his earlier books had non-African (often English) settings or were not specifically tied to a landscape or society, that is no longer so. About half the new poems are in fact concerned with the condition of Africa. Peters is now disgusted with current governments and sees the need for at least a moral revolution. In 'Rhun palms in the distance' (61) he accuses 'those who wear the crown' of finding 'the thing too big' ('thing' being always a pejorative word in Peters's vocabulary) and lapsing into a *laissez-faire* policy. The operation of such a policy allows both foreign and local business enterprise to make large profits. In 'I try to read a book' (62) he glances at the Scandinavian (largely Swedish in fact) packaged tourist trade into The Gambia, in which 'the nordic men trade us for small change'; in 'Two score and ten' (65) at the political ambition and trading activities of a youthful Gambian politician, Alhaji Momudu Cham.

It is a policy that leads to brutality and suppression. Even in writing about Soweto in 'Soweto, I know your anguish' (71), he equates the conditions in South Africa to those in many African countries and to the south of the United States. He finds the spirit of Soweto also

> . . . in my backyard
> where termites gather,
> in the offices of ten percenters

But his indignation turns also against himself, for he finds the same spirit 'in my envy of the next man' and ultimately in the heart of mankind, 'in my heart of gold'. Peters is by now using the rhetoric of Négritude but turning it against romanticism, complacency, and corruption.

'I am asking about the way ahead' (73) raises the question of the appropriate policy for the future, but does not progress beyond evidence of violence, inflation, unemployment, and corruption. 'Sanguine river' (75) is a retreat into the beauty of the River Gambia. It flows beside 'spruce cities like termite hills' and beside 'shanty town',

> But the river
> never falters
> stands erect
> waiting, waiting, waiting.

This is a peaceful interlude in the rage that Peters soon resumes. 'The tender landscape' (85) laments the commercial devastation of earlier beauty, with 'foreign cash' largely to blame. He rages against 'injustice and oppression', tribalism, 'blank indolence, incompetence', and lack of self-help; in short against, as he puts it in 'You shudder at the price', the immediately preceding poem, 'the inverted pyramid' that has been built by post-Independence Africa. The remedy, he says, lies in the hands of the people: 'we hold our destiny in rugged palms'.

Peters's fulminations offer few practical solutions; one would not expect poetry to display an economic blueprint. What he does offer is rage, dismay, bitterness, and deep disappointment in vigorous, almost shoutable lines. He opposes foreign capital, 'development', tourism, advanced technology, and large cities. He looks back nostalgically to a peaceful rural past, forgetting perhaps the disease and filth he points to elsewhere, but not rejecting 'the wholesome new' (poem 102). He is in no sense guilty of the complacency into which he accuses the politicians of falling. He believes in moral rectitude and self-help, and sees no way of establishing them in Africa unless the existing politicians are replaced. This programme of action comes to a head in 'Come down Sunjiata' (67), which, with a degree of political caution, he characterizes as a dream poem. In it he calls on the great thirteenth-century Manding monarch who established the kingdom of Mali (including the modern country of The Gambia) to return and establish 'Unity by the sword'. What we need he says is

... a mass uprising
from the Atlas to the Cape
to ravage the puppets,
perverts, Iconoclasts.

We need heroes worthy of the name.

Once again, as in 'Soweto, I know your anguish', he makes no distinction between white racialist South Africa and the independent nations of Africa, going in this instance north as well as south of the Sahara. The call is, I take it, for a moral revolution, or at most a bloodless revolution against the professional politicians, for Peters often inveighs against violence. This is the most outspoken of his political poems and even so it is incapsulated in a dream. He is, in fact, always hovering between the despair of reality and the hope of vision and prophecy.

In general, Peters offers moral solutions both to political problems and to moral problems. From the beginning of his career to his latest poems he advocates the virtues of truthfulness, altruism, self-discipline, self-help, and striving. The first poem in his first volume, *Poems*, ended with the word 'goodwill' and that partly sums up his moral outlook. But he also recognizes that the call and urge to *do* good are themselves seductive of genuine moral values. As he says in 'Sounds of the ocean' (*Satellites* 3),

The good is undone
by deliberation of effect.

Peters has always had a fastidious, almost puritanical distaste for drunkenness and sexual promiscuity. In 'After they put down their overalls' (*Poems*, p. 30; *Satellites* 53) he condemns workmen for drinking 'imported liquor' in open-air bars at lunchtime and going back to work with hangovers. In 'They dance wildly' (*Satellites* 37) he is disapproving of the way youth seek escape in drunken parties and casual liaisons. In 'I heard the Firebird's lament' (*Katchikali* 47) he fulminates against the policy of 'I'm alright Jack', 'doing one's own thing', and 'free love'. And in another poem from the same volume, 'The panelled walls' (51), he sees equally reprehensible failings in the smug elderly members of a club; they are complacent, inane, vindictive, and anti-intellectual.

In the 'New Poems' of the 1970s most of his moral fervour (as distinct from political outrage) is directed towards the young, but he maintains the kindly sorrowful tone habitual in his comments on youthful waywardness. There is now the suggestion that their lusting after an immoral and unproductive way of life is an example of Western corruption. When in the United States he visits a Navaho reserve and is saddened to find alcoholism, take-away food, and a mixture of hostility and servility: all of this is expressed in 'Here in the kingdom of the Navaho' (58). In 'What was the last word spoken' (68) he contrasts 'the bush vibrant in the rainy season', fecund with genuine life, with the superficial sterile desire to 'wear transistors like bracelets'. But as in most of his moral strictures, Peters does not exclude himself from questioning and condemnation. In the opening poem of *Satellites* (and *Selected Poetry*), he regards himself as being open to terror which 'grinds me corrupts me to fornication'. In 'A large house' (*Selected Poetry* 93) he examines his own retreat from the world, his large walled house with its records, books, gourmet food, and wines. He justifies them as things he appreciates and enjoys, he is never opposed to pleasure as such, only uncaring pleasure, but regrets that they cut him off from 'the fun and laughter' of humbler people.

The urge for warm human contact without surrender of the self runs through his poems. One of the earliest was 'She came in silken drapes' (*Poems*, pp. 10–11; *Satellites* 17; *Selected Poetry* 14). It is a surrealistic dream poem in which he sees Artemis, virgin goddess of the chase, brandishing not only a phallic symbol (a sword) but also, it would seem, an actual phallus ('that forbidden thing'). Like the goddess, the significance is 'veiled', confused, and contradictory. 'Love and loveless hate' are bound up together; the beautiful coral snake is poisonous; love is as alluring as the soft radiant rings of the planet Saturn. The goddess is both 'Butterfly' and 'Tyrant', and she inhabits the 'caves of Hysterus' (the word from which both 'uterus' and 'hysteria' are derived). Peters's fastidiousness comes out in the comment that love is a word 'A thousand times misused'. He however proposes to find true love through, but beyond, 'the phallic mound'.

The contrasting poem from the same collection is 'Clawed green eyed' (p. 26; *Satellites* 13; *Selected Poetry* 11). It is about a prostitute, 'Selling old boot' or the 'Prostituted fruit of Eve'. The harsh epithets give way at the end, however, to a softer, almost sympathetic touch as he sees the line of prostitutes along the edge of the park

> Like dancing caterpillars
> In folded leaves
> Softened by Social Conscience
> Hounded by prudes
> Friend of the falling star
> Victim of the lonely bed.

With the major exception of these two poems, sex and love are not important subjects in *Satellites*. Peters's next volume, *Katchikali*, contains, however, a number of poems on these subjects. 'Screams of childhood fright' (7; *Selected Poetry* 34) traces his attitudes to sex from childhood, through adolescence, to the present. After one or two characteristic precepts, such as 'Excitement only, perversion squanders vitality', he concludes that he now has a 'corrupted sense' of sex, hedged around with guilt to the point where 'healthy relationship founders' (the 'healthy' also, of course, being a characteristic word).

The next poem, 'Love is juxtaposed to the Ego', is an early one, which originally appeared in *Black Orpheus*.[4] Once again Peters is alert to the dangers of love. It 'stands between' the Ego and life, distorting both. It damages flesh and nerves, but in the end

> transmits the rapture of danger
> into a flowered eternity of years.

Long-lasting love-relationships and the eventual decay of passion are the subject of 'We have lived as if in vacuum cylinders' (12), 'These are the blades of grass' (27), 'Written on the scroll pages of this flower' (39; *Selected Poetry* 47), 'How to answer, speak, explain' (40), and 'And so this long affair' (55). It is perhaps because they contain painful hints of autobiography that all but one of these delicate and thoughtful love poems, together with 'She stood in the slanting light' (10), which concerns a briefer, evanescent love affair, have been excluded from *Selected Poetry*. All of them mingle love with greater or lesser degrees of regret, recrimination, pain, and, as so often in Peters, the sense of the lonely, suffering, but intact self emerging from the experience.

The love poems of 'New Poems' come towards the end. 'Your eyes close' (89) is his most explicit poem of copulation. But once again he has to mention 'shame or guilt', if only to convince himself that none are attached to this lovemaking. It does, indeed, have the positive virtue of clearing away 'shadows of suspicion'. 'Your walk is timeless' (90) is a light-hearted song with a good deal of rhyming. Its complaint is that his 'Wolloff cheri' has no sense of the value of money. 'You're tied to your star' (95) is almost as explicit as 'Your eyes close', almost as light-hearted as 'Your walk is timeless'. The half-amused complaint of the lover this time is that the loved one lacks facility with words and has to rely on 'electronic antennae' (presumably a cassette recorder) to explain what she has been doing.

Peters is, then, both passionate and balanced in his love poetry. Heart and head are in operation together. He has few romantic illusions. Love is not a matter of 'floating mermaids' he says in 'Mine is the silent face' (*Satellites* 5; *Selected Poetry* 4), but of 'anger and the passion of waves'. (In many poems his inner feelings are represented by the tumbling of the ocean, the deep throb of the earth, or the vehemence of wind.) But he recognizes that this tempestuous self is largely self-inflicted, for at the end of 'Mine is the silent face' he refers to 'this emptiness, this hell I invented' and in 'Nobody knows' (*Satellites* 8; *Selected Poetry* 6) he says that 'Self burns totally alone'.

The inner turmoil, the passionate searching, the sense of isolation never become maudlin or self-pitying. Peters has a deep-seated belief in the tonic effect of work and action. But the turmoil is constantly evident in his poems because of their tumultuous, seething, explosive imagery. In 'I want to' (*Satellites* 9; *Selected Poetry* 7) he says that 'The universe is my book', and that is certainly true in regard to the imagery he uses. There is nothing damply suburban or mundane in his imagery; it is always energetic and vigorous, and often elemental or cosmic. In the opening poem of *Poems* ('Open the gates', p. 1; *Satellites* 15) he urges the unobstructed or 'uninfarcted' heart to be 'Large and throbbing as the Universe', and he goes on to speak of 'bush-fires', 'stars', 'heaven', and the cleansing rain. The opening poem of *Satellites* (and *Selected Poetry*), 'Skyflood of locusts', uses vigorous imagery of 'trenches', 'Cannonade', 'Drilling', 'macerate', 'bleeding earth', a fire, and a 'deluge' in the first three stanzas and goes on to assert that 'Ecstasy and passion' are stronger than all such energies or events. Even music can be spoken of in this explosive way, as in 'On a wet September morning' (*Poems*, pp. 17–19; *Satellites* 36; *Selected Poetry* 25):

> The echo burst inside me
>   Like a great harmonic chord
>
> · ·   ·   ·   ·
>
>   Then the heraldic drums
> In slow crescendo rising
>   Crashed through my senses

Nature too is spoken of with the same furious quality, as in 'Sunrise drags me' (*Katchikali* 6; *Selected Poetry* 33), where the sunrise 'drags me out of bed, exploding sporadic blooms', or in 'Sound of rain on leaves' (*Katchikali* 9), where the sound of rain is likened to 'invisible hammers'. And the human body can be an image of the same kind, as it is in 'The world expands hydrocephalic' (*Katchikali* 30; *Selected Poetry* 43), where the world like a bloated body or brain is described as 'exposing central fires, tearing green arteries at source'.

The psychological unrest represented in all these images also expresses itself in the shark, crocodile, and snake imagery of *Satellites* and *Katchikali* and in the references to painters of psychological disturbance, Vincent Van Gogh (to whom 'Dear Vincent, thanks for sharing your soul', *Katchikali* 54, is addressed) and Francis Bacon (who is referred to in 'Eighteen: suicide appears logical', *Satellites* 31, and 'The man on the podium barks', *Satellites* 44). There are also explosive and tortured poems set within the context of a surgical operation or the treatment of a patient. 'Watching someone die' (*Satellites* 6; *Selected Poetry* 5) speaks of witnessing death as producing 'reinforced brutality to life' rather than any enlightenment; 'You lie there naked' (*Katchikali* 48) speaks of the surgeon as 'a maniac' creating 'a tropical storm' when a problem occurs during an operation; and in 'You talk to me of pain' (*Katchikali* 49; *Selected Poetry* 49) the patient's pain becomes a symbol of the surgeon's inner pain; but he has no way of removing the cause by surgery, no comprehension even of how the operation might be symbolic.

The doctor's life, mind and context are sometimes brought to bear on the subject of death, a major concern in *Katchikali*. 'Does death so delude us' (*Katchikali* 20) is a meditation on the compulsive fascination death exerts, conducted with a good deal of medical imagery. 'Isatou died' (*Katchikali* 21; *Selected Poetry* 38) and 'The world expands hydrocephalic' both refer to the death of a child. Isatou's death at the age of five is half welcome to her mother; but her father, 'through marble eyes', said

> 'Who spilt the perfume
> Mixed with morning dew?'

The attitude is ambiguous. The father's eyes are chill with loss, but not weeping, and his gnomic utterance is more like a monumental inscription on marble than a cry of grief. 'The world expands hydrocephalic' is a song 'of despair' in the face of death, seeking the appropriate 'tune'.

'Eighteen: suicide appears logical' (*Katchikali* 31) and 'I heard the Firebird's lament' (*Katchikali* 47) concern death in relation to adolescents, the first being about a disturbed girl's unsuccessful attempt at suicide, the second about a daughter killed accidentally in England by companions ' "larkin' about" '. In all of these poems Peters, with his characteristic honesty, confesses himself unable to get beyond grief and, sometimes, anger. He has no genuine source of comfort.

Among the poems of the 1970s, 'Twelve months to the day' (*Selected Poetry* 63) is a memorial poem. After a year, the death recalled does not produce the sharpness of grief of the earlier poems; there is more definition and description of the dead person. It is not dishonest adulation. There were two selves: 'A softer, kinder one' disclosed by 'disarming and spontaneous' ways and 'the darker one hidden from the world'. Peters's habitual convulsive, expansive imagery is used to characterize both the life and the death. There was a 'huge concern for self' that led to 'nights of thunder' in life; the death is likened to the uprooting of 'Great trees' and to a 'manic wrench'.

Peters's poems about life, death, the self, and love are generally as finely balanced as this. He thinks, he suffers, and sometimes he enjoys, but he does not arrive at solutions in matters concerning the individual. It is in the political poetry, especially in the 'New Poems' of the 1970s, that he is sure of himself, and that is because his attitudes are based on the moral values that he has always espoused. There is, then, in his work, a juxtaposition of personal uncertainty and guilt with certitude about the basis of individual and social morality. These two major elements in his work are linked by sharing a cataclysmic type of imagery that he brings to all subjects.

He is a poet without illusions. Though he believes in the personal and prophetic duty of the poet, he is doubtful that he will be heard. In 'Wings my ancestors used' (*Satellites* 4; *Selected Poetry* 3) he says that 'I am a trustee for the future' and 'the guidance is in me'. In the last of his 'New Poems', 'You're not listening' (*Selected Poetry* 104), he experiences the shouted word of the prophet ignored by the venal world amid polite chatter.

The centre of his poetry has shifted from personal poetry of the tortured soul, moral reproof, and occasional topographical poetry to denunciation of the governments of Africa. There has, however, been no major shift in his style. He has always written in neat external forms, letting the ideas dictate the poem. In dealing with what he considers the ineptitude and crassness of African governments, he has come to make more use of the strain of public oratory and his poems in this mode have perhaps a greater sense of urgency and energy. But these qualities existed from the beginning. He was always a poet of declamation and denunciation, with bold and furious images. It is just that recently he has given greater vent to this side of his work. Whereas in earlier work he ranged from The Gambia to Freetown to the Sahelian region to Africa as a whole to Europe and the world, there has been a concentration in the later poems on the continent of Africa. It is not seen as either especially wicked or especially virtuous, but as being in urgent need of political reform.

Notes to Chapter 3

1. *Poems* (Ibadan: Mbari Publications, 1964), p. 43. The poem is reprinted in *Satellites* (London: Heinemann Educational Books, 1967), pp. 73–4 (poem 42) but not in *Selected Poetry*. References to the volumes of Peters's poetry will be by the number of the poem, not by page number, except for *Poems*.

2. *Selected Poetry* (London: Heinemann Educational Books, 1981), poem 79 (pp. 109–10).

3. *Poems*, p. 29; *Katchikali* (London: Heinemann Educational Books, 1971), poem 4; *Selected Poetry*, poem 31.

4. No. 16 (1964), 30; *Katchikali* 8; *Selected Poetry* 35.

4 John Pepper Clark

▼▼▼▼▼▼▼▼▼▼▼▼▼▼▼▼▼▼▼▼▼▼▼▼▼▼▼▼▼▼▼▼▼

The mid-1950s represent a turning point in the history of West African poetry in English from derivate 'pioneer' literature, written largely in imitation of the models in British school text-books, towards new developments by younger writers aware of modern world writing and determined to draw both from it and from indigenous material and forms in order to establish new national literatures. Surveying such recently published monuments to pioneer literature as Dennis Osadebay's *Africa Sings* (1952) and R. G. Armattoe's *Deep Down the Blackman's Mind* (1954), the Gold Coast writer Davidson (Abioseh) Nicol commented: 'Since modern poetry is not widely read in West Africa, the European influence felt by these poets is that of the nineteenth and early twentieth century before T. S. Eliot's *Waste Land*.'[1] But he recognized the new spirit, and commented ruefully that trying to keep up with all the new work was 'like trying to catch an accelerating train' (p. 121).

Nicol himself was one of the new breed of poets and so was Gabriel Okara in Nigeria, whose first poems appeared in 1957. But they were soon to be shouldered aside in energy and proliferation by even younger poets such as John Pepper Clark. Clark published his first poems in *Beacon* and *The Bug*, two University College, Ibadan, magazines, in 1958, and his first volume of poems preceded Okara's by a decade and a half. With Okigbo's *Heavensgate* it was, in fact, one of the first volumes of poetry devoted to work by a single author to be published in Nigeria (for Osadebay had been published in England).

Its forty poems included a number of works that Clark chose not to reprint in his second volume, *A Reed in the Tide*.[2] The second volume, in fact, printed only sixteen of the forty poems, together with two of the six parts of the long poem, 'Ivbie'. Clark clearly found the task of selection painful, for in 'A Personal Note' prefaced to *A Reed in the Tide* he compared it to surgery on oneself and said 'What to cut, and what to save out of a body of poems that has come to represent more or less part of my own self, will always remain with me an unsettled issue' (p. vii). Yet he performed the task with great skill, and I believe there are few readers who would regret the omission of the rejected poems.[3] Some are obscure, some impenetrably private, some have over-assertive sound-patterns or are prisoners of their own sound pattern, some have fine lines but irremediable flaws in concept or construction, some depend heavily on rather laboured and prosaic similes, and some are too

closely based on their literary models. Others, though not subject to
these faults, are slight and self-absorbed vignettes: four of them, 'Pub-
song', 'The Water Maid', 'Easter', and 'The Outsider', were rescued
for Clark's definitive retrospective collection, *A Decade of Tongues:
Selected Poems: 1958-1968*.[4]

Like his close friend at this time, Christopher Okigbo, Clark was
experimenting with various styles. Like Okigbo, he was prepared to
risk naïvety or sentimentality for the sake of a striking effect. Many
of these early poems are, then, apprentice works. It should be
recognized, though, that the earliest are not necessarily the least competent. One of the best pieces he ever wrote was 'For Granny', one of
his earliest adult poems (it was published in *Beacon* 1, No. 2 (1957),
21).

The one surprising omission from *A Reed in the Tide* was the
long poem in six movements, 'Ivbie', which had previously been
published in *The Horn, Beacon*, and *Présence Africaine* as well as at
the end of *Poems*.[5] *A Reed in the Tide* printed only the fourth and
sixth parts, but the whole poem was resuscitated for *A Decade of
Tongues*, where it appears (pp. 23-32) with the sub-title 'A Song
of Wrong' and with explanatory shoulder-notes. 'Ivbie' was the
one clearly political poem in Clark's first volume and as such is the
precursor of the American poems forming the second part of *A Reed
in the Tide* and of the poems about the Nigerian crisis in the later
volume, *Casualties*. Its omission from *A Reed in the Tide* occurred
at a time when Clark was ill-disposed to poetry that could be seen as
politically involved. With critical discrimination he therefore selected
from this aesthetically flawed poem only the two most presentable
movements.

The meaning of the title 'Ivbie' is explained in the first note to
the poem in *A Reed in the Tide*: 'Hands-over head signal and cry by
women at a time of great loss or wrong for which there can be no
remedy or justice' (p. 39). The subject is the conquest and domina-
tion of Africa by Europeans. The opening question, 'Is it not late
now in the day ...?', is a rhetorical one, for it is obviously too late
to undo the destructive work of the invaders from 'far-fabled
country'. They have brought their own institutions and technology,
treating indigenous 'occult groves' with 'alien care and impunity'.
Their tourists have given superficial self-satisfied glances at 'the
thousand intricacies' of the subject people. They have photo-
graphed sacred objects, plundered rare and revered works of art, cut
down forests, enslaved the people, exported oils and minerals,
imported their own smug religion, and, somewhat less reprehen-
sibly, established mission hospitals. The second note on 'Ivbie'
in *A Reed in the Tide* (p. 39) refers to a passage in section II
which does not appear in this volume. The archetypal missionary's wife, 'Mrs Gamp', is said to act as a nurse and midwife in the
hospital:

Sweet Mrs Gamp, not a coward,
Followed her man into the wild
And wiping gentle hands on her eyes,
Without bias,
Delivered amid cries in the mission ward
A wisdom-teethed child (*Poems*, p. 46)[6]

The point is that the hospitals were used as a means of indoctrination, encouraging the development of a new generation of children who were metaphorically born with the teeth of Christian wisdom, an image of detestation in its literal meaning, as Clark says, 'among several Nigerian peoples'.

The third movement contrasts the cosmic nature that the invaders impute to their mission and message with the materialistic reality of their presence. They represent themselves and their culture in imagery of cosmic storm, analogous to the appearance of an indigenous deity such as the mother-goddess, Oyin, who was once accompanied by 'weird-splintered flame' over 'a wood-awninged lake'. But now such imagery, whether to accompany the manifestation of an indigenous deity or the foreign god who supplanted the indigenous gods, is obsolete. The effect of cultural invasion is the death of all religion and its replacement by the materialism symbolized by a society where 'Austin Herefords go toot/Tooting in mad rush for loot'.

The fourth movement plaintively and with a touch of sarcasm inquires whether the 'communal gods at the gate' slept while the invaders' 'whiff of carrion' blew into the village. The odour comes from 'An unlaid ghost' entering the village surreptitiously, despite the warning prophecy of Oyin, the creator-mother of the Ijaw people. This poison will—and Clark uses another image very germane to the perpetually moist Niger Delta country of his homeland—though seeming a mere trickle, become a flood, dissolving all the old civilization. The great goddess, Oyin, who sees all this in the future, is even herself distorted by the vision, for she takes the shape of a bearded owl, a beard being 'a terrible aberration for a woman among the Ijaw', as Clark says in the Notes to *A Reed in the Tide*.

The fifth movement presents the poet as irresolute about what he should do. Quotations from *King Lear* and *Hamlet* reinforce the image of the Niger 'spinning whirlpools': the poet can neither rest nor take decisive action. He is a 'bastard child' of the Niger, for he is heir to the heritage not only of the Ijaw but also of the invaders.

The sixth movement is addressed to the 'missile-hurled' invaders, enjoining them to 'Pass on' and leave behind 'unhaunted/An innocent in sleep of the ages'. Applied to Africa, Nigeria, the Ijaw, or the poet himself, the conclusion is somewhat facile. He admits in this same section that 'Magic chords are broken', and presumably could not be reinstated even if the destructive agent could be induced to pass on. The omission of the fifth movement from *A Reed in the Tide* to some extent masks this contradiction.

The shorter poems retained from *Poems* may be considered to fall into five groups. The largest is a group set in the country of the Niger Delta. In quality they represent a set of related poems comparable to the 'Casualties' group of Clark's next volume. There are four of them: 'For Granny', 'Night Rain', 'Abiku', and 'New Year'. They depict a warm family relationship amid the rain of the delta country, barely kept out by thatched roof and mud floor. Outside, at night, owl and bat perch in the sacred *iroko* tree, the traditional haunt of witches, and *abiku*, the spirits of children who keep returning in a cycle of birth and death to plague their mother, may be abroad. (The scene is mostly a night one in these poems.) The poet speculates on the relation between person and person, person and life, and on the family scene or on nature as a metaphor for life.

In 'For Granny (from Hospital)' he thinks back to the meaning of a childhood incident in a dugout canoe on a kind of pilgrimage (for they are accompanied by 'pilgrim lettuce' floating down the flooded stream). He offers two alternative explanations, one more mundane, the other more metaphysical. Perhaps granny hugged the boy to her because the sound of the turbulent waters reminded her of the 'endless dark nights of quarrels' in his father's 'house of many wives'. As with 'pilgrim lettuce', the natural surroundings offer a kind of pathetic fallacy that bears on the human situation. The quarrels are as unnecessary as the waters are 'needless' to the stream. The alternative explanation is that the falling stars, despite their vast journey, cannot match the human depths represented superficially by the 'shallow silten floors' of the house, raised just above the level of the muddy waters. The stars' path is transparent; the human depths silted and dark. It is a poem with hardly a word out of place, and its dialectical style and final question opening out on eternity are quite worthy of Yeats at his best.

'Night Rain' moves outward from the comforting security of the house (protected from the dampness of rain by a mother's industry, experience, and ingenuity) into an image of the whole country. As in 'For Granny', the effect is delicate and understated: it comes about through the 'drumming' of the rain on the roof taking on the characteristic of drums beating over the whole land, a land, as Clark rather sentimentally and uncritically concludes, 'of the innocent and free'. The final line is much more applicable to the brothers in their mother's hut than to the expanded sense of the whole land.

'Abiku' again has an image of a warm enclosed household successfully combating incessant rain. The speaker conducts a dramatic monologue with an *abiku* who has plagued the household. At first he seems rather off-handed in suggesting that the *abiku* might as well stay outdoors if he does not find the house comfortable. This is, of course, merely a cunning stratagem to try to terminate the cycle of coming and going. In his argument, though, he comes round to the stability and desirability of the household, which causes him to try another tack, an open, unservile invitation to come in and stay. This is followed by a trace of threatening in the assertion that the *abiku* is easily recognized by the mutilations inflicted during his earlier visits. Then the invitation is renewed, with a note of pleading for the *abiku* to recognize the injury he is doing to the mother:

> Then step in, step in and stay
> For her body is tired,
> Tired, her milk is going sour
> Where many more mouths gladden the heart. (p. 5)

O. R. Dathorne has pointed out that here Clark 'incorporates literal translations of Yoruba names that are given to *abiku* children: for instance "Malomo", which means "step in and stay", and "Arcad'Ojo", which means "her body is tired".'[7]

'New Year' is a less successful attempt to use the understated metaphoric technique of 'For Granny' and 'Night Rain'. It tries to move from a scene of two reeds, on the bank of a stream at the end of a flood season, to two people, cut off from the busy life of the stream and from each other. The wind blowing them becomes, rather unsubtly, one of 'world-blight', a term that clashes with the use of the stream as an image of the world.

A fifth poem might be associated with this group because of its night and water imagery and because of the dialectical style that brings it close to 'For Granny'. It is 'Horoscope', a piece in which the intricacy of the sentences and the artillery-like quality of the diction seem at odds with the triteness of the thought. All the poem is saying is that it is inconsistent to believe in the physical power of the heavenly bodies and not in their psychological power.

The second group of poems consists of works not about nature or, directly, human beings, but about pictorial representations. 'The Imprisonment of Obatala' derives from Susanne Wenger's batik painting of the subject and 'Girl Bathing' from works by Monet, notably, no doubt, *La Grenouille*. Thirdly, 'Agbor Dancer', though not attributed to a source, certainly creates the effect of being a description of a statue or painting.

'The Imprisonment of Obatala' seems imprisoned in its own rigid rhyme scheme, which produces substantial obscurity. The first stanza is the only one really based on the painting. It comments on the ominous 'stick-insect figures' threatening Obatala. The second and third stanzas contain neither a clear account of the imprisonment of Obatala nor any significant interpretations of its meaning. All we are left with at the end is a sense of injustice and menace conveyed by some striking but dislocated images.

'Girl Bathing' is an odd collocation of Négritude symbolism, centred on woman as an emblem of traditional Africa, and of indefiniteness about whether the girl herself is African at all, granted the source in Monet and her 'porcelain skin'.

'Agbor Dancer' also has Négritude elements: the girl dancing, the 'throb of a drum', the 'ancestral core', and her 'communal call'. The poet ends by confessing, rather disingenuously, that he cannot 'answer' the call he has depicted. I suggest that the scene is described from art rather than actuality because of the isolated sense of the dancer against the green backdrop of the forest; there are no crowd, no musicians, no heat, no dust. The figure seems abstracted from reality, as if dancing to a drum in the mind.

Another group closely akin to these picture poems consists of three picturesque or tableau poems, 'Fulani Cattle', 'Ibadan', and 'Return of the Fishermen'. 'Fulani Cattle' suffers from the same forced intellectuality and occasional forced diction as 'Horoscope'. It opens with the kind of obvious simile ('Contrition twines me like a snake') that is found more often in the poems not reprinted. But it does succeed with its implied comparison and contrast between the cattle and people of Nigeria. Both form clans, both have a chief's stool for regulation and order (though just what is meant in the case of the cattle is not clear), both suffer. What the animals have, however, is patience and fortitude, reminiscent of the 'Why bleat, oh why bleat!' of 'Ivbie' IV. The poet's speculations on the source of these qualities is a little trite: he thinks it could be because their feelings are anaesthetized or because they are content at least to get some rest. The close, with its forced jocular rhyme on 'prevail' and 'tail', introduces yet another flaw to this frequently anthologized poem.

'Ibadan' is a memorable miniature, like a slightly extended Japanese *haiku*. 'Return of the Fishermen' also has something of the miniaturist's art. Returning us to the delta area in scenery, it is almost like a child's painting, full of vivid colour and movement. Its three strophes, with their intricate linked rhyme-scheme, portray three scenes in the fishermen's return, the last offering a welcome home. All the imagery is of jabbing movement: the paddles in the water, the sun rapidly sinking, even the village and quay 'breaking' on the sight.

The last two groups of poems are derived from English poetic models, one drawing on a Blake–Wordsworth–Tennyson tradition of naïvety, the other on a Gerard Manley Hopkins tradition of self-delighted word-spinning. The first group, 'Tide-Wash', 'Hands Over Head', and 'Streamside Exchange', all use material from the Niger Delta within English literary forms. 'Tide-Wash' could be interpreted either in political or in personal terms, the swirl of water being the euphoria either of Independence or of love. In either case it has disappeared into the sand, leaving the participants exposed. 'Hands Over Head' seeks to achieve the unnerving contrast that Blake and Wordsworth often achieve between the naïvety of a ballad measure and the tragedy of the events described. It is, however, too clotted with historical and anthropological detail to focus attention on the pathos and horror of the events. 'Streamside Exchange' (which is similar in form to a Nigerian children's game) offers, in the bird's reply, the fatalistic acceptance of the cycle of events that occurs in several of these poems. It is a genuinely simple, lyrical, and profound little poem.

'New Year' and 'Ibadan Dawn' are the only two Hopkinsesque poems salvaged from the first volume. I have already discussed 'New Year' as a Niger Delta poem, ignoring its patina of echoes from Hopkins's terrible sonnets and 'To Margaret'. 'Ibadan Dawn' announces itself as 'after *Pied Beauty*', and it is an interesting exercise in the breathlessness, word-coining, and clotted quality of Hopkins's poem. It cannot by its nature, however, be anything but an apprentice piece.

The second half of *A Reed in the Tide* consists of sixteen poems dating mostly from the period when Clark spent a year (1962–3) in the United States. *America, Their America* is his prose account of that visit, cruelly reviewed by Wole Soyinka under the heading 'A Maverick in America', where he characterizes the author and his account as 'crude, adolescent, self-pitying, and self-congratulatory'.[8] Seven of the poems in *A Reed in the Tide* were first published in *America, Their America*.

Not all the sixteen poems in the second half of *A Reed in the Tide* are, however, about America. The section begins with five poems and ends with a sixth that are either personal or concerned with Nigerian politics. 'Flight across Africa' is another picturesque poem, in which the body of Africa, seen from an aircraft, is compared to a skeleton, picked free of flesh, no longer fit for a sacrifice. Though the imagery of preparing an animal for sacrifice at a shrine, washing away the entrails in a stream, is vivid, it is not intellectually well integrated to the poem. If traditional Africa has been already thoroughly sacrificed, there will be no call to wash away anything. And this *non sequitur* leads directly into the confused personal and symbolic image of the plane's passage from the land of Africa to the Atlantic Ocean.

Then follow two political poems, pointing forward to Clark's next volume. 'Emergency Commission' reworks, with much surer hand, some of the imagery from the rejected poem 'Tree' (*Poems*, p. 32). It refers to the split in the Western Region's Action Group party in 1962, the two factions being headed by Chief Obafemi Awolowo, the virtual founder of the party, and his former deputy in the party, Chief Samuel Akintola. Awolowo had moved into Federal politics as Leader of the Opposition, leaving the premiership of the Western Region to Akintola. When the party sought to purge Akintola, disorder broke out in the Western Region House of Assembly and a constitutional crisis over who should form a government ensued. The Federal Government, dominated by Northern politicians, with whom Akintola was in sympathy, intervened, and later set up a commission of inquiry into the financial affairs of the Region's statutory corporations. In due course it found evidence of manifest corruption in the handling of state funds by several politicians. Awolowo's moves against this politically motivated manœuvre left him open to a charge of seeking to overthrow the Federal Government.

'Emergency Commission' contents itself, however, with pious expressions of disapproval at how trusted men could be so treacherous (symbolized by the cock crowing), 'rotten', and inconsiderate of ordi-

nary people's interests which they were supposed to serve. As the poem
was published in *Black Orpheus* (No. 13, 1963, p. 23) only a few months
after the commission's report had been released, it was politically pru-
dent of Clark to leave the matter at this point.

The last poem in the volume, 'The Leader', is concerned, at least in
part, with Chief Awolowo. In the 1950s, after returning from a few
years' legal training in England, Awolowo had done a great deal towards
the inauguration of a united independent Nigeria. As founder of the
Action Group party in 1951, acknowledged leader of the Yorubas,
Premier of the Western Region, and later Leader of the Opposition in
the Federal Parliament, he had seemed impregnable to the tongues of
enemies ('iguanas'). Now, however, he had been sentenced to a long
term of imprisonment, in part because of the machinations of his former
lieutenant ('Nearest of kin'), Akintola.[9] He is trussed up like a captured
alligator, for his jaws—his newspapers, parliamentary seat, and other
means of expressing his opinion—have been shut. The poem stands, of
course, beyond these local and transitory circumstances, but as with
'Emergency Commission' the local origin seems clear. Both poems
seem to have been written while Clark was away from Nigeria during
a year which covered most of the salient events at home, but 'The
Leader' was not published until 1964 (in *Ibadan* No. 19, 1964, p. 48)
and it could therefore afford to be somewhat more explicit.

'His Excellency the Masquerader' may be directed against Nigeria's
first indigenous Governor-General and, later, first President (from 1
October 1963), Dr Nnamdi Azikiwe. He performed a delicate balancing
act between rival factions while in office, often seemed indecisive, and
sometimes dressed up for official occasions in the uniform of a Field-
Marshal or gave press conferences on his official yacht. Alternatively,
it could be directed against the new Western Region Governor appointed in the wake of the constitutional tangle of 1962. Chief Joseph
Odeleye Fadahunsi, a businessman, took office on 1 January 1963, and
swore in Akintola's new coalition government the same day. He had
been National President of the NCNC (formerly National Council of
Nigeria and the Cameroons, then National Council of Nigerian
Citizens), a party that, although basically Igbo, might be considered to
have had some support over the whole country rather than merely in
one region.

Whether or not this is the background Clark had in mind, the poem
suggests that the man appointed to a high state office is seen as a 'ford'
or 'bridge' between north and south in Nigeria (symbolized by 'sand'
and 'swamp'), that is, he is supposed to bring harmony between the
Hausa-Fulani interests of the north and the Yoruba and Igbo interests
of the south. Yet the bridge is insecure, with bolts loose and rust
showing. Unlike the masks worn in towns like Ojoto, this masquerader
has no human solidity behind his public appearance: there is only wind
(words) and straw (indecision). The poem, beginning with *rime riche*
(serve/serve; stands/stands) passes through decreasing assonance (drop/

grip, brown/sand), to no terminal sound-patterning at all: the hopes for genuine service and efficacy from His Excellency have petered out.

'A Child Asleep' is a picturesque poem, but with more eventfulness and more dialectical ratiocination than those in the first half of the volume. It is a meditation on a very young child feeding from its mother and then falling asleep on the sand. Its rotund appearance reminds the poet of the Buddha, who also 'Sat so in dust', but unlike the child he was silent and penetratingly intellectual. By contrast, the child, feeding 'dropsically' just as it desires from the mother's breast ('fullness of sap science cannot give') attracts flies in the evening light. Concentrating on the child, the poet fails to notice at first that it has relieved its bowels on the sand and has pulled off the stump of its umbilical cord. This takes the poet back to the light image with which he began: the child is now 'Tumbling head over heels into arms of light', its own independent human life and enlightenment. Despite occasional reminiscences of other poets (for example, 'feeding on desire' from Eliot), this is one of Clark's most successful combinations of the picturesque and the dialectical: the two modes are combined from the beginning.

'Who Bade the Waves' is another attempt in a similar vein, but it tries to combine and superimpose too many images for a clear outline, either static or narrative, to emerge and carry the dialectic. It is, furthermore, a much more introspective poem. Clark begins with superimposed images of the horsemen of Bornu, King Canute, and an American rodeo, relying on 'stands' to suggest 'strands' and 'sands'. It is a daring combination, and its general import is clear: Clark does not see himself as such a theatrical and masterful person. His heart, unlike that of a stallion or a caged lion, turns inward, not outward. Yet though psychologically wounded, he is a survivor, and he cries out for release, as if trapped by fallen stones in an earthquake. (For Clark, as for Okigbo, stones are a common image, but Clark, unlike Okigbo, does not stick to their Yeatsian symbolic meaning of hardness of heart.) The way of deliverance offered by Christ leads to the drinking of the cup of bitterness to the dregs, to crucifixion, and to death. Such a way of abnegation seems not to allow for the animal life of the body, with its unthinking, unheeding desires. Such a way is a way of rhetorical windiness, whereas Clark feels a passion like boiling stone. This is an ambitious and provocative poem, self-centred yet uncertain and open-minded.

The ten poems about the year Clark spent in the United States include a number that are journalistic and hastily written. In *A Reed in the Tide* the sequence begins with two that do not appear in *America, Their America*. 'Las Palmas' (omitted from *A Decade of Tongues*) is a miniature in the same style as 'Ibadan'. 'Boeing Crossing' is a continuation of 'Flight across Africa', with a similar jauntiness of personal reference. It falls into two halves, the first chiefly a piece of description of the aircraft and its passengers, the second more ruminative. After comparing the mythical journeys of Sinbad and Jonah, Clark, rather inconsequentially and banally, asks those who believe in such myths to pray that modern travellers, able to bend time, should not lose their common sense. The third of the American poems that is not taken from *America, Their America* is 'Cave Call', a similarly joky, but less reflective, poem about a New York subway ride from Times Square to Washington Square.

'Three Moods of Princeton' is the first of the seven poems extracted from the prose volume, some of them being accompanied in *America, Their America* by a prose explanation. 'Three Moods of Princeton' (which was dropped from *A Decade of Tongues*) offers one spring and two winter vignettes, the first with reminiscences of Yeats, the third with a final line from a popular anti-nuclear-war song. 'Cuba Confrontation' is a rather obvious satiric piece about the U.S. diplomatic and military bluff over Cuba in 1961-2. 'Home from Hiroshima', its companion piece about American politics, is a more subtle satire about the profits of peace and war and how fragile a presidential-inspired peace is. The American eagle is said to have turned to 'the olive Shoot', the placement of 'Shoot' at the beginning of a new line giving a sinister interpretation to the apparently peaceful words. But the eagle of aggression is still rampant over America and may, as Clark says in a wittily ambiguous last line, cause 'The wild west [to] wreck the world'.

'I Wake to the Touch' arose, according to Clark, out of a dream involving his brother in India and James Meredith, the first black student at the University of Alabama.[10] James Meredith seems to have been lost in the transition from dream to paper and his place taken by a hand 'as Mortal and fair' as, apparently, the 'livid' serpent!

Clark calls 'Service' 'a little song' (*America, Their America*, p. 191/193) written after getting a meal from a slot machine. 'Two Views of Marilyn Monroe' (the third poem to be dropped from *A Decade of Tongues*) offers in the first part the complaint that American girls make themselves look dowdy and in the second part a trite reflection on the consolation of women. 'Times Square' was written, he says, in the Port Authority Bus Terminal in New York City after a night spent seeking for 'lasting warm contact'. He calls it a 'wail and yawn like a lost dog baying the moon' (*America, Their America*, p. 217/219). Despite its many imaginative lines, it is ultimately self-pitying and inconsequential.

Essentially light, occasional poems such as these were to find a place among the 'Incidental Songs', Part II of Clark's next volume, *Casualties*.[11] But the major part of that volume is the impressive political sequence, 'Casualties', where he seems to have found a focus for his poetic gifts. *Casualties* was published in 1970, only a few months after the end of the Biafran War. In the Notes to the volume Clark, hurt, as is also evident from the poems, by the loss of many friendships during the war, takes great pains to distance himself from all but one of the political and military events before and during the war. This is a disingenuous statement, for in the eyes of some of his former friends, Clark was an active Federalist who justified the detention of Wole

Soyinka for most of the war and became, as a popular phrase had it, General Gowon's 'Poet Laureate'.[12] What Clark seeks to do in the Notes is justify his own 'neutrality' at a time when so many of the best-known Nigerian writers in English were actively and vociferously pro-Biafran. At the same time he offers an interpretation of the events of 1966 and after, obtained in part from Major Emmanuel Ifeajuna, whom he characterizes (in contradiction to press reports of the time) as the leader of the coup of 15 January 1966, and from General Gowon.

Apart from the fable-like use of animal imagery to avoid naming some of the main actors in the political drama, these are direct poems of statement and reflection. The Notes do not make all the identifications. Major Chukwuma Nzeogwu, the most extrovert of the five majors (or 'hunters') responsible for the 15 January coup, is clearly identified as the 'cockerel'. The victims of the coup are less readily identified: the Sardauna of Sokoto is 'the lion in his den', 'Fallen in the grass' that is characteristic of the northern Nigerian landscape; Chief Akintola is the 'rogue elephant' or 'jackal', 'Fallen in the forest' of Western Nigeria; Sir Abubakar Tafawa Balewa is the 'vizier' or 'shepherd-sheep' abducted by Major Ifeajuna from Lagos 'by the sea'; and 'His castrate ram', or 'the bull without horns', 'spilling bags of bills All the way to a shallow grave' is the Federal Minister of Finance, Chief Festus Okotie-Eboh, who lived in Lagos around the corner from Balewa's official residence. One intended victim who escaped was 'the alligator', 'the old master of the stream', 'the high priest of crocodiles', or 'the hyrax', Major-General Johnson Aguiyi-Ironsi, who emerged from hiding after the killings and as General Officer Commanding the Nigerian Army formed a military government. His régime lasted for only six months, a time that Clark characterizes, in poem VII, as the silting up of a mighty river, and as highly favourable to the interests of the Igbos. Ironsi, a drunken, indolent, incompetent, full of promises, as Clark sees him, was replaced in July 1966 by Yakubu Gowon, seen by Clark at the time as the saviour of the country.

The twenty-eight poems of 'Casualties' do not tell the story in chronological order. 'Skulls and Cups', the second poem, is concerned with events in the second half of 1967, after war with Biafra had broken out; 'Vulture's Choice', the third poem, takes us back to a fable representing the need for the coup of 15 January 1966. It is hard to see a strict logical order for all the poems, except at the beginning and end of the series, where the first two and the last two poems offer highly personal details and interpretations. Other personal poems punctuate the more generalized ones: notably X, XII, XVII and XIX. Many of the other poems are cast in the form of animal fables, of either a narrative or ruminative kind. XI is a dramatic discussion; XXIV a poem about a photograph; and XXVI a satiric song.

Almost all deal with death or the loss of friends. The animal imagery of the game-hunt is supplemented by plague imagery, of rats, mice and locusts, and, more importantly, by an image-cluster of faces, sun and song that acts as a motif for the series. It is announced in the first poem, 'Song':

> I can look the sun in the face
> But the friends that I have lost
> I dare not look at any.

The sun, as distinct from the night when the coups and many of the massacres occurred, can be a favourable image, but is more often represented by what are, by implication, false suns; faces are ambiguous, for many have turned from friendship to enmity, or exist no longer; and actual (as distinct from imagined) song is always sinister or destructive (as it tends to be in Eliot's *The Waste Land*).

In poem IV, 'The Burden in Boxes', about the mounting death-list under Ironsi's régime and his apparent indifference to it, the sun is an ambiguous image, for it contains the ill-considered applause that gratifies the General's vanity. In the darkness of cold storage are the coffins, emitting 'ominous music'. In VI, 'The Cockerel in the Tale', the sun is also ambiguous, because it is associated with another theatrical figure with whose character Clark is out of sympathy. In this witty poem, Nzeogwu, the cockerel, executes the Sardauna of Sokoto in Kaduna ('the desert end of a great road') and also Chief Akintola (in Ibadan). In the morning he crows about the dawn of a new régime to the news media of the world, though 'uncertain then Where the sun should rise'. This is followed immediately by 'The Reign of the Crocodile', the implication being that Ironsi, who had been intended for execution by the majors, is an unexpected and false sun to rise from the night of killings. At the end of this poem, Clark writes that when Ironsi 'came to centre stage',

> The people cried for a song,
> The song was in the street,
> But like the ham he was,
> He sat down to a party,
> Called in his cronies, and
> Not one knew the song.

Here the song is, unusually, a favourable one, but there is no one to sing it. The actual music of this sequence is always ominous.

'What the Squirrel Said', poem IX, has the 'horns' of war blowing down forests. 'Leader of the Hunt', the next poem, ends with a reiteration of the sun and friendship motif from poem I. 'Conversations at Accra' has the A speaker, Ifeajuna, wanting to blow a horn that will call the people to national unity, but the horn seems to be broken: at any rate he is unable to produce the music of reconstruction—like all favourable musical references this one remains notional.

'July Wake', poem XIV, has references to the setting sun, symbol of the curfew imposed by the military government and of the end of life that seems so imminent to many people. The man hunted by the military in this poem is 'uncheered by faces', for all citizens are afraid to help or, indeed, to stir after curfew.

'The Rat in a Hole', expressing Clark's personal fear, refers to another false sun, the rising sun emblem accepted as its national symbol by the newly proclaimed Republic of Biafra in the east, 'Calling all to thunder' as Clark, a pro-Federalist, puts it. 'The Flood', poem XIX, again expresses personal fear, this time with glancing reference to the poet's 'Song', which here proves inadequate to still his fear.

'Death of a Weaverbird', poem XXII, is a tribute to a fellow poet and friend, Christopher Okigbo. His voice, clear 'as the siren's', is both seductive and premonitory. Clark imagines him dying with a song in his throat directed against his adversaries and proclaiming the inevitability of his own death as a fitting, if tragic, end to his life and career.

'A Photograph in *The Observer*' concerns young soldiers being medically examined before being sent to the front line. They enlisted 'honeycombed in the sun', full of the joy of life and adventure. But the war-machine of night overtakes them, just as their own warped image of the enemy is one seen only in darkness. This poem leads on to another based on a newspaper report and photograph, this time of the execution of two Federal officers for war-crimes against civilians, at sunset, 'the glare before dark'.

'Party Song' seems to refer to the mindless unawareness and inactivity of the politicians before the first coup and of Ironsi's staff before the second coup. The song is in reality a death-song, accompanied, though the party-goers do not realize it, by the drums of war.

In 'The Casualties', poem XXVII, Clark refers to the envoys of Biafra, seeking support in foreign capitals for a cause that other countries could not understand. It is true that the poem could be interpreted as referring to envoys of both rival governments, but there are, I think, good reasons for rejecting this reading. Clark's sequence of poems has a number of references that can be seen as hostile to Biafra and to Igbo solidarity. The 'locusts' and 'grasshoppers' of 'The Locust Hunt', poem XIII, that is, the foreigners out of their own homeland who are hunted down and massacred, are largely Igbo, and the imagery is not flattering. 'Exodus', poem XV, again referring to the massacres of Igbos and their flight back to their own homeland, contains the charges that the Igbos were proprietorial in their occupancy of important positions in the nation and over-intellectual and impatient. 'The Rat in a Hole' equates the rising sun of Biafra with a call of 'all' to war. Even 'Dirge', poem XVIII, though a mild and compassionate work, is not quite whole-hearted in its plea for protection of the Igbo. Those who have themselves madly cut down trees (this seems to apply to those who have committed atrocities on both sides of the clan conflicts) should be punished (turned into 'charcoal'), 'But let us not cut down the clan!' The 'But' can suggest that what Clark is advocating is a limit to justified killing that stops short of extinction of the whole clan. This is, no doubt, a very uncharitable interpretation, but it is not an impossible one. Even

'Death of a Weaverbird' attributes to the dead Okigbo a bellicose vindictiveness. The one poem on this subject that is even-handed is probably 'The Beast', poem XXI, when it refers at the end to the circumstances where

> blood calcifies into boulders
> For brother to hurl against brother.

The background to 'The Casualties', poem XXVII, is, then, that of a Federal partisan. (Certainly many commentators on this volume expressed great hostility to the political poems, largely, I suspect, on grounds of politics rather than literary qualities.[13]) But there is another intrinsic and another extrinsic reason why in this particular poem Clark intends to refer to the Biafran envoys. The intrinsic reason is that he calls them 'emissaries of rift', and from his Federalist point of view, amply expressed in the original Notes, it was the Biafrans who were the secessionists, the rift-makers. The extrinsic reason is simply that Federal Nigeria, already having diplomatic representation in the important capitals of the world, had little need to send out special envoys. It was the Biafrans who had to establish a network of new diplomatic links.[14]

These emissaries are scornfully spoken of in the poem as 'wandering minstrels . . . beating on The drums of the human heart'. Once again, the music is false and, indeed, horrific, as in this case it masks the destructiveness of the guns. But this piece of partisanship gives way to the generalized statement, applicable to both sides: 'We fall, All casualties of the war'. And the reason given is in terms of facial imagery:

> Because we cannot hear each other speak,
> Because eyes have ceased to see the face from the crowd

The final poem, 'Night Song', is conducted largely in terms of faces, music and the sun, including a variation on the thematic line brought through from the first poem (also a 'Song'). The faces now are haunting in their number and intensity; the sun is blotted out; song is distorted by war. Then the last strophe summarizes Clark's view of events from the first coup to the time of the Biafran War. The imagery is first that of song. The five majors began a song one night that should have been the prelude to a festival (an image taken up from poem VII) for the whole of the 'three hundred tribes' of Nigeria. Instead it brought death to 'cantor And chorus', the majors as the cantor, the people of Nigeria as the chorus. Then the metaphor changes to one drawn from architecture, reminiscent of what Major Ifeajuna said in 'Conversations at Accra'. In that poem he referred to his plan for replacing the four regions of Nigeria, in which the North was unduly influential, by fourteen states:

> Out of four unequal pillars
> To a barn like bedlam,
> One taller than the rest

Together, I sought to build
A new estate of fourteen wings

Now, in 'Night Song', Clark speaks of 'the crash of columns and Collapse of rafters' as an image of what actually ensued. But out of the ruin arises a saviour, General Gowon, who both takes up the lost song and allows the new national house so often dreamt of to appear, 'Firm upon the ground', with a mansion (one of the twelve states into which Gowon divided Nigeria in 1967) for the Igbo who 'followed ghosts Into the forests of night'. Or, to take a less partisan interpretation, the mansion is a heavenly one, a place of honour for those who died, on whichever side.

A Decade of Tongues includes an 'Epilogue to *Casualties*' (pp. 88–9), written some years later after a visit in 1974 along the road that led to the former Biafra. It is the 'unnatural Disaster that is war' that affects the poet, the seemingly needless loss. He pauses at Onitsha, birthplace of revolutionaries (Ifeajuna), elder statesmen (Azikiwe), and reluctant administrators (Ukpabi Anthony Asika, the Igbo political science lecturer appointed by Gowon to the most unwanted post of all, administrator of the East-Central State that had been recaptured from the Biafrans). Beyond Onitsha, formerly the largest market in West Africa, are the towns whose names were associated with the last-ditch stand of the Biafran high command as they were forced further east, making hypocritical statements about fighting 'to the last man' while preparing to leave by air from the last available air-strips. Five miles east of Onitsha is Ogidi, birthplace of Chinua Achebe, the most notable literary partisan for Biafra as Clark was for Federal Nigeria. Achebe spoke bitter words about Clark during the war, and Clark thought that he might 'never forgive, never forget' because of the 'wrong in his own heart'. Onitsha itself holds the poet, however, with its tottering houses, torn bridge, and evidence of human and commercial tenacity. His final image suggests, though indirectly, that the cause of the war was the relentless competitiveness of foreign interests. They are symbolized here by the cathedral spires of rival Christian denominations (Anglican and Catholic) still seeking to capture the souls of those who dwell, like biblical sheep, in 'eastern pastures'.

The whole sequence of 'Casualties' is outspoken political poetry. Like the most enduring poetry of this mode, however, it rises above its partisan origins. The image of the confessedly fearful poet, unable to protect himself by song, surrounded by the furious game-hunt of insurrection and reprisals, and by the fire, flood, or thunder of a civil war that threatens to destroy not only him but a whole nation, is an abiding one. Poem leads on to poem or reflects back on an earlier one to give some sense of order. And all through runs the cluster motif of face, sun, and song.

The remainder of the volume consists of occasional poems, three from his homeland, eight from the African and Indian part of his 1968 round-the-world trip, in which he did some proselytizing for the Federal cause. The first is 'Incident at the Police Station, Warri', based in part on the painting by Piero della Francesca, *The Flagellation of Christ*. As with Clark's earlier poems deriving from paintings, he freely departs from the pictorial details. Piero's painting has no crowd, though it does have 'three very important Looking persons', traditionally identified as Prince Oddantonio da Montefeltro and the evil ministers who connived at his murder. Nor, of course, does the painting have gallants 'Asking the girls to more wine and song'. Typically, Clark has superimposed the Nigerian scene of a beating at a police station and the fifteenth-century painting, just as the painter himself superimposed first-century Jerusalem and fifteenth-century Urbino.

'The Lagos–Ibadan Road before Shagamu' is another 'picturesque' poem, in part derived from a newspaper account of a fatal bus crash. Most of the remaining poems are imagistic miniatures, except for two longer picturesque ones on India, 'The Players' and 'Bombay'. Both revert to the mood of quietism bordering on fatalism that was characteristic of *A Reed in the Tide*. Players, crowds as 'itinerant' as the players, and the city of Bombay are all trapped in a 'routine' that is inescapable. The beggar-boy's only thrill is the sight of a rupee; the girl has a restlessness in the eyes that comes of boredom, fatigue, and insecurity, not creativity or zest; and Bombay itself is a place where 'nothing seems new'.

The tenseness of 'Casualties' has passed. After the emergency Clark has relapsed into the somewhat detached observer of his first volume of poems. In between had intervened the journalistic vigour of the American poems and the committed, often tragic, documentaries of 'Casualties'. Now in a sense, though with increased mastery of technique, he was back where he began, but now even more isolated, lacking the close family warmth that he could once retreat to. Apparently realizing this, he turned from poetry to dramatic and scholarly activities.

Notes to Chapter 4

1. 'The Soft Pink Palms: On British West African Writers—An Essay', *Présence Africaine* No. 8/9/10 (June–November 1956), 108–121 (p. 117).
2. The volumes referred to are *Poems* (Ibadan: Mbari Publications, 1962) and *A Reed in the Tide: A Selection of Poems* (London: Longman, 1965).
3. Gerald Moore and Ulli Beier, eds., *Modern Poetry from Africa* (Harmondsworth: Penguin, 1963, 1968) do, however, retain three of Clark's rejected poems, 'Olokun', 'Easter' and 'Cry of Birth'. 'Olokun' is also selected in Wole Soyinka, ed., *Poems of Black Africa* (London: Secker & Warburg, 1975; Heinemann Educational Books, 1975), pp. 43–4.
4. London: Longman, 1981. They appear on pp. 12, 14, 21, and 22 respectively.
5. *The Horn* 2, No. 2 (1958), 2–15 (with an introduction by Abiola Irele); *Beacon* 1, No. 5 (1959), 28–32; *Présence Africaine* No. 57 (1966), 284–91; *Poems*, pp. 44–51.

6. Reprinted in *A Decade of Tongues*, p. 26, with the reading 'wisdom-toothed'.
7. O. R. Dathorne, *The Black Mind: A History of African Religion* (Minneapolis: University of Minnesota Press, 1974), p. 287.
8. *Ibadan* No. 22 (June 1966), 59–61.
9. There were, of course, other close associates who went over to Akintola's party; on the other hand, at least one 'Onitsha' pamphlet, *Martyrdom of Chief Obafemi Awolowo* by Adio 'Mosanya (Yaba: Pacific Printers [1965]), p. 20, uses the analogy of Peter denying Jesus to refer to the sentencing of Awolowo by his fellow Yoruba, Mr Justice George Sodeinde Sowemimo, the Asalu of Oba Abeokuta. Sowemimo, in delivering sentence, expressed regret that he had no alternative under the law: 'My hands are tied'.
10. *America, Their America* (London: André Deutsch, 1964), p. 64; (London: Heinemann Educational Books, 1968), p. 66.
11. *Casualties: Poems 1966–68* (London: Longman, 1970).
12. For one viciously unfavourable view of Clark's activities see Wole Soyinka, *The Man Died*, Appendix C. It should be remembered, though, that Clark and Soyinka had clashed in print as early as 1966 over Soyinka's scathing review of *America, Their America*.
13. See, for instance, Thomas Knipp, 'Militancy and Irony: The Mood of West African Poetry in the Seventies', *Ba Shiru* 8, No. 1 (1977), 43–55, which contains, *inter alia*, an account of Wole Soyinka's opinion, expressed at the first meeting of the African Literature Association, Austin, Texas, March 1975. Michael J. C. Echeruo had earlier said 'I think *Casualties* is a disaster. It's sheer journalism ...' and Kalu Uka, 'I think *Casualties* is rubbish': *Dem Say: Interviews with Eight Nigerian Writers*, ed. Bernth Lindfors (Austin: Occasional Publication, African and Afro-American Studies and Research Center, The University of Texas at Austin, 1974), pp. 14, 72.
14. The extent and wastefulness of Biafran diplomatic effort is reflected in S. O. Mezu's novel, *Behind the Rising Sun* (London: Heinemann, 1971; Heinemann Educational Books, 1972), Eddie Iroh's *Forty-eight Guns for the General* (London: Heinemann Educational Books, 1976), and John de St Jorré's 'Nigerian Civil War Notebook', *Transition* No. 38 (1971), 36–41.

5 Taban lo Liyong

▼▼▼▼▼▼▼▼▼▼▼▼▼▼▼▼▼▼▼▼▼▼▼▼▼▼▼▼

The writings of Taban lo Liyong raise in an acute form the question of what poetry is. If poetry were solely lyrical, concerned with the song-like expression of emotions, then Taban would not be a poet, for his verse is made up of gnomic philosophical utterances, rhetorical shouts, and repetitive lists. Where the Cameroonian poet Mbella Sonne Dipoko will alter, and in particular condense, his prose utterances before presenting them as verse, Taban, who writes highly rhythmical prose, sometimes seems merely to divide it into lines or strophes and call it poetry. Where the Ghanaian poet Atukwei Okai seems aware of the danger of endlessly repeating a refrain or a structural formula of words in a rhetorical poem, Taban's tolerance of repetition sometimes knows no bounds.

Like Mazisi Kunene, Taban is a philosophical poet, prepared to make poetry directly out of belief. But his combination of substance (largely from Friedrich Nietzsche) and form (reminiscent of Heraclitean fragments, Blake's gnomic sentences, Wyndham Lewis's 'blasts', and, indeed, Nietzsche's own aphoristic style in *Human, All-too-Human* and *Thus Spake Zarathustra*) is unique. His advocacy of Nietzsche's concepts of progress through the fusion of opposing tendencies (Taban's 'synthesism'), the nature of frenzied creative energy, the élite Übermensch or Superman, and the dangers of rationalism (including orderly form) have made him an outsider to many literary circles. He is a person admired for his intellect and warmth of personality, but often deeply suspect because of his alien and uncongenial ideas. African poets in English are often expected to develop political ideas within a fairly narrow band of liberal or left-wing orthodoxy, whereas Taban conforms to no expectations, not even his own.

The cult of the Superman has made him quite shameless in talking about himself and his family in both prose and verse. He examines the meaning of his father's life and death, castigates his wife for infidelity, laments his loss of custody of his two sons, and discusses his own personal and literary ambitions. If the Freudian notion of creativity being the attempt to sublimate neurosis or the Jungian notion of it as an anodyne for inner distress and tension have any plausibility, it is in the work of people like Taban. And as an outstandingly intelligent and introspective person, he is aware of this. *Meditations* (London: Rex Collings, 1978) is 'Dedicated to people with strong complexes of one kind or another'; and in it he justifies neurosis because it 'lifts people up to another level, beyond society, *ahead* of society' (p. 146). He notes that 'Somewhere in my make up, I share epicycles with the mad' (p. 17) and 'It is madness of a sort' (p. 31). But it is not only in madness that he feels an affinity with Nietzsche; he also suggests that 'Without syphilis, without malignant derangement, can a man ever amount to anything?' (p. 146) and announces that, in this sense, 'Ladies and gentlemen, I have syphilis' (p. 147).

The short-breathed forms adopted by Taban allow him to try out propositions, even the most outrageous and shocking, to see where they lead. Because his senses of fact and of fiction are so intermingled, he sees no inconsistency between, for instance, advocating physical suicide, advocating metaphorical suicide by the cessation of writing, or advocating fortitude and resistance to depression. Each is a possibility, each an idea worth entertaining. As a result, when he seriously advocates practical policies (as, for instance, in *Thirteen Offensives Against Our Enemies* [Nairobi: East African Literature Bureau, 1973]) he is likely to be treated as a jester, prankster, impossible idealist, or self-appointed irritant rather than as an imaginative thinker of the unconventional and even the unthinkable.

Wole Soyinka once said that Taban lo Liyong 'is not only an extravagant poet but an extravagant personality'.[1] The extravagance is self-recognized; Taban is a restless spirit wandering among ideas. As he says in 'An Excerpt from an Essay on Uneven Ribs: A Prelude':

> Let's reduce the prominence
> We have laid to an obedience classical
> And let's leave the mind to wander free
> To worlds unheard of.[2]

He is not, however, optimistic that his call will be heeded, for 'Deep down in man there dwells immobility, the supersonic barrier man will never overcome' ('To Susan Sontag, with Love, Part II', p. 63).

Frantz Fanon's Uneven Ribs (1971) was Taban's first volume of poems, though it had been preceded by his often impish and individualistic renderings of Luo songs in *Eating Chiefs* (London: Heinemann Educational Books, 1970). He had begun to write in 1964, the year in which his father died and in which he married. In *Meditations* he refers many times to the traumatic quality of both events:

> I am an immediate extension of the chemicals in my father. A secret thread joins us. When it snapped, I knew the ground had been cut under my feet. I have been off balance, ever since. The resulting restlessness is this. (pp. 126-7)

To please his father he had been an obsessive, omnivorously reading student. After his death, he turned from political science to English literature as his subject of study. To vindicate his father and to please, or at least to cope with, his wife, he became a writer.

His own summary of the main literary influences on his style is '*Pickwick Papers, Tristram Shandy, Don Quixote, Gargantua and Pantagruel*, Erasmus's *In Praise of Folly*' and Walt Whitman,[3] all rather rambling episodic works, fizzing with ideas, but randomly organized. Taban delights in such spontaneous, unfettered works and despises tight literary organization as 'Aristotelian', a frequently used pejorative word. In the first article in *The Last Word*, for instance, he justifies writing an essay that was not 'coordinated, controlled, or sequential':

> So what? Isn't each writer an arbitrary maker, ordering or re-ordering the world? . . . if I were on my way to a wedding feast, and were offered a mariner's tale, I would forgo the feast.[4]

Or, as he twice says in *Frantz Fanon's Uneven Ribs*:

> I'd rather be bright mad
> Than dull and well. (pp. 35, 42)

The easiest poems to approach in *Frantz Fanon's Uneven Ribs* are perhaps those that most closely resemble the style of Okot p'Bitek: the short dramatic monologue, 'Uncle Tom's Black Humour' (pp. 66–71); the short conversational narrative, 'Telephone Conversation Number Two' (pp. 72–8); and the two long dramatic monologues, 'The Marriage of Black and White' (pp. 96–114) and 'Student's Lament' (pp. 117–46). 'Uncle Tom's Black Humour' begins as a Négritude celebration of blackness, part serious, part parody. At 'because i labored hard in the fields' (p. 67), the scene seems to change from Africa to the United States, and the speaker from an African proud that his people were responsible when 'shaky french cabinets stumbled and fell' to an American black proclaiming his sexual vigour and his outstanding achievements. Then at 'have you known a confirmed culprit' (p. 69) the speaker seems to change again to an American black who justifies remaining in apparent subordination as an 'Uncle Tom', satisfied to be 'a permanent parasite in permanent dependence' because, on the whole, it is a better life without responsibility. In this third section the diction changes: there are no more references to Shakespeare's Caliban or Othello and there are a few touches of Southern dialect, such as 'chillun' and 'sumthin'.

The poem has, then, a protean speaker, suggesting that even in simple poems Taban is too brimful of ideas to be easily satisfied with consistent characterization or scene. It also has much of his characteristic aphoristic quality, as in

> well mr i admired your gun
> but you could not my magic

or

> sweets or gold
> i fill my purse

And, though this hardly needs saying, it is an amusing poem.

'Telephone Conversation Number Two' bears little relation to Wole Soyinka's well-known 'Telephone Conversation', except in so far as both telephone calls were abortive, but Taban could not resist the random association. The tale of an intercepted attempt at a sexual adventure is told straightforwardly, with occasional inversion of word order, perhaps to give a sense of the stateliness of the mock epic. At the end, though, Taban tries to interpret the encounter, offering the consolation that it was a useful, untaxing experience for a writer.

'The Marriage of Black and White' approaches more closely, in both subject and style, to *Song of Lawino*. Taban imagines himself as the speaker, married at his parents' behest to Lucy (the actual name of his wife), but now, again in accordance with his parents' wishes, seeking a second wife. Much of the poem is addressed to Beccie (or Becky), a white American girl, apparently of German extraction. Taban's address to her enables him to espouse his characteristic 'synthesism', though in a somewhat bizarre way. One of the attractions he holds out to Beccie is that she should choose his third wife for him:

A Chinese or a Russian, or one from France
Will do for me:
For my guests come from near and far.

Ours is the meeting place
Of people and thoughts
We derive our strength
From an openness of mind
And an attitude which says
The best also comes from left and right;
Take from each the good in it
Tell him to throw away the chaff. (p. 99)

With a quite close approximation to Okot (but without the vigorous animal imagery), he goes on to praise Ugandan dances by contrast with effete Western ones and, in section II, buxomness and strength in a woman.

Hyperbole and the mock-heroic emerge strongly in section III, where the speaker boasts of his sporting and intellectual prowess (in training for the Olympics and 'The harder race—the decathlon of the intellect') and praises the genetic advantage of the marriage of enemies. In section IV he rejects Nietzsche's condemnation of the mingling of races; indeed, he advocates mingling as being best suited to

A world shrunk by Orville and Marconi
A world that knows no boundary,
A world in flux,
With the colour disc in full swing
Blurring the primaries,
A world betterworsened by
I-it. (p. 108)

His sense of rhythm causes him to substitute 'Orville' for 'Wright' or

'Wright brothers' (the first aviators). His breadth of reading is hinted at in the 'I-it', a parody or secularization or extension of the Jewish theologian Martin Buber's concept of 'I-Thou'. Buber had used 'I-Thou' as a formula for dialogue between the individual and God or one individual and another. Taban explains what he means by 'I-it' at the end of section V, where he says that for children in contemporary society,

> The new 'it' has preoccupied them
> More than 'us'. (p. 111)

Section V almost loses the sense of dramatic monologue, of the speaker's attempt to persuade Beccie, and becomes instead the 'pop philosophy' of which he acknowledges himself a writer in 'An Excerpt from an Essay on Uneven Ribs: A Prelude' (p. 47). He ranges over his ideas on freedom, mother-fixation, and the raising of children.

Section VI returns to the appeal to Beccie, in a mock-heroic vein as if he were Aeneas and she Lavinia, daughter of Latinus, king of Latium, whom Aeneas married. The analogy, hinted at a few times in the poem, is particularly apt in view of the argument about strength arising from the marriage of enemies.

The appeal brings the poem close once again to the pleas and arguments of Okot's Lawino. What is different, however, is the wide range of literary and historical reference and the serio-comic tone. Right to the end, Taban leaves open the question of whether all this is fantasy, fabulation, sublimation, a comic sketch, or a serious possibility.

'Student's Lament' is offered as meditations arising from the response to Taban's prose essay, 'Négritude: Crying Over Spilt Milk'.[5] The essay attacks Négritude as a romantic empty doctrine based on falsehood (that Africans are homogeneous and quite different from everyone else) and weakness (that pride should stem from African non-achievement in technology). He also attacks the base of the American Pan-African movement by pointing out that American Negroes are the product of European as well as African genes and are thoroughly Americanized in culture. He believes that 'inward looking philosophy suffocates' (*The Last Word*, p. 198) and that the way forward is to embrace whatever is useful (including Western technology) irrespective of its origins. This is the 'synthesism' or cultural borrowing advocated throughout *The Last Word*.

'Student's Lament' is concerned largely with attacking the obtuseness and venality of African politicians (with several guarded thrusts at existing heads of state, including President Julius Nyerere of Tanzania and his concept of 'African socialism') and defending the critical rôle of students, for Taban had been put down as a mere student who should not criticize his elders. He derides the folly of an isolationist foreign and cultural policy and the obscurantism of ill-educated, self-satisfied politicians who mumble shibboleths such as *harambee, Uhuru,* or *ujamaa.* He berates the double standard that encourages casinos for the

rich but closes the brothels of the poor or that wastes money on spectacular but useless projects. Daringly, he suggests that 'the skipper'
needs 'overhauling' (p. 132), but pragmatically accepts that such an
action is 'ruled out'. He is no radical, though: he accepts that the
anarchistic abolition of government, the breaking of the 'social con-
tract', would be either futile or impossible; and a revolution would
merely transfer power and wealth from one group to another. Like
Lenrie Peters, he favours a moral revolution, a government concerned
for all the people, especially the needy. He has little sympathy with the
Romanticized past of Négritude nostalgia. Like Dennis Osadebay,
whose lines,

> Don't preserve my customs
> As some curios
> To suit some white historian's taste

he had quoted with approval in *The Last Word* (p. 197), his own advice
is to

> Shed no tears
> For vanishing exotica. (p. 139)

Action is needed, however, to criticize and condemn the venality of
politicians and it is the students who should carry it out. 'The poor', he
says, must 'be promoted' (p. 143) to release untapped energies into the
task of government. The poor were made use of by the current ruling
class in the bitter struggle to independence, they 'hid in the mountains
Under Kimathi and Oloo' (p. 144) during the Mau Mau campaign, but
they have not been rewarded.[6] Instead, the old slogans are mouthed,
and students are vilified.

The short lines are again reminiscent of Okot p'Bitek, and to some
extent so is the stream of invective and the occasional sense that this is
a translation. But again Taban has a much wider range of reference and
of ideas. His aphoristic style, exemplified in

> When the poor man curses
> The rich man's stomach aches (p. 130)

or

> I am searching for a world
> Where the savant is no servant (p. 131),

alternates with illustrative anecdotes, like that of the beetle and the
grasshopper (p. 130) or the cock and the eagle (p. 132). These anecdotes,
like those of Okot, are often beast fables. The occasional inversion of
idiomatic word order ('The injunction wise', 'freed we became') seems
to be adopted mainly to achieve a more decisive rhythm in these short
lines.

These 'meditations' do not, in all, amount to a coherent policy. That
is not to say they do not make good sense or that individual passages

are not trenchantly argued. But the moral basis, humanitarianism, is neither cogently argued for nor presented in compelling rhetoric. As a philosopher, Taban is not rigorous enough, as a 'pop philosopher' not vehement and persuasive enough. He leaves the tenor of his ideas to be carried by such tepid lines as:

> Give equal valence
> To the words I,
> *It* and *They*. (p. 133)

As with most criticisms one can make of Taban, it has been anticipated by him. In 'The Throbbing of a Pregnant Cloud' (pp. 20–32), a poem largely about the difficulties he experiences in saying what he wants to in an effective way, he admits that world-weariness has sapped some of his early vigour:

> But many a day has passed
> And our sights are red
> And no more terms are left
> With which to call
> The word BLOOD (p. 21)

Earlier in the poem he had called his thoughts the 'musings of a ghost on a spree' and 'Visitations on grounds familiar' (p. 21). In section IV he explains his struggle with appropriate language:

> I have strived to say the things that are new
> But the things that are new take long to understand (p. 22)

And in section XII he comments on the acidulous nature of his affection and laughter:

> I kiss
> With a bite
>
> And joke
> With corrosion (p. 27)

The melancholy with which this section ends,

> One thing I know
> My best days are over (p. 28),

is a frequent theme in this volume, for Taban alternates between elation and despair. In other books he sometimes contemplates suicide; here the depth of his depression is expressed in a nihilistic attitude to society, the contemplation of a return to animality. That is the conclusion of 'An Excerpt from an Essay on Uneven Ribs' (pp. 50–1) and it is touched on, though somewhat ambiguously rejected, in 'Student's Lament' (pp. 134–5). In 'To Susan Sontag, with Love, Part II', he sums up the feeling that gives rise to this attitude in the adage, 'What is progress but a Victorian figment of the mind?' (p. 63).

Alongside this depression, however, exist the high spirits of 'The Best Poets' (pp. 36-40), in which he imitates in language and lineation what he is saying, and writes pastiches of e e cummings, Ezra Pound, and concrete poetry. What he says here so jauntily about his own poetry is, I think, true: he is a poet of thoughtful statement with concern for rhythm and shape on the page but for no other formal qualities. Taban once told Heinz Friedberger that his literary training had been in fiction: 'I write poems,' he said, 'mainly if I want to illustrate a certain point or if a sudden emotional outburst comes in me which I have to record in writing.' When the interviewer suggested that these narrative poems might be called 'ballads', Taban replied, 'Some are ballads, except that I am not very good at singing, and therefore that ballad quality which has to do with the singing is not there.'⁷ This is, in fact, the major difference between the versification of Taban and Okot: Okot is a singer and his verses are musical.

The gaiety and energy of 'The Best Poets' are found also in the more serious tributes to 'Gloria Bishop' (pp. 79-80) and 'Helen Elizabeth Westeastian'. Gloria Bishop, as he explains in more detail in *Meditations* (pp. 120-2), was an American teacher who aroused through her abundant sexuality his interest in literature, especially Walt Whitman. Helen Elizabeth 'Westeastian' was an art student, the illegitimate daughter of a white American woman and a South Korean cook, as he explains in *Meditations* (pp. 144-5). He met her when he was a student at the University of Iowa, and found her intellectually sympathetic and stimulating. She loved her nominal father, an American G.I., but he detested her as a constant reminder of his wife's infidelity. Hence, Taban can say for both Helen and himself that 'we wish dad were around to steady things' (p. 94).

The energetic drive of these poems is apparent also in 'Laurels for Carmichael in Prison' (pp. 89-91). Stokely Carmichael had graduated from Howard University, Washington, D.C. (where Taban studied for his B.A. degree) in 1964 and from 1966 to 1967 was chairman of the Student Nonviolent Coordinating Committee (SNCC). His activism for black rights landed him in gaol, and the poem compares his militant methods with those of more moderate and older black leaders, including Martin Luther King and Whitney Young. The main questions Taban asks about correct tactics are answered in favour of Carmichael, who would 'Call a spade a spade' without respect for the sensitivities of people like Everett Dirksen, the Republican minority leader of the Senate in the 1960s who, though a conservative on most issues, gave vital support to the Civil Rights Act (1964) and the Voting Act (1965). The final questions are clearly rhetorical: the judgment has already been made through the argument of the poem.

Taban's second volume of poetry, *Another Nigger Dead: Poems* (London: Heinemann Educational Books, 1972), is a much slighter work. It has politico-philosophical poems ('bless the african coups', pp. 1-7; 'the filed man laughed and said', pp. 8-9; 'to miss li', p. 10; 'there goes my son', p. 11; 'with purity hath nothing been won', p. 12; and 'blood iron and trumpets', p. 13), personal poems ('i was weaned from my playmates right in the womb', p. 14; 'i walked among men in america', pp. 54-8; and 'when some people dig', pp. 59-61), a large number of brief meditations or passing thoughts (pp. 17-53), and the impenetrable prose *conte-à-clef*, 'Batsiary in Sanigraland' (pp. 63-72).

'Bless the african coups' may be considered to derive in part from Taban's reading of Nietzsche, especially, of course, his first book, *The Birth of Tragedy* (1872). Taban treats tragedy as essentially national rather than personal or cosmic, though it may be experienced 'when your child dies' (p. 1) as a result of national turmoil and it also 'teaches us that we are not the lords of this world' (p. 3). But Taban, like Nietzsche, has an optimistic view of tragedy: it can exist only where hope, yearning, and the desire for greatness are found; it is extinguished by such poverty-stricken doctrines as existentialism, the theatre of cruelty, the theatre of the absurd, and materialistic science. And, in a stunning finale, he points out that it is also annihilated by callousness.

'The filed man laughed and said' is a more jocular, but no less serious poem. The filed man is a representative of bureaucracy (with its filing systems), of predatory government (as if with filed teeth), and of ideological fanaticism (as if filed right down to a minimum or marching in file). He is an advocate of nationalization by the corporate state, the one-party state, and entrenched government. The absurdity is that he sees no absurdity in nationalizing (and hence perpetuating and institutionalizing) poverty.

'With purity hath nothing been won' adopts some of the rhetorical patterns of Ezra Pound's Canto 45 ('with usura hath no man a house of good stone'). It is a prelude to the ironic war song 'blood iron and trumpets'. Both are examples of Taban's full-blooded dramatic espousal of a point of view that he rejects but wants to experience and examine.

'I was weaned from my playmates right in the womb' contains a good deal of bizarre advice, but also some personal revelations. The bookishness and the outsiderhood that he attributes to himself from childhood are true, and the ending is a brilliantly condensed summary of the way the world has treated him:

> i brought doubt into the world
> the world doubted me instead
> such is fate
> master confuser (p. 16)

The second autobiographical poem, 'i walked among men in america', is even more revealing. The story told here in sequential form is also referred to fragmentarily many times in *Meditations*. His wife, Lucy, was 'a homegirl' from Acholiland who had gone to England to study: 'she has finished all the knowledge That they teach in Bristol

And London', as he puts it in 'The Marriage of Black and White' (p. 98), and then come to America. Knowing little of her, but respecting her educational background and his father's efforts to secure her for him, Taban married in 1964. They had two sons (Umbi and Kica, as he tells us in *Meditations*, p. 157). In 1968 they returned to East Africa, and Taban, disappointed at not being offered a position at Makerere University College, joined the staff of the University of Nairobi. After six years of marriage, his wife left him, taking the two boys. The poem is a lament against injustice, ending with an imprecation against those who do not practise humility. Like most of Taban's personal poems it reveals deep hurt, some self-pity, and a great desire for warm, untainted human affection.

'When some people dig with hoes' is another lament against injustice. It begins with a broad social scope and gradually narrows down to the individual speaker, so downcast and burdened by his own existence that he cannot bear to think of anyone else's problems.

The aphorisms are in an elevated biblical language, of the kind often used by Ezra Pound or T. S. Eliot. The lines on cynicism and humility (p. 22) are reminiscent of Pound's Canto 81 (containing the famous 'Pull down thy vanity' passage); the lines on clarity (p. 40) recall Canto 84 ('There are distinctions in clarity'); the play on word and world (p. 31) recalls Eliot's 'The word within a word unable to speak a word' ('Gerontion'); and 'his highness the masquerader' (p. 35) recalls John Pepper Clark's poem, 'His Excellency the Masquerader'. Intelligence, learning, scepticism, and humanity are evident in almost all these epigrams; very few fall flat.

Thirteen Offensives Against Our Enemies (Nairobi: East African Literature Bureau, 1973) consists mainly of political essays in prose. There are, however, three poems, 'The Common Man is a Parasite' (pp. 21-7), 'Colonial Atavism in a Neo-Blackman's Head' (pp. 37-40), and the long sequence of 'Ancient Egyptian Poems' (pp. 45-70). All three are in long, Whitmanesque lines full of declamation, parallelism, and rhetorical repetition.

'The Common Man is a Parasite' is not for the most part directed against the object its title would suggest. It is largely about the unholy alliance between African writers and politicians and, apparently without irony, in praise of the civil service. Politicians and writers are said to be of the same kind: they have gone to the same schools, they have the same expensive tastes, they are equally cynical. Writers are in opposition only in order to take the politicians' seats at the next revolution; their conferences are mirror images of the politicians', except that the manifestos against South Africa are more literate. The second half of the poem is largely devoted to praising the civil service for its dedication and practical achievement. As he said in the essay 'Eleven Steps Towards African Development', 'a sound, competent administration guided by a code of honour stressing responsibility, initiative for visible results is the greatest possession any country could have' (p.

15). The sense of the need for honourable conduct as the key to good government is one that he had also expressed in 'Student's Lament'. There too he had expressed faith, derived in part from Carlyle and Nietzsche, in the value of hard work. His aphorism in section VII, 'Greatness is work' (p. 25) summarizes a good deal of the writing of these two mentors. From that aphorism he is then poised to launch an attack on those who do not satisfy what Carlyle called 'The Gospel of Work'. The unemployed, 'the common man', is called here a 'parasite', deserving to be exploited by politicians and forced to work.

That is the straightforward reading of the poem. With Taban, however, the tone is rarely devoid of some undermining irony. It is provided here by the apparently favourable use of 'Uncle Tom' and 'Gunga Din' as models to be followed (p. 25) and by the last line of the poem, where he suggests that the policy he advocates will be not only for the good of the common man, but 'ours as well'. Now Taban is quite capable of taking pejorative terms like 'Uncle Tom' and turning them upside down (as he does in 'Student's Lament') and on the whole that is what I think he is doing here. But he had earlier, in a pejorative sense, called his beloved father an 'Uncle Tom' who, because of his 'religious respect for the white man', 'had to die'.[8] The poem is for the most part to be taken at face value, but, as is so often the case, Taban has not quite convinced himself that he does not want to say the opposite, or say that what he has written is in jest.

'Colonial Atavism in a Neo-Blackman's Head', one of Taban's most prosaic poems, poses no such problems of intention. It states very clearly, in relation to the proposal to establish a national religion, some of his most deep-seated beliefs: that African culture is not hermetically sealed from the rest of the world, that it is and always has been the product of many sources, that it is multifarious rather than homogeneous, that religion is often a tool of government, and that black governments often act like former white colonial ones.

'Ancient Egyptian Poems' takes up the main complaint of 'Student's Lament': that Taban and people like him, the tellers of truth, the incorrupt, are not listened to, but are despised and persecuted. In this later poem, however, there is a much more pervasive sense of national corruption; he now feels that the derision and condemnation are deliberate state policies to stifle opposition. The 'special force guns' (p. 46), the 'media of communication' (p. 47), and the 'C.I.D.' (p. 48) are used to deal with dissenters and visionaries. 'Fear is before me today', he says (p. 50), 'For now it is a sin to fart, shit and crap' (p. 56). He himself is denigrated: 'Look, my reputation stinks' (p. 55); and he is tempted to leave Africa. Section 11 is a dialogue about this kind of escape, but he says that 'I fear to let myself go into the Western World, cold and austere without a hope of any return' (p. 57) and he comforts himself with the hope that 'The weather is likely to change' (p. 57).

In *Meditations*, in a passage addressed to his dead father, he expands on his attitude to the possibility of leaving Africa for America:

I am not fleeing to America, because America has enough. If I am
to go elsewhere, let me go to a place where I will have the scope to
do much to an appreciative audience.

Flight to America is a worse death. The dead culprit pursues his
shadow into the land of the electric light where the shadows are so
substantial you never really see the moon. (p. 156)

He did, in fact, go to Papua New Guinea, though such a possibility is
not raised in 'Ancient Egyptian Poems'.

The major value he does hold to here is that of education, the need
for which is vigorously stated in sections 8, 15, 16, and 18. Lack of
education is in this poem and elsewhere one of the criticisms he makes
of politicians, though more important to him is their failure to take heed
of the advice of those who are well educated.

Confidence in his own education makes him, here and elsewhere,
anxious to do something memorable. In section 11 he argues with
himself that 'If thou diest now, who will remember thee?' and 'I fear
not death but death in obscurity' (p. 57). In *Meditations*, in the passage
just quoted, he contemplates going somewhere 'where I will have the
scope to do much to an appreciative audience'.[9] Such an ambition is the
gist of the sustained copulation metaphor of section 20, where the wife
can be interpreted as literature or fame which he tries in vain to serve
until he draws on the strength of his mother and father. It is to them
that his thoughts turn so often in all his writings; at times it can seem
almost like infantile regression, as if, with all his learning, his personal
and social strength had not developed beyond adolescence.

Sexual metaphors, especially substitutionary, thwarted, or perverse
ones (masturbation, rape, impotence) and the embarrassing emissions
of the body abound in this poem. So do images suggesting that 'Man is
but an animal' (p. 64): animals, insects and bugs, parasites, and raven-
ously eaten food. There is also one image that well expresses his own
concept of himself in an uncomprehending, unappreciative world: 'I
love darkness ploughed through by the fast-moving car' (p. 59). And
another image of himself leads him to doubt whether the Nietzschean
Superman can be realized:

> Humanity ties me down
> The superman is just a mirage
> Unless he is the social capitalist. (p. 65)

The 'Unless' introduces a possibility based on Taban's distrust of
political ideologies (other than moral ones) and his belief in political
and economic salvation through eclecticism, the combination, for instance, of socialism and capitalism.

Ballads of Underdevelopment (Poems and Thoughts) (Kampala: East
African Literature Bureau, 1976), offers further discursive rhetoric
and aphoristic observations about subjects he has dealt with before.
Nietzsche lies behind much of the book still, though it is now a

Nietzsche who is often placed in historical context or criticized for inconsistency. The values remain much the same: workers are needed more than writers, eclecticism is a more sensible economic and cultural doctrine than nationalism or Pan-Africanism, Taban has 'shouted hoarse' but is 'not yet heard' (p. 31). Yet there is perhaps a new disillusion and cynicism. The image of rats (and of many other animals) pervades these poems, often being used as a symbol of activity in ignorance, conduct ruled by superstition, or achievement within puny limits, as in

> How a rat will pass through life
> Without ever knowing its name is Ratty (p. 50)

or

> How to calculate the price of rats
> And cut each others throat over a swine or two
> While giants in millions count
> And order about traders in vermins (p. 41)

The poem that is begun by this second quotation is realistically pessimistic about the economic state of Africa in relation to the Western world, though the reason it offers is in terms of the neglect of his own formula for economic eclecticism: 'Synthesism is quite around the corner' (p. 41). Potential is neglected, though it lies dormant till a time when

> Many more are the things we shall learn
> And those we shall enjoy
> When our noses are sharp enough
> And the eyes learn to read unwritten poems
> And the smallest sigh reaches the ears
> And our skins can sense the forces around
> And our imagination
> Can conjure games past and to come. (p. 61)

Granted his Nietzschean belief in the superior importance of action to poetry, it is not surprising that Taban adopted a hortatory, urgent style suggesting the labour and sweat of the workman rather than the polished elegance of the artist. Like Ezra Pound he unashamedly makes poetry out of his own emotional life and his economic ideas, and like Pound he arrives at a stage of disillusionment; of not having achieved his high ambition. He never loses the sense of being a jester, an entertainer, and the fabulation that flows from this rôle sometimes serves to veil his own true feelings or beliefs in a confusing swirl of contrary ironic indicators. Deep emotion is beyond him in poetry; it is hard to imagine any reader being moved to grief or ecstasy by his work. The emotions he deals with are social ones: the object is a class (like politicians, poets, civil servants, or the poor) or at best the representative of a class (notably, wives). He seems always to be addressing an audience, always to have his voice raised, always to be adopting the rôle of sage or pedant. It is not that he is doctrinaire. He does have a few favourite ideas, it is true, but with most other ideas he is prepared to juggle them, to examine them in all lights, and to wonder whether they are true or false. His mercurial imagination takes him to extreme positions, verging sometimes on a sceptical nihilism, but it just as quickly brings him back, for he is at heart a 'synthesist'. His adoption of the rôle of jester, irritant, or the perpetual leader of the opposition can make him seem devoid of any commitment except to contrariness, and it has certainly produced for him enemies and detractors who remain implacable in their criticism even when Taban himself has moved on with a jest from the position that gave offence. The result is that he is his own worst enemy when he wishes to be taken seriously. Some would deny that he is ever serious, but I have tried to show that he does have a fundamental core of belief and commitment. He is even more introspective than Dennis Brutus or Lenrie Peters, and his introspection has an air of shameless exhibitionism about it. His restless quick-wittedness, the mobile intellectuality that enables him to play with a proposition and turn it inside out, can seem like Brutus's sensitive and nervous awareness of all the possible approaches to an issue, but where Brutus seems to be striving for truth, Taban often seems to be striving only for effect or for self-display. He cannot convey the emotional sincerity of Brutus, and perhaps he rarely wants to. He differs from Brutus too in not having found a task suited to his exceptional talents; his striving to be a Nietzschean Superman has not succeeded.

Notes to Chapter 5

1. Address of the Co-ordinating Secretary (Wole Soyinka) to the Inaugural Meeting of the Union of Writers of the African People, Accra, February 1975, in *African Currents* No. 2 (Summer 1975), 19–22 (p. 19).
2. *Frantz Fanon's Uneven Ribs* (London: Heinemann Educational Books, 1971), p. 50.
3. See *Meditations*, pp. 22, 122.
4. *The Last Word: Cultural Synthesism* (Nairobi: East African Publishing House, 1969), p. 8.
5. *East Africa Journal* 3, No. 8 (November 1966), 7–14; reprinted in *The Last Word*, pp. 187–206.
6. The attitude expressed towards Mau Mau here is a dramatically effective one, but not Taban's own. His own view is that they were 'thugs' and that Kikuyu acquisitiveness did not end with Mau Mau; see *Meditations*, pp. 136–7.
7. *Cultural Events in Africa* (London: The Transcription Centre) No. 57 (1969), pp. I–III (p. II).
8. This was in an article written in 1970 in response to the unfavourable *TLS* review of *The Last Word* and *Fixions*. It was published together with the original review in *Ghala* (special literary issue of *East Africa Journal*) 8,

No. 1 (January 1971), 38-40, and in *Thirteen Offensives*, pp. 113-19 (p. 117).

9. This is not empty boasting. His work in the University of Papua New Guinea, if not always 'to an appreciative audience', was vastly stimulating to students and staff.

6 Kofi Awoonor

▼▼▼▼▼▼▼▼▼▼▼▼▼▼▼▼▼▼▼▼▼▼▼▼▼▼▼▼▼

In politics and philosophy, as well as in the theory and practice of literature, Kofi Awoonor is a syncretist. He amalgamates all experiences, whether personal ones or the collective experiences of Africa, in order to produce a single vortex of images. Africa for him is a continent and a notion that draws into itself, appropriating and adapting, the whole of human life and history. As he said in an address at the University of Washington:

> Africa continues to expand, change, adapt—not into a so-called universal construct determined by a Euro-Christian order, but inclusive of it, in spite of it, engulfing the historical and religious experience of Islam and its sociocultural impact. It restates all its complex personality in terms of its authentic inevitable historical reality—in response to global imperialism, expansionist communism, corporate capitalism and superpowerism, technology and consumerism, the expanding dimensions of political amorality, all pulled into an essentially African frame of things governed by laws that are endemic, capable of growth and elimination.[1]

This attitude is syncretism in an African framework, to be distinguished from the universal syncretism of, say, Taban lo Liyong or Michael Echeruo, both of whom are trenchantly criticized earlier in this lecture for using 'universal' as, in Awoonor's opinion, a euphemism for 'European' or 'Western'.

From the African vortex, the artist as visionary, acting on behalf of his community, selects and shapes material 'in the journey towards a harmonic order' (p. 142), the personal expression of which is 'the ecstasy of unabandoned being' (p. 141). Out of syncretism comes the journey towards unity, unity of philosophy or religion and union of being. The artist, 'the one who renews the cosmogony' (p. 142), operates as 'priest, shaman, farmer, fisherman, true teacher' (p. 142), suffering

> moments of 'madness' that will shatter the so-called perceived reality. The models exist in the artist-carver, poet cantor, drummer, dancer, diviner, and healer. All the momentary crisis points of 'madness' are overstepped, conquered, subdued, for an ultimate calm which only defines the next phase of energetic takeoff. Danger and joy are part of this circular progression with periodically assertive moments (immeasurable by a stop watch as the Roman calendar) of human progress. (p. 142)

This view of the artist explains a good deal of Awoonor's own practice in writing. It explains the ceremonial incantatory quality of much of his poetry, the formulaic element, which as in most religious or other ritual utterances can seem either profound or, because of the necessary degree of generalization, empty and hollow. It explains the sense the poetry creates of being simultaneously about visible reality and a metaphysical understanding of it. It explains why so many of the poems in his first two volumes seem interdependent, as if they were simply different handfuls lifted from a common source. It explains his use of multiple images, often drawn from widely differing sources, to focus on the exact nuance of meaning he wants. It explains his invention of new forms that ignore conventional boundaries between, for example, verse and prose, or narrative and ritual. It explains why the central figure of Amamu in his experimental prose work, *This Earth, My Brother* (London: Heinemann Educational Books, 1971), is thought to be insane by those unable to share his vision.

In a note in his first volume, *Rediscovery and Other Poems* (Ibadan: Mbari Publications, 1964), Awoonor (or George Awoonor Williams as he was then) says that he began writing in 1949. The notion of cultural synthesis is, however, one that came gradually to him. His first published adult poetry, 'The Sea Eats the Land at Home', 'Songs of Sorrow', and 'Song of War',[2] was largely derived from Ewe dirges, laments, and battle songs, which he learnt in part from his grandmother, Afedomeshi, and translated into English. 'Songs of Sorrow' has many lines of virtual translation from the work of Henoga Vinoko Akpalu, the originator of the modern style of Ewe dirge. It begins by talking about Dzobese Lisa, the Creator God or Fate of Ewe belief. The immutable fate destined for each person is said by the Ewe to be like the chameleon, whose sudden changes and foul-smelling faeces are a significant metaphor for fate.[3] Obviously regarding these poems as apprentice work, he chose not to include them in *Rediscovery*. In that volume, however, and in his second, *Night of My Blood* (Garden City, New York: Doubleday, 1971), several poems draw on the two early 'Songs', incorporating whole lines and passages from them. Some other poems, Awoonor tells us, were first written in Ewe and subsequently translated into English. One example he gives is 'I Heard a Bird Cry', broadcast in Ewe in 1961, and then translated into English some time later.[4]

The first stage of Awoonor's progress towards cultural synthesis was, then, to rely heavily on Ewe oral poetry as his main source. The second was the bringing together in a single poem of material from the Ewe tradition and the European tradition in which he had been educated. Material from the two strands is set down side by side to emphasize a clash of cultures. Gerard Manley Hopkins, W. B. Yeats (in mythic and political ideology as well as in the creation of a mysterious mood of cosmic immanence), and T. S. Eliot are the major modern writers from whom he draws, but there is also a pervasive influence of the Bible.

Awoonor's first and second volume both contain several examples of each of the first two stages in his work. *Night of My Blood* does, in fact, reprint about two-thirds of the poems in *Rediscovery*. The ten not reprinted have been disowned by Awoonor as 'not finished works' and 'bad poetry', and he has said that he is glad *Rediscovery* is out of print (*Palaver* interview, p. 54). Two of the omitted poems are, however, readily available in Moore and Beier's *Modern Poetry from Africa*: they are 'Lovers' Song' (2nd ed., p. 102), an example of the first phase of his work, and 'Easter Dawn' (p. 103), an example of the second.

Night of My Blood contains one long poem, 'Hymn to My Dumb Earth' (pp. 82–95), that Awoonor regards as representing a third phase in his development, the synthesis of cultures rather than the juxtaposition of them as in the second phase. Here the material from each culture reinforces rather than opposes that of the other. Bud Powell, the jazz pianist; the crucified Christ; the childless villager; the man saddened by the venal politics of independence all merge into one, in much the same way as several of the disparate characters in *The Waste Land* merge into Tiresias. Awoonor says of his poem that:

> The Bud here, the Christ image, the person who is left almost totally bereft of any love or any support, is what we see again and again. We have seen him in the earlier part of the poem, 'I have no sons to fire the guns ...' There is no opposition between these two—the 'I' of this section and the 'Bud' of the other. The Biblical echoes reflect the same thing. 'My God gave it to me, this calabash,' comes straight out of an Ewe song and coincides very well with, '... the Lord did not/let the cup pass away.' He will have to drink it. This is what I think suggests a groping, a journey towards unity. (*Palaver* interview, p. 54)

The only other poem that might be put into this third phase is 'The Return from Bali' (*Night of My Blood*, p. 61), which seeks to assimilate the way of life in Bali to that of Africa, ending with the traveller's goodbye or invocation of peace on those remining (*selamat tinggal*).

The largest group of poems in *Night of My Blood* consists of those of the first phase, which use the material of Ewe songs as their staple. The imagery is frequently of travelling, especially by water, and more especially on the ferryboat of death. Solemn rites are encountered along the way, there are gates and gate-keepers, there are altars for sacrifice, there is perfume and incense, there are songs and drumming, there are fires for cooking. The moon and stars shine, as the voyager looks towards the coming dawn. The crow and the vulture perch and observe. Flesh peels away from bones, nature putrefies, and death, with its attendant tears and drums, is never far away.

The central object of the journey in these poems is the achieving of communal and individual harmony or unity. In 'Exiles' (p. 23) the exiles are lost souls who have disturbed the former harmony: they have 'Slashed, cut and wounded their souls', leaving a 'mangled remainder

in manacles'. 'Desire' (pp. 24-5) concerns 'the bewildered The wanderers' who 'lost their way homeward'. In 'The Consummation' (p. 27)
the search is for some way of unifying the rituals of birth, circumcision,
death, and eternity. And in 'Rediscovery' (pp. 36-7), the title-poem of
his first volume, unity in and with death is achieved:

> there shall still linger here the communion we forged,
> the feast of oneness which we partook of.

It is a feast that unites the living and the dead, the historical past, the
present, and the future. It is a metaphysical communal unity that
sometimes touches on either the migration of the Ewe people several
centuries ago from the upper reaches of the Niger to their present home
on the coast of Ghana, Togo and Benin, or on their resistance to colonial
power in the nineteenth century. More generally, the journey, with its
pervasive imagery of the moonlit, wind-tossed sea, is a journey into the
tradition of Ewe poetry, especially dirges and laments. Ritual imagery
of purification abounds: the purification is for the purpose not of cleansing from sin but of achieving readiness and unity.

The first poem in the collection concerns the poet's equipping himself
to be the spokesman for such a journey. He is aware that his personal
god of song, the Hadzi voodoo that every Ewe musician has, is at
present unfit to inspire him. The bringing of the god back to health is
itself a process involving a journey, an unaccompanied journey across
water to a shrine dedicated to the god of healing. The poet is himself
unfit to enter the shrine facing the god, but is made to come in ignom-
iniously with his backside first. The cure prescribed by the god of
healing is another journey, back 'to your father's gods', which have
been 'violated' by neglect. The announcement of the remedy and the
poet's obvious intention of following it is itself sufficient to cause the
god of songs to 'burst into songs', which the poet is 'still singing with
him'.[5]

The 'journey homeward' as the second poem, 'Exiles' (p. 23) makes
clear, will for some exiles, who have 'committed the impiety of self-
deceit', be a bitter one. They will never feel at home, for they have
dismembered their souls and will be, like the unresting ghosts, the
'night-revellers', doomed to eternal restless waiting. The search, even
for the poet, will be a long and difficult one, as 'Desire' (pp. 24-5)
indicates. He will listen to the communal sea and to his own individual
soul, he will look into the 'scattered ashes from forgotten hearths' and
'in the fireplace where mother's cooking pot hangs'. He will need to be
sceptical of the myths both of 'past travails' or of 'future glories', in
other words of the kinds of self-deceit inherent in Négritude, or as he
puts it in an interview with John Goldblatt:

> the setting up of a false myth in response to another false myth
> [colonialism]. . . . Our ancestors were as barbarous and cruel and as
> devious as anybody else's ancestors. And there was no Golden Age

in Africa any more than there was one anywhere else. The corruption of Africa is an aspect of its humanity. To deny that corruption—that we sold people into slavery and did all the usual horrible human things—is to suggest in a way that we were not human.[6]

What he can be certain is true, however, is his childhood memories, such as that of newly washed clothes, smelling of camphor, taken out from his grandmother's box.[7] The emphasis on humanity as an ultimate value is as characteristic of Awoonor as of Dennis Brutus. The 'resting place' that is the object of his search is not in another world, though it may involve communion with the spirits. It is in this world and its values, as 'In My Sick Bed' (p. 26) makes clear.

The longest and most complex poem of this first phase is 'I Heard a Bird Cry' (pp. 42–53). It is a long lament, partly addressed to 'my people', partly an expression on their behalf, partly an assertion against them, partly an interior monologue. Most of the recurring images—tears, fetish bells, drums, songs, the journey by canoe, mad dogs, the dunghill, birds, the evil snake, the harmattan, rain, and flood—are concerned with loss, destruction, or death. There is the loss of sovereignty to the white man, who with the 'voice of a gun' (p. 47) has destroyed 'the walls of my father's house' (p. 43). His culture has swamped the indigenous one: his clothing has to be put aside before the ceremonies of the ancestors can be undertaken (p. 45), but it has permanently subverted the 'rich men' of the land, who insist that it be worn to any feast that they give (p. 52). The speaker, a younger man, has to remind himself that he was there when the ceremonies were performed; although he wishes he had 'stayed at home' (pp. 48, 49), he is not prepared to be insulted for his inexpert participation in the ceremonies but returns the sarcasm he has been subjected to (p. 45). Later, he finds that as a poor man he is not listened to (p. 49), but he derides the lack of charity of the rich, their neglect of the starving poor, and insists that he has 'The singing voice . . . from the gods' (p. 51) and will not be silenced. Within this 'song of sorrow' (pp. 48, 49), there is, in fact, a good deal of invective, especially towards the end. It is directed against the powerful and rich ('the swooping eagle', p. 47; 'The drunken dogs', p. 52); the naïve faith in the Christian saviour (p. 52); and the equally naïve faith in independence or political reform (pp. 52–3). Much of the poem is, then, devoted to asserting the truth and validity of his own vision, as the refrain, 'Hush! I heard a bird cry!' indicates.

The tears, so prominent in the first half of the poem, gradually abate, so that at the end the poet can adjure his heart to 'be at rest' and can look forward to the feast which 'is ready for us'. The relative optimism of the ending has not been argued for; it has simply emerged out of the emotional drift of the laments, imprecations, and exclamations that make up the poem. The whole poem has the atmosphere of a dream-vision, in which the poet alternately is submerged in the communal personality and emerges to assert his own identity as singer or as critic of society.

The title poem, 'Night of My Blood' (pp. 54-7), is by comparison much more straightforward. It celebrates the historical migration of the Ewes, particularly the Anlo group. It is a miniature national myth, oddly accompanied by references to the passover and by the use of a phrase from Gerard Manley Hopkins's poem, 'No worst, there is none', 'Comforter where is your comforting?' (pp. 54, 55). The crucifixes referred to are not biblical, but presumably refer to the 'dakpla' of the Yewe cult of thunder worship, the cross worn on the back by initiates— Awoonor says that the cult is 'still very powerful among the Anlos' (Duerden interview, p. 47).

One of the finest poems of the first phase is the noble tribute to Christopher Okigbo, 'Lament of the Silent Sister' (pp. 74-7). Amid the familiar imagery of moonlight, drumming, and a canoe on the river, Okigbo is envisaged as coming into Awoonor's part of the river, cutting away the raffia gates that enclose him. Okigbo is represented as a poet with a voice

> Strung clear as the gong of the drummer boys
> Bright burnished like the glint edge of
> the paschal knife . . . (p. 74)

Awoonor modestly represents himself as unready and unprepared for Okigbo's uncompromising brilliance, for 'My flood had not risen then' (p. 76). But Okigbo's cry, as he pressed on to his death, released the waters of poetry in Awoonor, and the poem ends in tumultuous, almost sexually excited, ecstasy.

The poems of the second phase sharply juxtapose the old and the new ways, with no particular liking for the new but a recognition nevertheless that they have to be accommodated. 'The Cathedral' (p. 25) speaks of the replacement of 'a tree' by 'A huge senseless cathedral of doom'. 'The Anvil and the Hammer' (p. 29) speaks of 'the flimsy glories of paved streets' alongside the 'tender and tenuous' traditional culture. The new culture is ugly ('The jargon of a new dialectic'), where the old is spoken of with tenderness and affection ('sew the old days for us').

The third phase poem, 'Hymn to My Dumb Earth', abjures the use of stock responses to the dichotomy between the old and the new. It uses material from a multitude of sources including his earlier poems, and the tone with which any fragment, old or new, is used has to be deduced from the context. There are quotations from the Bible, nursery rhymes, Christian hymns, spirituals, political slogans, Andrew Marvell, Thomas Gray, T. S. Eliot, Dylan Thomas, the original words of the Ghana National Anthem, and a modern Anlo anthem. The largest number of quotations come from Christian hymns and the Bible, for, as Awoonor says, 'My soul is locked in alien songs' (p. 92). Many of the quotations are distorted to the reverse of their original meaning. 'O, come all ye faithful', the Christmas hymn, becomes 'O, Come all ye faithless' (p. 86); T. S. Eliot's 'fear death by water' in *The Waste Land* becomes 'fear death by guns' (p. 90); the Lord's Prayer becomes 'Our Father who art in heaven/do whatever that pleases you' (p. 92).

The poem is a complex image of a beloved and beautiful land to which the poet is destined to return in death, thus paying his debt. But it has been ill-served by its conquerors and rulers, so that 'the land was covered with blood' (p. 82); political and business affairs are like 'chameleon faeces' (p. 83); relative fights relative and all fight against the interests of the nation (p. 88); politicians mouth slogans (p. 89) and look after their own interests. The only 'redemption' (p. 91) (in 1968, when this poem was written, the word did not have the tainted political overtones of its later use in the 'National Redemption Council', though the former President Kwame Nkrumah had been known as the 'Osa-gyefo' or 'Redeemer') is to return to the life-giving rivers of the land itself.

Images of madness, disorder, death, and excrement abound. They go alongside precepts about the prudence of remaining silent and quiescent in such a society; to accept that 'Everything comes from God'. But opposed to this strain of images is a set of musical ones, mostly of black jazz musicians such as Thelonius Monk, Bud Powell and Coleman Hawkins, heralding a return of the Messiah or the road to Mecca. They are accompanied by images of dispossession (Esau) and sacrifice (Bud Powell, Christ and the poet), for the future has in it images of war (pp. 86–7) and of peace (p. 88) which alternate to the end of the poem. The ending itself, as with so many of Awoonor's poems, combines peace, death, and a return to the traditions and the land of one's ancestors. The last line, 'Everything comes from God', has now lost its cynicism: it is possible for the poet to believe that in regard to this event it is a true dictum.

'Hymn to My Dumb Earth' was written in 1968, after Awoonor had left London, returned to Ghana, and then gone to live in the United States. His third volume of verse, *Ride Me, Memory* (Greenfield Center, New York: Greenfield Review Press, 1973), is about America, Afro-America and Africa. It opens with 'America' (pp. 9–10), which relates his expectations of America in images of cowboy films and some lines from Archibald MacLeish. The next two poems, 'Harlem in Summer' (p. 11) and 'Harlem on a Winter Night' (p. 12), present the brutal and pitiful realities of America. Ironic contrast is also the chief mode of the ten 'Long Island Sketches', which are mostly concerned with people or incidents encountered on Long Island, particularly in Stony Brook, where he was teaching at the campus of the State University of New York. Awoonor presents himself as saying very little, but being in turn irritated, charmed, or numbed by the behaviour he encounters. He says that in some quarters he was considered 'stiff and British' (p. 19) as a teacher, though his own impression of his classes is one of liveliness and informality.

The repressed violence in some of these poems finds an outlet in the five 'Songs of Abuse' (pp. 20–23). They draw on the Ewe tradition of poetry of abuse or *halo*. The object is to be outrageously but humorously vindictive about physical characteristics, motives, and actions, to make every line an almost embarrassingly direct attack. The ten 'Hymns of Praise, Celebration, and Prayer' (pp. 24–8) are also composed of brief, separate utterances, but they are quite often gnomic in content and the poems are puzzlingly mixed in tone. Images of violence and of peace are used to characterize nature, society, politics, religion, and the individual soul, for 'Where there are gods of war, there must be gods of peace' (p. 25).

The first hymn speaks of his mind as a 'strange burden town' (p. 24), burden here referring to a load, the substance of a message, and the refrain of a song. Through this town passes 'A band of noisy music men' who are greeted and celebrated in the remaining pieces. They include individuals such as Dennis Brutus, remembered street pedlars from his homeland, a feminist, and a woman on Hydra; and incidents such as American wars, both overseas (Korea and South Vietnam) and civil, and senseless slaughter throughout the world, often fired by religious principle. Arlington, in poem IV, is the name both of a cemetery in Boston commemorating Bostonians who died fighting the British in the War of Independence, and of the National Cemetery where America's honoured dead have been buried since the Civil War. As such it is a name associated largely with the dominant white majority in the United States. Memphis is the name of the town in Tennessee where in an unprovoked attack on blacks in May 1866 white residents killed 46, wounded over 70, raped women and burnt churches and schools. 'Was there not a dirge sung at Arlington and Memphis?' Awoonor asks (p. 25), emphasizing his theme of the universality both of hatred and of love. Awoonor's conclusions from his representation of the human condition are that 'Love shall leaf these winter trees' (p. 27); that there is a consolation in nature: 'the moon came out and she stopped crying' (p. 28); and that there is a persistence and continuity of life: 'tomorrow too the sun shall rise again' (p. 28).

'Afro-American Beats' (pp. 29–33) is a celebration, in the same style as 'Hymns of Praise', of American representations and memories of Africa. It has sections on the black American jazz singers, Nina Simone and Roberta Flack; the great alto saxophonist, Charlie Parker, his successor, John Coltrane, and the trumpeter, Miles Davis; the black writer Maya Angelou who worked in Ghana from 1963 to 1966 and whose autobiography, *I Know Why the Caged Bird Sings* (1970) Awoonor had apparently recently read; Fred Hampton and Malcolm X, the Black Panthers, and other references concerned with the murder of blacks, both in America and Africa, such as Ulundi (the final decisive battle of the Zulu War in 1879 when Cetewayo's forces were defeated), Memphis (1866), Sharpeville (1960), Elisabethville (during the Katanga secession movement, 1960–63), and Alabama (scene of many protests against segregation and discrimination in the 1950s and 1960s);

Ralph Ellison's seminal novel of black consciousness, *Invisible Man* (1952); and Langston Hughes's long crusade as a black poet. With 'ears to earth' (p. 33), black Americans can be one with Africa; with understanding, black Africans like Awoonor can see in black Americans 'the light [that] shone from your dark beautiful soul' (p. 32).

Sorrow and death continue to be recurring concerns in the simple imagistic 'Etchings from My Mind' (pp. 34-5). Echoes of Hopkins ('Summer's sorrow'), T. S. Eliot ('death in mountains ... single night motels', 'At the final hour'), and Dylan Thomas ('festival of ... ears of corn', 'this 37 year old chill') reinforce the natural hieratic, ceremonial stateliness commonly found in Awoonor's work.

The second and shorter subdivision of *Ride Me, Memory* is called 'African Memories' and deals with reminiscences of his family and of himself. 'My Father's Prayer' (p. 39) presents two contrasting images of the relationships between Awoonor and his father, the first as dutiful son, the second as wayward rebel. He told the students at the University of Washington in 1973 that

> My father belongs to the old school; even though today he and I are very great friends, we used to quarrel a lot when I was a younger man, simply because I was very much like him. We had a clash of will all the time. (*In Person*, p. 157)

The sense of a tradition to be carried on by the poet in spite of the collapse of ancient values is strong also in 'My Uncle the Diviner-Chieftain' (p. 40). 'To Sika' (pp. 41-2) is addressed to his eldest child, recalling an accident in London and painfully searching his own soul about the conflict between his duty to and love of the child on the one hand and the powerful necessities of his adult concerns on the other. It is a humbler and perhaps more loving poem than Dennis Brutus's explanation to his children, 'For My Sons & Daughters'. 'When My New Passport Came' refers to the refusal by the Busia government to grant him more than a one-year extension of his passport, thus forcing him to return to Ghana at the end of that time. Meanwhile he wittily contrasts the politically motivated limited renewal of his official identity with his personal renewal in the daily cycle of the forces of nature. His home-coming too is seen in natural terms as the sloughing off of a dead skin no longer needed.

A different kind of homecoming, the return in death to the land of spirits, is the subject of 'To Those Gone Ahead' (pp. 45-7). He recalls his maternal aunt; his cousin and childhood companion, Dede; his maternal grandfather, Nyidevu, whose totem was the hippo. Their departure was honoured with customary ceremony, from which Awoonor, now in an alien land (typified by 'winter birdsong and a yellow moon'), seems cut off.

Though in many ways this lament, like the rest of the poems in this volume, seems to have a clearer outline of imagery and a less dream-like drift of thought and emotion than the earlier poems, its subject and many of its images revert to those of 'Songs of Sorrow' and 'A Dirge' (*Night of My Blood*, p. 63). Awoonor's American experience had made him readier to use contemporary references and given him the confidence to mingle traditional, literary, and original imagery together, but it had not altered his fundamental subjects or mood. He simply became more explicit, placing less reliance on the automatic hypnotic effect of traditional materials.

This loosening and clarification in the texture of his poetry continues in his next volume, *The House by the Sea* (Greenfield Center, New York: The Greenfield Review Press, 1978). It opens with a poem, 'Poems, Fall '73' (pp. 2–3) in which he speaks of *Ride Me, Memory* as 'My bird held captive these centuries' which, 'Fluttering its wings for a lack of direction and basic hesitation' flies into the 'glass windows' of American indifference and incomprehension. The poems of the first part of *The House by the Sea* seem often as if they were deliberately written to avoid this fate. They proceed in vivid spurts of reminiscence and end often with a cynical or sentimental line or strophe. They are poems to win applause at a public reading. By that I do not mean they are insincere; it is just that their shape has been dictated in many instances by a sense of the right emotional curve to affect an audience.

Many of them are concerned with brutality, especially racial brutality, and more especially the slavery experienced by Africans and Jews. They are scornful of deliberate ignorance, cautious unwillingness to become involved, or specious claims of neutrality, especially when mouthed by fellow-writers. They are vehemently opposed to American intervention in the affairs of other countries, whether in Allende's Chile, Castro's Cuba, or the shifting politics of Bolivia. They yearn wistfully for tenderness and humanity while celebrating the feats of those who have seized liberty by force or deploring injustice and oppression in Africa and elsewhere.

A similar juxtaposition of opposites occurs in some of the love poems. 'After the Exile and the Feasts' (pp. 10–11), for instance, is full of violent contrasts. The 'blue night streets' become dark 'at scarcely afternoon'; there is the 'purgatory of allies and comrades'; the 'hands of your care' are 'callousing', for they make 'survival and betrayal . . . one'; the available wings or 'fans' are those of 'gassed birds'; 'guitars' in the Mexican border town of Nogales 'vomit' their cheap songs; his life seems like 'mine fields' in which he is the last soldier left; his 'hurrahs' are of 'defeat'; and the lovers' sexual and intellectual communion reminds him of 'the howl of booted dogs fleeing the pavement of our minds'.

Awoonor had lived in England and the United States for nearly eight years. As the time approached for him to return to Ghana, many of the poems took on a complex air of nostalgia, fatalism, and self-assertion. 'Departure and Prospect' (pp. 17–19) speaks of his desire to return to 'my ravished earth', to face up to accusations or rumours, and to refuse any alien rôles wished on him, though without denying his foreign experiences. It is a dream poem like 'When Going to Jail' (p. 19) which follows it. But, as 'Of Absence' (p. 21)—one of his more blatant 'recital' poems—makes clear, his primary love is 'the drummers of my home-town'. His homeland, in the widest sense, Africa, is prey to unjust government within and falsification without. It is a victim both of the South African régime and of cultural colonialism from Europe, typified by Négritude, the Sartrean concept of 'black Orpheus', and the view of Africa as one of the circles of Dante's hell (p. 27). In the narrower sense, of Eweland, and in particular the Anlo Ewe country of the Keta lagoon where he grew up, his homeland was once prey to foreign infiltration, typified several times by references to the Bremen Mission (the North German Missionary Society); in 'play that game we played' (p. 15), for instance, he recalls a childhood game of jumping on the horizontal marble gravestones of the German missionaries who had built a church at Keta.

The attitude to Eweland and to Africa is thus a complex rather than naïvely sentimental one. It is sometimes reflected in the poems that celebrate his American friends, notably the poets and writers named in the dedication to the volume. 'So he comes now the clown' (pp. 22–3) and 'An American Poem' (pp. 29–31), for instance, both see these warmly appreciated friendships against a background of African, Amer-ican, and world history, consciousness of which keeps breaking into his personal pleasure at American companionship.

Awoonor returned home in 1975 to take up a position in the English department of the four-year-old University of Cape Coast. Within a few months, at a time of rumours of a coup against Colonel I. K. Acheampong, Chairman of the Supreme Military Council, he was arrested. No charges were laid, for there appears to have been some doubt in the minds of the authorities about finding a charge on which he could be adjudged guilty. A special decree was promulgated to define the new crime of giving shelter to or aiding the escape of an alleged coup leader, and to impose the severest punishment. Awoonor was charged in August 1976 with harbouring Brigadier Kojo Kattah, a friend since childhood, and the ringleader of an alleged plot against the government. Awoonor admitted welcoming him to his house but said he was not aware that he was wanted by the government. Awoonor was found guilty and sentenced in October to twelve months' imprisonment. He was, however, released almost immediately, perhaps in recognition of his long period of confinement, perhaps as a result of the representations of international organizations. Many of the poems in the second part of *The House by the Sea*, 'Homecoming', were written during his detention in Ussher Fort Prison. It is the 'house by the sea' (p. 54) of the title, though he says 'I cannot see the damned sea because of old caked walls built by Dutchmen' (p. 50); it is not the 'dream house' of 'Departure and Prospect' (p. 17) or 'the house by the sea' (p. 58) at the 'ferry port' of death. It is, as he wryly remarks in 'The Wayfarer Comes Home' (pp. 64–78), 'the house of Ussher'; the reference is, of course, to Edgar Allen Poe's story, 'The Fall of the House of Usher'. In this prison he thinks often of freedom, of the landscape outside that he cannot see, and even of the 'chattering bluejays of Kalamazoo' (p. 46), left behind in America. Amid his boredom he holds to the optimistic belief that 'the abscess that hurts the nation' (p. 40) will one day burst and that love will eventually produce again 'the miracle of the world' (p. 39).

The most ambitious poem of the whole book is 'The Wayfarer Comes Home: (A poem in five movements)' (pp. 64–78). It is his most self-confidently relaxed poem, one where he has at last achieved mastery of his materials, one where the overt struggle to achieve synthesis has been replaced by unselfconscious achievement. It is a poem of homecoming, less in the physical sense than in the spiritual. Home is Eweland, stretching from Ghana across the mountains of Togo, and in the wider sense the whole of Africa. In prison himself, he recalls in the first and last movements the struggle against oppression in Soweto, which had come to a head earlier in the same year.

Home and its entire spiritual meaning is personified as the beloved one, loved 'since conception' (p. 65) except for a period when she was lost 'among the high grass of infancy'. This refers no doubt to the vehement attempts of the mission schools, Presbyterian and Roman Catholic, that he attended to subvert him from his ancestral beliefs. Subsequently he came to the city from his homeland (his 'sinning time', p. 64) and later searched in foreign places for an understanding of what the land meant to him, though without success, for 'you were another spirit of another time and place' (p. 66). Now, in his prison cell, he celebrates the spirit of his homeland, and because he is a poet whose task it is to express such meanings, he can be elevated and inspired by the spirit to identify himself with his ancestors and their history: he can become 'king of the mountain', 'the lion that roamed the violent shores', and even 'the ferryman of the river', mediating between life and death.

The second movement elaborates on the battle of Datsutagba in 1866 between the Anlo Ewe and armies from the neighbouring peoples raised by the British against the Anlo as a punitive measure. The battle, fought in the fan-palm forest between the River Volta and the Anlo island town of Anyako on the Keta lagoon, was very even, and although the Anlo retired first they regarded it as a Pyrrhic victory for the British-inspired forces. This, then, is the epic fight between the Anlo leopard, lured from his forest home to the banks of the Volta, and the British lion.

At the end of the movement, a proverb introduces a passage on divination by the casting of gourd seeds. Here the poet assumes another of his rôles, that of prophet or diviner, but the means used, the seeds, act as a link in the long chain of fertility symbols in the poem, beginning with salmon and turtle in the first movement and going on to harvest images and images of fecundity in the later movements.

Eggs, the fruit of the palm, pods, seeds, and harvest are the prevailing images of the third movement as the poet prepares to take on another rôle, that of fetish priest at a shrine by the Keta lagoon, his homeland. Alongside these images are those of death, funeral rites, and burial, so that the ceremony to be performed by the poet is obviously bound up with both life and death, symbolized by pod and shroud.

In the fourth movement, the speaker is the land, the beloved, speaking to the poet as 'Wayfarer'. The traveller is tired, footsore, and hungry. Awoonor may be recalling a walk of eleven miles that he made with his mother as a small boy of about five,

> singing merrily at the beginning of the journey. Soon my feet started to hurt and tears flowed before I made the sound of weeping. Then the journey would be long and weary for me. (*The Writer in Modern Africa*, p. 117)

His lover, however, awaits him, bidding him change 'your cripple's crawl' into 'a warrior's gait' (p. 73). She too experiences confinement and suffers from the fact that 'our gods are maimed by native and foreign cudgels' (p. 75).

The final movement is a celebration of the land of his birth and upbringing and of Africa. It is also a fervent proclamation that freedom and justice are near at hand. He recalls the slave plantation and the fishermen on the Keta lagoon, the forests and mountains beyond the land of the Ewe, the 'wizardry' (p. 77) of ancestry from which he has sprung. He recalls also the suffering of Soweto and announces that 'the festival time has come', 'the dance has begun', and 'the heap slags [perhaps intended as 'slag heaps'] of the raw cities will burn' (p. 77). Then, linking this prospective battle with that of Datsutagba, he refers to 'stalking the evil animal' and 'the sanctity of the ambush', for in the forest the Anlo ambushed their enemies on three sides. The poet's last rôle, then, is that of single-minded warrior, and in what appears to be a daring local reference to his own political struggle as an Ewe in Ghana, he says that 'the swamp beneath the hills shall receive the evil animal' (p. 78).

As with the earlier long poems, this one gains much of its effectiveness from being the culmination of earlier attempts at some of the material. Awoonor writes poetry as some composers write an opus, using similar thematic material from work to work and ending in a large-scale composition that draws on some of the earlier ones. He tries out ideas, particularly, in this instance, in 'Found Poem' (pp. 49–50) and 'Sea Time, Meaning a Pledge' (pp. 58–60), and then brings the whole complex of his current ideas together in 'The Wayfarer Comes Home'. The earlier examples in *Night of My Blood* still contained gaucheries, naïve sentimental passages, and awkward construction. These evidences of poetic insecurity have almost entirely vanished from 'The Wayfarer Comes Home', partly because of his maturity as a poet, his assimilation of his materials, his confidence in his own voice rather than that of other poets (whether Ewe or European), his control of the earlier tendency to diffuseness of subject, and his ability to find a subject and situation where he could write directly about his own condition (which he does without self-consciousness or self-pity), his rôles as a poet, and his dedication to the land of the Ewe and to Africa. The reverential ceremonial hush of earlier poems is largely absent now: instead there is a sharpness and clarity in the imagery such that it no longer needs to be smothered in ready-made ritual incense. Awoonor's deliberate syncretism, that carefully adopted apprenticeship, has now merged into his own authentic poetic voice. He has achieved an assimilation of materials that Christopher Okigbo, despite his more intense dedication to the craft of poetry, never did.

Notes to Chapter 6

1. Tradition and Continuity in African Literature', in *In Person: Achebe, Awoonor, and Soyinka at the University of Washington*, ed. Karen L. Morell (Seattle: University of Washington Institute for Comparative and Foreign Area Studies, African Studies Program, 1975), pp. 133–45 (pp. 140–1).

2. *Okyeame* 1, No. 1 (1961), 59–61; *Modern Poetry from Africa*, ed. Gerald Moore and Ulli Beier (Harmondsworth: Penguin, 1963, 1968), pp. 78–81 (1st ed.), 98–101 (2nd ed.).

3. Awoonor reprints and discusses 'Songs of Sorrow' in his volume of essays, *The Breast of the Earth: A Survey of the History, Culture, and Literature of Africa South of the Sahara* (Garden City, New York: Anchor Press/Doubleday, 1975), pp. 203–8. He goes on to discuss 'A Dirge' (pp. 208–9), 'I Heard a Bird Cry' (pp. 209–13), 'Song of War' (pp. 213–15), and 'At the Gates' (pp. 215–16).

4. See 'Interview with Kofi Awoonor' in *Palaver: Interviews with Five African Writers in Texas*, ed. Bernth Lindfors *et al.* (Austin: African and Afro-American Research Institute, The University of Texas at Austin, 1972), pp. 47–64 (p. 48). Awoonor says that he translated it 'about six months' after writing it in Ewe, when '*Black Orpheus* requested some of my poetry'. But it was not published in *Black Orpheus* until No. 15 (1964), pp. 23–31. It is possible that the 1961 date given for the Ewe broadcast is wrong.

   It is in this interview that Awoonor discusses (pp. 52–4) the three stages of his development towards cultural synthesis.

5. For Awoonor's own comments on this poem see the 1968 interview with Dennis Duerden in *African Writers Talking: A Collection of Interviews*, edited by Dennis Duerden and Cosmo Pieterse (London: Heinemann Educational Books, 1972), pp. 37–50 (pp. 47–9).

6. 'Kofi Awoonor: An Interview with John Goldblatt', *Transition* No. 41 (1972), 42–4 (p. 43).

7. See Kofi Awoonor, 'Reminiscences of Earlier Days', in *The Writer in Modern Africa*, ed. Per Wästberg (Uppsala: The Scandinavian Institute of African Studies, 1968), pp. 112–18 (p. 116).

7 Wole Soyinka

▼▼▼▼▼▼▼▼▼▼▼▼▼▼▼▼▼▼▼▼▼▼▼▼▼▼▼▼

In view of Wole Soyinka's increasingly vehement commitment to Pan-Africanism, it may seem perverse to characterize his poetry as a synthesis of African and Western elements. But Soyinka has never been the crude kind of Pan-Africanist who denies the Europeanized part of Africa's history. His poetry, though it shows signs of a struggle to emphasize its African origins, remains deeply indebted, at least for its form and many of its references, to the tradition of English literature.

His earliest extent work, written at school and university,[1] provides few hints of the mastery of his chosen medium that he later attained. It does, however, provide evidence of his characteristic tense, jumpy ebullience and his sense of the louring violence of humanity. The early poetry is full of nervous energy darting about with little regard for decorum or uniformity of tone. When he compiled his first volume of poetry[2] Soyinka omitted not only the obviously juvenile work and some of the light-hearted occasional pieces but also some early poems that had been much admired and anthologized. They were 'The Immigrant', '. . . And the Other Immigrant', 'My Next Door Neighbour', 'Telephone Conversation' and 'Requiem'.[3]

It is easy to account for the rejection of the first three.[4] They are acute, sometimes malevolent, social satires, clever but heartless. The jaunty, venomous lines, with their two or three beats each and occasional lines of one or four beats, are in a flexible, conversational rhythm that makes good use of the possibility of expanding then snapping shut on the triumphant closure of a witty one-beat line. The black expatriate in England in '. . . And the Other Immigrant' haughtily keeps up professional British standards of dress while half-starving himself, because he is scheming towards the senior civil-service post he will gain back home. He is contemptuous of all ' "riff-raff" ' and 'All whiteness in a face'. He congratulates himself on the sound intellectual reasons for his self-confidence:

> Let pedants tease their pompous heads
> While to my repertoire I add
> (The sound, if not quite the spirit of)
> Our new-coined
> Intellectuals' slogan—
> Négritude.

The movement towards the sting at the end is typical of these poems. So too is the touch of half-rhyme ('heads', 'add'). So too is the flexible style that can encompass in its conversational eclecticism even an eighteenth-century iambic tetrameter like 'Let pedants tease their pompous heads'. But probably more important as a reason why such a poem was unacceptable to Soyinka for perpetuation in a book is that its tone and point of view wobble. In trying to pack in too many thrusts, he sacrifices uniformity in the point of view. The parenthetical line, 'The sound, if not quite the spirit of', cannot be considered the opinion of the immigrant: it is an authorial comment by Soyinka. The tone even of 'repertoire' and 'new-coined Intellectuals' slogan' is not quite right: this language is too perceptive and self-critical for the foolishly complacent immigrant: again it is Soyinka intruding.

The tendency to pack too much into his lines will remain characteristic of Soyinka's work. So too will the sense of superficially polite behaviour masking volcanic thoughts. In 'The Immigrant', the central character thinks of using a knife on the face of the English 'native girl' who has snubbed him at a dance palais. In 'My Next Door Neighbour', the spinster in the basement flat seizes as her life-support system on a prurient observation and hatred of the prostitute who lives above.

The bitterness and venom of these poems will recur, but in the poems Soyinka has chosen to collect they will be placed in a context of understanding pessimism about humanity rather than one of clever exposure. 'Telephone Conversation' is an almost flawless satire, witty, humorous, and with a beautifully judged pace. Soyinka tired of it, partly no doubt because of the frequency with which he had performed it in public, partly because he was in danger of being identified with it to the detriment of attention being given to his more subtle and serious poems. There is also the consideration that as a satire of contemporary society it has dated in a way that the more generally cultural poems have not. Just as the brand-names in the novels of, say, Ian Fleming, Cyprian Ekwensi and Charles Mangua gradually become obsolete, so too do similar details in the two 'Immigrant' poems and even such details as the telephone with 'A' and 'B' buttons in 'Telephone Conversation'.

The finest of the excluded poems is 'Requiem', characterized by Donatus Nwoga as 'a requiem to a dead love'.[5] It is a poem that might well have found a place in the 'For Women' section of *Idanre and Other Poems*, perhaps alongside 'Song: Deserted Markets'. The tone is extremely complex. As in most of Soyinka's serious poems, the reader has to be alert to the end: no nuance of mood can be forecast or taken for granted; the intellectual pressure, reassessing and developing an understanding of the mood, persists to the end. The speaker is still haunted by the memory of the girl he loved, whom he took to his 'thorned bosom' and wounded. At present the memory is fresh, his 'resolve' only 'tamed'. But he knows that time will make 'longings crumble too'. That self-comforting thought is, however, immediately followed by a wild stanza of insane release, in Shakespearian imagery and language. Applying the gruesome truth of actual bodily decay to the body that metaphorically represents the love he once experienced, he addresses the termites (or, as an English poet would have said, worms):

> Then may you frolic where the head
> Lies shaven, inherit all,
> Death-watches, cut your beetled capers
> On loam-matted hairs. I know this
> Weed-usurped knoll. The graveyard now
> Was nursery to her fears.

It is a poem very far from the complacency and assurance of the rejected satires, but still Soyinka excluded it from his first volume. *Idanre and Other Poems* is a very carefully composed book, a *livre composé* that works up to a crisis in the title poem. But 'Requiem' would not be out of place either in mood or in imagery. Its imagery of dawn and evening, earth and air, blood and dew, grain and ashes, ritual and ceremony is reflected in the poems included in the volume. Had Soyinka placed it in the 'For Women' section, however, that section would have been expanded to disproportionate length. The possibility of upsetting the delicate balance between the sections must have been one reason for its exclusion.

One other possibility is that Soyinka considered its imagery of ritual and ceremony too exclusively Christian and/or personal. The last of the six movements uses the imagery of the cup of sorrow that Jesus prayed might be taken from him. The fourth movement speaks of a ritual cupping of the lovers' hands together so that earth might sift through. On the other hand, the ritual significance of dry air and rain is in accordance with Soyinka's usage in *Idanre and Other Poems*.

I do not want to suggest for one moment that Soyinka is later averse to using Christian, Graeco-Roman or personal imagery. What he does, however, is integrate any such imagery into the pervading imagery of Yoruba belief. The first stanza of the first poem in *Idanre and Other Poems*, for instance, has a glancing reference to the iron spears or staves (*asen*) that are the commonest symbol of Ogun, the Yoruba god of iron. Soyinka manages to assimilate into such Yoruba myths material from his very extensive fund of learning. Like many of the greatest poets in any language, he is a myth-maker. And like all successful myth-makers he begins from existing myths, which he develops and rejuvenates by introducing 'foreign' material. This is, of course, the essential mode of any living tradition, whether myth, ritual, religion, custom or artistic performance. (By contrast, Achebe's Ezeulu in *Arrow of God* destroys himself and his religion because he inflexibly follows the letter of the ceremony of which he is guardian rather than its purpose.) A *griot* or praise-singer develops and expands the material he inherits; a play that continues in the repertoire of a company is adapted to new social circumstances in later performances; Yoruba religion accommodates new phenomena like electricity to the responsibilities of the existing gods (allocating electricity, of course, to Sango, the god of thunder and lightning). But it is not only in orally transmitted traditions that creative change and adaptation, often of a profound kind, may occur. A great artist may achieve the same result in the written tradition. One has only to think of English poets whom Soyinka admires, Blake and Yeats. Like them, Soyinka is a myth-maker of something radically new. Like them, he is eclectic in his sources. Like them he has a basic myth into which other elements are subsumed.

Soyinka's myth is not something merely created by and confined to the poetry, nor is it something that relates outside its expression solely to the life of the poet. It is a myth about Africa today, and sometimes, more generally, about humanity. Its poetic elements, drawn from Africa and from Europe, parallel the materials that are used, and must be used, to shape current African society.

I have called it a myth, but it is really a set of myths, developed by Soyinka as his ideas have changed, though frequently making use of similar elements. Even with a myth, however, neither the scene nor its meaning will remain static, for Soyinka is essentially a poet of kinesis. Granted his belief that modern Africa can assert an identity only by drawing on a selection of its history, it would, indeed, be inconsistent for him to think that that amalgam would itself not be subject to change.

Soyinka as a myth-maker on the grand scale is comparable with only two other African poets in English, Christopher Okigbo and Okot p'Bitek. They too hold in tension in their poems material that is African and material derived from Europe. Their purpose, too, is the same, for they share the recognition that modern African society draws both on its African history and on European elements, and they represent this dual (or, more accurately, multiple) origin in their poetic materials. There are differences, of course. Okigbo's poetry sometimes resists interpretation away from its clearly personal reference to the broader African one. And Okot p'Bitek finds no place for European philosophy or religion in Africa and expresses his myth in the kind of social satire that Soyinka carefully eschews. One other African poet, Dennis Brutus, began a kind of myth, centred on the troubadour. But despite the accomplishment of many of the poems about this figure, Brutus apparently came to think that the myth was too personal and that the matter of modern Africa should be expressed in direct unadorned rhetorical poetry intended for oral delivery.

Such poetry is, of course, at the furthest remove from Soyinka's *Idanre and Other Poems*. Soyinka writes difficult, condensed poetry, in which individual poems may not yield their meaning unless placed alongside others. This volume can, indeed, be interpreted as an assembly of myth-making materials leading up to the fully developed myth of the title poem. A fairly small number of images and scenes is repeated, with incremental additions of meaning, up to the final poem. This is not to say that Soyinka has a limited number of images. He is, on the contrary, constantly fecund. But one set of images provides a theme that can be ornamented by more ephemeral images.

The central image in this volume, as in a great deal of Soyinka's mature poetry is Ogun, the 'God of Iron and metallurgy, Explorer, Artisan, Hunter, God of war, Guardian of the Road, the Creative Essence' in the Yoruba religion, as Soyinka puts it in the Notes to *Idanre*. Although not the chief of the *orisa* or 'ministers of Olodumare' (that is, of the 'owner of heaven')—the chief is Orisa-nla, as Soyinka explains in another note—Ogun is perhaps the most assertive, the one whose power is most obvious in the world, the one most to be feared.

> Ogun is a crazy orisha who still asks questions after 780 years
> Whether I can reply or whether I cannot reply,
> Ogun please don't ask me anything

says one of the *oriki* or praise-songs.[6] He is the chief deity of Abeokuta, the town on the River Ogun dominated by grey boulders, near where Soyinka was born. At his shrines iron staves (*asen*) are planted in the ground.

Asen provide the core of a set of very frequently used images for Soyinka. The dawn, a time sacred to Ogun, is commonly seen low on the horizon through a screen of grass and palm-trees, described as spikes or spears. Soyinka also makes frequent use of all kinds of aery filaments—spiders' webs, fronds and feathers—that resemble wires, of whose manufacture Ogun is the presiding deity.

The first section of *Idanre and Other Poems* is 'Of the Road', five poems about dawn and the road, both sacred to Ogun. In these five poems, dawn and the road are associated with the sexual energy of sunrise, creativity, iron and death. It is possible, of course, to find many analogies in Soyinka's other work to these image clusters. His play *The Road* (1965) is one obvious source. Another is his novel, *Season of Anomy* (1973), where section 4, 'Harvest', begins with the scene:

> The sun filtered through in yellow shafts, weightless insubstantial bamboos, organ-pipes which yielded to contact with the car, ran lightly over the panels, ran through the windscreen and played on their faces.[7]

'Dawn' has for some readers been a dragon guarding the gate of Soyinka's poetry and deterring entry. It is a carefully contrived poem, consisting of a single sentence followed by an exclamation, arranged in diminishing verse-paragraphs (five, four and three lines) separated by single lines. The syntax is rather Latinate, with many almost absolute phrases referring to the palm, some inversions of word order, and the subject and verb ('The lone intruder/steals') reserved till near the end of the sentence. (Dylan Thomas often poses similar difficulties.)

Once this is understood, the poem yields its meaning more readily. Soyinka is writing a 'celebration of the rites of dawn', seen in terms of a theophany in which the sun rapes a lone palm tree, 'tearing wide The chaste hide of the sky' that has previously enfolded it like a 'night-spread' (that is, the bed-spread of the night). It 'steals' up on its (more or less willing) victim, first faintly illuminating various parts of the palm before rapidly overwhelming it in the glory of a god. The palm is seen as if just stirring, resting on its buttressed trunk as if on an elbow. 'Spring-haired', a notorious difficulty, I take to mean covered in the hairy filaments produced in the spring or growing season, with 'spring' hinting also at the springing of an arch, such as the buttressing root provides. The filaments will obviously pick up and reflect the first rays of light. The various other parts of the palm are then described. Beyond its 'head-grains' are the 'spikes' or 'fronds' primly protecting the reddish kernels that sprout above them. In the theophany, the red kernels seized by the sun give promise of fructification.

But if the images reminiscent of the *asen* of Ogun here are used to draw attention to the creative element of the god, the next poem, 'Death in the Dawn', draws attention to his destructive element. The common time for such destruction has been set in the first poem. The second begins with the words 'Traveller, you must set out At dawn'. Again, a few details are picked out in the faint light that is rapidly (in Nigerian latitudes) succeeded by dawn. The traveller is enjoined to watch the feet of those beginning work in the field; they are 'cottoned', because they are wrapped round either with literal cotton rags to keep out the winter cold or by the white mist.

The traveller, Soyinka himself, as the head-note makes clear, has a white cockerel fly against the windscreen of the car and die. But this propitiatory offering to the God of the Road is without efficacy. The death can, indeed, be interpreted as a 'Perverse impalement', for it fails to stop man's insatiable desire for technological progress. But the road has another victim to reap, a driver killed a little farther along. The traveller addresses him 'Silenced in the startled hug of Your invention', the invention being at the same time the actual smashed car, the symbol of man's hubristic technological progress, and something which, as it is made of iron, is the product of technology, and is intended for the road, Ogun himself has helped to create. The 'You', in other words, applies to the killed man, mankind in general and Ogun. Technology and 'Progress' are here seen as something likely to be destructive, but as they are within the province of Ogun they have also a creative aspect. One of Ogun's attributes, according to Soyinka, is that

> He is 'Lord of the road' of Ifa; that is, he opens the way to the heart of Ifa's wisdom, thus representing the knowledge-seeking instinct, an attribute which sets him apart as the only deity who 'sought the way', and harnessed the resources of science to hack a passage through primordial chaos for the gods' reunion with man. The journey and its direction are at the heart of Ogun's being and the relationship of the gods to man.[8]

In the poem, Soyinka's own reaction mimics or mocks the contorted grimace of the dead man, as he thinks of his own human involvement in death and envisages himself as the dead man.

The notion of man's inventiveness is picked up at the beginning of 'Around Us, Dawning', but here the invention is an aerial 'beast', a jet. Dawn, the invention, and death are again linked, as the mountains seem to reach up *asen*-like lances to pierce the bold intruder, and the poet feels himself at the centre of the life-giving and life-destroying explosion of the sun.

'Luo Plains' is a more descriptive and less dramatic poem than the others in this set. It has some splendid images, as in the description of brilliant shafts of sunlight piercing through cloud: 'Molten silver Down cloudflues of alchemist sun'; or in the extravagant conceit in the first paragraph of a line of egrets being like a 'Plague of comet tails' or providing with its wings ('pennants') an aerial line on which whole worlds (not just the earth) seem to pivot. The sense of vast space, of the cycle of time and of imminent danger could not be better conveyed.

'In Memory of Segun Awolowo' brings us back to Nigeria, the setting of the first two poems. It is an epitaph on a friend, the eldest son of Chief Obafemi Awolowo.[9] Segun Awolowo died in a road accident, attributed by Soyinka to Ogun 'of seven paths'. The poem ends with an image of restless wandering spirits, 'Grey presences ... Adrift from understanding', who complain about the capriciousness of Ogun. In this poem, the road, the sun, harvest, iron and death form an association with the other poems in the group.

Dusk and darkness replace dawn as the setting for the four poems of the second section, 'Lone Figure'. Death is even more pervasive than before, though not to the exclusion of notions of creativity and fructification. Each poem is concerned with a visionary dreamer, who is now dead. The account in the New Testament gospels of the life of Jesus in the week from Palm Sunday to Easter Day pervades this set of poems, sometimes in overt expression, sometimes indirectly. 'The Dreamer' uses images of Jesus on the cross; 'The Last Lamp' has overtones of Holman Hunt's painting, *The Light of the World*; and 'Easter' refers obliquely to several details from the biblical story, with even a reference to the slaughter of the innocents (the subject, incidentally, of another painting by Holman Hunt). 'The Hunchback of Dugbe' is more doubtfully linked to the Christian Holy Week cycle, but it may be that the deformed visionary is to be seen as analogous to the small man, Zaccheus, who, to gain a better view of Jesus on his Palm Sunday progress to Jerusalem, climbed a tree.[10]

Soyinka is characteristically concerned with the effects of such mythical stories. In 'The Dreamer' he speaks of the 'fruit' that comes after the flower of the dreamer's words. The boughs of the tree will be 'bowed to earth' as 'A girdle for the see'. The sense hinted at here seems to be the world-wide spread of Christianity, its assumption of the world as its see or diocese, and the resultant dissension and disputation that has arisen within the organized church. There is Yeatsian imagery of stones, tumult, thrones and 'incense on the sea' at the end, reminiscent of the Byzantium poems and of Yeats's vision of the Christian era ending in chaos.

In 'Easter' he adverts again to 'future decadence' and, in another image derived from Yeats, to the 'Decay [that] Caulks earth's centre'. But this apocalyptic imagery is subordinated to the image of the spurned dreamer, the rejected or neglected poet, who allows himself to become intoxicated by the easy and painless gift of the blown frangipane blossoms and to ride his 'winged ass', a combination of the winged horse of Pegasus, the ass on which Jesus rode as a symbol of humility, and the ass as an emblem of folly. He rages, unable to accept the children's Christian way of the palm, its yellow fronds plucked only after one has passed through the danger of the spikes (the crown of thorns).

'The Hunchback of Dugbe' is about another rejected dreamer, a deformed lunatic in Dugbe Market, Ibadan. Soyinka begins by wondering how this solitary outcast spends the night; in the end he comes to believe that his spirit, not sighing, but silent, walks about in the ghostly motley of light and dark. The middle stanzas describe how this has come about: he has been killed at night by a cement-mixer truck, its rotating bowl like a 'vast creation egg' producing 'lace curtains' of pebbles inside itself.[11] This machine comes to rest over the body of the hunchback and his 'crossed cassava sticks', with its bowl still rotating, thus creating the illusion that 'the world Spins on his spine'.

The hunchback as spirit has his own enclosing womb-like load described as a matrix, with which is associated another symbol of fecundity in the 'Pigeon eggs of light' that dance about it. Once again, Soyinka has raised the possibility of creativity being achieved by the dreamer, but again it remains as potential rather than achievement.

These three poems contain perhaps more glances at English poetry than any others in Soyinka's work. I have referred to the Yeatsian echoes, but there are also such touches as the Shakespearian 'walks in motley' at the end of 'The Hunchback of Dugbe' and the Tennysonian opening of 'Easter'. They are difficult and ambiguous poems, overloaded with possibilities and deficient in clear statement. It is particularly noticeable how dreamlike the syntax is; it seems to float in moody description rather than come to an indicative statement.

'The Last Lamp' is a simpler, more uniform and better poem. It uses the image of a lantern getting dimmer as it passes away downhill from the observer and, as its bearer stops, seeming to gather her shadow around her. The bearer has the 'patient stoop' of generations; she is an old woman, apparently a market woman, at the point of death, which she meets with her habitual patience, knowing that she cannot have peace. The dreamer's rage in 'Easter', which follows, thus provides a spirited contrast. Neither dreamer has peace, but one of them, the old woman, not Wole Soyinka the poet, has patience.

The third section, 'Of Birth and Death', sums up a persistent strand of the first two, but does so with considerable ceremony and ritual.

There are numerous attempts to propitiate the bringer of death, beginning with 'Koko Oloro', the children's propitiation chant. Children are, of course, particularly vulnerable, as the *oriki* of Ogun recognizes ('Ogun kills the child with the iron with which it plays') but if Ogun's protection can be attained it is inviolable:

> The lion never allows anybody to play with his cub
> Ogun will never allow his child to be punished.[12]

Koko oloro is the pot filled with berries and kola nuts offered by children at the shrine as they sing this song.

'Dedication' is a propitiation ceremony for Moremi, his daughter, reminiscent in some ways of Yeats's 'Prayer for My Daughter'. He uses in the ceremony a number of symbolic substances: earth as giver and supporter of life and receiver of death; the yam as symbol of fecundity and domesticity; the air as a support above storms; peat as something ageless and incorruptible both by day and night; peppers for sweetness and venom in the tongue; palm-flesh within thorns (as in 'Easter'); palm oil for fecundity; honey for bringing happiness to others; camwood for affection and love; white chalk for perfection; antimony for relations with the spiritual world; salt to avoid tears; rainwater for purity and fecundity; and fruit, a repeated symbol of fecundity.

This is followed by two poems about the death of children, one deeply anguished, one reflective. 'A Cry in the Night' begins with a mother who has given birth to a still-born child pounding her head on the earth, that earth which, at the beginning of the preceding poem, was said to be life-supporting. Her intention may be to effect some kind of propitiation, but she will be unsuccessful, for no sympathetic manna-like scales will fall from heaven's scars. Heaven is quite unmoved and unaffected; just as the *abiku* is in a later poem of this set. The body is hastily buried, the woman, broken in spirit and physically retching, is folded 'harshly' by the night.

'A First Deathday' begins by describing a contrary experience of birth: 'We triumphed then upon the wails of birth'. But the triumph is ultimately that of the child, Folasade, when, exactly one year later, she dies. She avoids further earthly life, which would take her ever more remotely away from the secret of existence; instead she runs happily to her death with a last breath of mockery, like an *abiku*.

'For the Piper Daughters (1960)' is an earlier attempt at the propitiation and benediction of 'Dedication'. It was originally published in *Ibadan* No. 12 (1961), p. 28, as 'For Three Children' (with only one 'never' in the last line). It is an exuberant poem (like 'To My First White Hairs'), but it nevertheless contains many elements of Soyinka's belief that good is always associated with evil. What he recognizes in the Piper sisters is spontaneity, and in the end he wishes that they may dance, pray, and sing with enjoyment and without deliberation, so that for him they will never grow old. It is Soyinka's familiar notion of the natural adaptation of an organism to environment so that it continues to maintain its basic properties.

With 'Abiku' in this alternating pattern of moods we are back to the world of childhood death. The practice of propitiation is seen this time from the point of view of the *abiku*, the child returning repeatedly to the world only to die early and grieve the mother. Soyinka's *abiku* alternately taunts the mother with the ineffectiveness of the standard ritual propitiations and precautions and then commands and cajoles her to take these traditional measures.[13] The placing of bangles on the neck and ankles of the *abiku*; the offering of goats, cowries, palm oil, ash and yams; the branding of the child with the pattern of a heated piece of snail shell for subsequent recognition; the deep burial of the body; the repetition of the act of conception: all are futile. All such measures point, indeed, to a repetition of the cycle of conception and death. The act of coition is obliquely conveyed in imagery of moisture, dew, spider's webs, wine froth and night. Into the door of 'The way I came' comes the 'Suppliant snake', which, with a cry, the mother unwittingly kills. (Soyinka may have been led to this usage by familiarity with the Elizabethan English locution of killing and dying for detumescence.) Then after this mood of heartless inevitability and almost impish malice, the last stanza suggests just a touch of self-pity by the *abiku*. In the womb he 'moans'. But this slight relief of mood is almost immediately taken away, for while he moans he is turning the fertile egg-yolk into a burial mound. The effect is tautly produced by the short last line of the stanza, 'Mounds from the yolk'. In this poem, the first three lines of a stanza normally contain four strong beats, the last line only three. This final shortening is a characteristic pattern in Soyinka's stanzas, throwing particular weight on to the last line, which is often rather gnomic. It is especially useful in intensifying a mood of melancholy, fear, hatred or mockery.

'To My First White Hairs' is a light-hearted self-mocking interlude, calling for the onset of the 'sham veneration' provided by white hair. 'Post Mortem' continues something of the same mood of amusing but bitter mockery that began with 'Abiku'. Again the sense of futility and inevitability is evident. The 'masked fingers' of the dissectionist will not in fact learn 'how not to die'. In *Season of Anomy* there is a similar, more extended scene, in which the dissected brain is described as 'a fallen meteor: craters, ridges, a network of irrigation channels [forming] a microcosm of the world from which it had fallen' (p. 223) and the doctor comments 'We learn much about the human body here you know. Unfortunately . . . we don't seem to have learnt much about the human mind' (p. 224). At the end of the poem there is a mock paean in praise of grey, here associated with dissection, sleep and death. Grey is in fact the prevailing colour in this whole volume, which on the whole lacks words of colour. It is brought to the forefront in the next section but one.

What follows immediately, however, is 'For Women', a section that contains several poems in rhyme. Soyinka has turned away temporarily from the contest with the gods over life and death to explore the possibilities provided by relations between men and women. They range from the casual insignificant sex of 'Song: Deserted Markets' through two poems metaphorically describing the act of coition ('Her Joy is Wild' and 'In Paths of Rain') to a poem set near childbirth ('Psalm') and one at childbirth ('To One, In Labour'). 'Black Singer', 'Bringer of Peace' and 'By Little Loving' stand a little outside this pattern, the first being about song as an expression of the pain and wounding that are elsewhere expressed through sex; the second an analysis of the nature of the peace that a woman can offer; the third about an abortive experiment of removing oneself from company and sex.

Seeds, grain, wine and rain are the prevailing images of this section, as pain is the prevailing mood. 'Song: Deserted Markets' is set in Paris, presumably in the district of Les Halles, formerly the chief market and brothel area. The 'Seeds' that fill the gutters are thus both waste produce and the waste of unproductive love making. In one of Soyinka's characteristic contrasts, the next poem, 'Psalm', again using imagery of grain and harvest, is addressed apparently to a pregnant woman beloved by the father of the child she is carrying. He is joyous, solicitous of her welfare and ecstatic about the mystery of coming birth.

'Her Joy is Wild' transfers this ecstatic mood to a woman who begs the poet for an exuberant and savage act of love-making, of the kind normally associated with a woman wishing to conceive her last child. It is a frenetic, unrealistic mood, ignoring 'the wispy moments' of doubt; she even has a ('blind') vision in her love-making that the act is the killing of a 'senile chieftain'. The poet puts aside his doubts and unshells the nut of the future by participating in coition and the conception of a child. The ecstasy this time, then, is seen as spurious and as having an uncertain outcome.

'Black Singer' returns to something like the mood of 'Song: Deserted Markets'. The song is full of imagery of wounds and promises and it seems 'indifferent' to the way it is received by listeners: it just runs away and is lost in the night.

If the woman in 'Black Singer' makes little personal contact, the woman in 'Bringer of Peace' engages very closely with a man and his passions. The question is whether the effect is lasting or merely superficial. The man's peace (or, perhaps more exactly, accommodation with the world) is represented by fire, which protects him in 'unguarded moments' and serves to 'hold the beast at bay'. Woman's peace is like light rain, soothing the earth, and damping down, though not extinguishing, such fire. It is only 'a tacit lie of stillness', for its effect is only a temporary cessation of 'the python's throes' or a temporary bringing to rest of 'the bowstring's nerve'. It fails to reach the wild beast within man, the 'inborn howl', the constant struggle to break through the civilized surface. The fire is on the surface, and that is all that a woman's peace can touch.

'To One in Labour' returns to the mood of 'Psalm'. Despite the unusual and even, to some readers, repulsive imagery of a queen ant perpetuating life at the expense of her lovers, the feeling is one of tenderness. The womb is likened to an ants' nest containing a queen. Around her are her dead lovers—the unfertilized human eggs, or perhaps past affairs, now dead. But in 'the silent shrine of pain' the death-dealing process is contracting as the life-giving one comes to fruition. It is a more sober poem than 'Psalm' because of this assertion of the necessity for death to be associated with life.

'In Paths of Rain' is in one sense a more sober rendering of the act of coition than 'Her Joy is Wild', but this time without any sense of the factitious or false. It also, however, rehearses and sums up many of the other strands in this section, including the child-birth of 'Psalm' and 'To One in Labour'. Much of the imagery can be simultaneously applied both to coition and parturition, with their sense of tension and ultimate release. In addition, there are glances back at some of the propitiation symbols of 'Dedication' in the references to antimony, kernels and ash at the end. Yet amid these reiterated images, there are probably as many new and startlingly apt images as in any of Soyinka's lyrics, most of them concerned with bright, mysterious flickering light (fox-fires, a heart stimulus to a hare used in an experiment, glow-worms, flecks of mica and antimony, and 'lantern sanctuaries'). It is an arcane and captivating poem, which might well have ended this section.

But Soyinka wanted to take up some of the concerns of 'Bringer of Peace' again, and he does so in 'By Little Loving'. This poem has a title in common with and a superficial resemblance to a poem by Thomas Blackburn, whom Soyinka met when he was studying at Leeds University. It is in stanzas of four lines with the outer lines ending with something like Wilfred Owen's three-quarter rhyme or assonance. This use of rhyme can easily produce a sense of disappointment or incompleteness, and it is intended to do so here, particularly as the first of each pair of rhyming words tends to have a jaunty connotation and the second a melancholy one (sought/drought, hailed/howled, hate/hurt, for instance).

As an attempt to assuage pain, Soyinka tries to cut himself off from human contact. He knows that the best remedy is to express hate as a counter-balance to the wounds of love, but instead he tries to provide a store of peace. This proves, however, as factitious as the woman's peace in 'Bringer of Peace'. As in that poem, the emotions burst out from within. More importantly, perhaps, and this is a point not made in 'Bringer of Peace', by allowing the fire to die down he had aborted the birth of the phoenix by denying it the pyre on which to immolate its worn-out self. This section ends, then, with an assertion of the poet's need for emotional involvement, with all its pain and hurt, if the creative spirit (conventionally symbolized by the phoenix) is to have means of expression.

'I Think It Rains', the opening poem of 'Grey Seasons', uses rain as a symbol for the release of creative energy.

> I think it rains
> That tongues may loosen from the parch

he begins; and in the third stanza he looks forward to rain washing away 'These closures on the mind'. The rain will not merely release creative energy, however; it will interact with it, imposing its own pattern. It will produce its own 'skeins' or 'searings' on our desires and longings; it will at times be 'unbending'; and it will with some pain 'Bare[s] crouching rocks' in the poet.

The circling ring of grey ash before rain is touched on in various other poems of this section. So, more generally, is the season of rain and resulting fruitfulness, the season of Ogun, whose presence has already been established in the *asen*-like imagery of 'Rain-reeds' in 'I Think It Rains'.

In 'Prisoner', however, there is no rain, but only wispy smoke by day and a sandstorm by night. The moist grey smoke swirling over the closely cropped grass represents the ordinary hours of life from which the apparent wisdom of old age is built up. The sandstorm represents a dramatic happening in life, the seizure at night of a 'companion'. But the drama of the storm subsides, the man is imprisoned. As he has no burning cause to sustain him, he is destined to a life made up of empty grey hours.

Greyness in this poem has a quite different connotation from its creative/destructive connotation in 'I Think It Rains'. 'Prisoner' is, in fact, a very negative poem, as can be seen by noting the number of negations in it: 'do not ... not ... not ... not ... Nothing ... lacking'. Greyness here is repetitive meaninglessness.

The next two poems make no overt reference to 'grey', but they take up some of its associations. 'Season' is a harvest poem: the rain of the grey season may be assumed to have fallen; it is now dry, and the corn is ripe and ready for harvest. The sign of its ripeness is an ambiguous one: rust, reminiscent not just of a golden-brown russet colour indicating that the corn is ripe, but also of the spotty fungal disease, rust, that so readily attacks and wilts crops of this kind. The vigorous imagery of the growing season, occupying the middle of the poem, with its pollen, dances, arrows, streaks of light, rasping and piercing, is supplanted at the beginning and end by the languid imagery of wilted plumes, tassels, long shadows and wreathing smoke. The last line, then, 'The promise of the rust', is ambiguous and uncommitted in tone: the promise may turn out to be either 'ripeness' or 'the germ's decay'. Decay and death are always associated with fruitfulness, just as in 'Psalm' the woman's ecstatically celebrated pregnancy is seen as 'the ruin of [your] cornstalk waist'.

In 'Night' there come together elements from both 'I Think It Rains' and 'Prisoner'. In 'I Think It Rains' Soyinka recognizes that the coming of inspiration involves some pain for and alteration in the poet; in 'Prisoner' the central character is possessed and bound wholly by a grey essence. In 'Night', Soyinka surrenders entirely, though not without fear, to something that is painful and dangerous, but not debilitating. Night, having jealously overcome a rival, the luminescence of the sea, similarly drains the poet of all other thoughts, at the same time heightening his senses so that they pain him. But in this tense, receptive state he recognizes that he is vulnerable to the spirits of the night, that is, living death, perhaps madness.

The sense of preternaturally heightened sensation as a prelude to receptivity of something destructive is carried over into 'Fado Singer', which describes and reflects on the effect created on the poet by a wrenchingly powerful performance of popular songs in Portuguese by Amalia Rodriguez. In this moving and witty tribute to her, Soyinka represents the songs as overwhelmingly sensual, so much so that eternity seems annihilated and no escape from the senses is possible. The cosmic umbilical cord (with its witty hints of a chord fingered on the guitar and of the vocal cords) is severed by the singer; she embodies only human pain and not divine hope; and the result is the tyranny of the flesh, a different, but equally imprisoning kind of grey: 'grey melodic reins'.

By this stage in the volume, the prevailing note is of pain, vulnerability and the need to make heroic efforts to resist overwhelming forces that would betray the self and bring it to the verge of madness. That is as good a preparation as any for the six poems of 'October '66', written about and during a period of what Soyinka elsewhere called genocide. In the Northern Region of Nigeria, occupied chiefly by Hausa-Fulani people mostly adhering to the Moslem religion, there had been living a substantial minority of Igbo people who had left their own Eastern Region because of its close settlement and limited opportunities. They were traders, professional people and civil servants. In the Northern Region they were often regarded as too clever by half, infiltrators who would not only monopolize trade and the civil service, but would also scheme to shift the balance of power in the Federal Constitution of Nigeria away from the populous and politically dominant North. To some extent, they were also disliked or despised because most of them professed Christianity. In May 1966 there had been massive attacks on Igbo people and property in the North, set off by the belief that the political coup of January 1966—which removed the Federal Prime Minister, Alhaji Sir Abubakar Tafawa Balewa; his fellow Northerner, the powerful Alhaji Sir Ahmadu Bello, Sardauna of Sokoto and Premier of the Northern Region; and the Premier of the Western Region, Sir Samuel Akintola—was an Igbo plot to seize power. The counter-coup of July which removed the Igbo, Lieutenant-General John Aguiyi-Ironsi, as Head of State and installed Lieutenant-Colonel Yakubu Gowon, a Northerner (though not a Hausa-Fulani), did not assuage the hatred directed against the Igbos still in the North. Though many had already fled to the Igbo homeland, fresh massacres broke out at the very end of September and carried over into October. Many of the Igbo, consolidating now in their homeland in south-eastern Nigeria, feared that even this would not satisfy the Northerners and that they would be subjected to a war of liquidation.

Soyinka had many friends among the Igbo intelligentsia. Like many Yoruba, he had his own reasons for being suspicious of the Northerners, their feudalism and their hold on the Federal Government. They had been instrumental in precipitating the Western Region crisis of 1962 and in having the Yoruba Chief Awolowo indicted; they were suspected of inflating their census figures in 1963; and they had helped manipulate the corrupt election in the Western Region in October 1965 so that the Northern sympathizer, Chief Samuel Akintola, was returned as Premier. Arising from this last incident, Soyinka was tried on a charge of holding up the Western Region Studios of the Nigerian Broadcasting Corporation at gunpoint and making an illegal broadcast as a substitute for a taped victory speech by the Premier. Although he was acquitted two months later, there could be no doubt that he was deeply troubled by the political conditions of Nigeria, and fearful of further Northern initiatives.

Nigeria had been under military rule since the January coup. All troops were placed on alert at various times, as massacres and riots occurred and civil war or complete civil disorder seemed imminent. Soyinka begins 'October '66' with two poems in which the subtly defined imagery he has built up through the rest of the volume seems in disarray. In 'Ikeja, Friday, Four O'Clock' he describes truckloads of soldiers, seen near the Lagos airport, as an insubstantial 'mirage of breath and form'. So debased and corrupted are the times that the earth will drink not rain, but blood from these soldier 'gourds'. They are being sacrificed as 'A crop of wrath' on the false altar of war, not at the behest of any god.

The image of the false crop is taken up in the title of the next poem, 'Harvest of Hate'. Here again the travesty of the carefully established symbols of Soyinka's poetic world is expressed. The libations and offerings appropriate to the October harvest are all perverted this year. But Soyinka realistically recognizes that this is not some sudden mischance or aberration. He had, indeed, left open the possibility of national self-destruction in *A Dance of the Forests*, the play commissioned for the Nigerian Independence celebrations in 1960. Here he offers a stanza of relatively straightforward political analysis:

> Now pay we forfeit on old abdications
> The child dares flames his father lit
> And in the briefness of too bright flares
> Shrivels a heritage of blighted futures

Soyinka managed to get away from Nigeria for a few weeks,[14] and the next poem, 'Massacre, October '66', embodies the reflective mood possible for someone removed from the immediate conflict. He is in Tegel, a northwestern suburb of Berlin, walking by a lake.[15] He begins with a romantic, idyllic scene, which he later abrogates. There are willows that break up the sunlight, the surface of the water reflects the light like stained glass, and Soyinka looks through the coloured fragments to try to find his own thoughts in the uniform brown silt of the bottom. But nothing happens: 'The lake stayed cold'. Instead of mentally swimming in it, he finds himself swimming instead in the colourful flush of autumn leaves that swirls around in the air like leaves of paper containing messages.

But the waves thrown up by boats on the lake mock the hollowness of this 'idyll sham'. He turns to a solider, though also hollow, image, as he walks over acorns and listens to the unique sound each one makes as it cracks, as if it might aspire to being an image of the uniqueness of each human skull.

Continuing his meditation, he reflects that he will crush fewer acorns than the number of skulls being crushed in Nigeria, yet for both there seems no end to the supply. Then he tries to think himself out of his misery by turning away from the stained-glass windows of the lake to admire and, though a stranger, to feel love for a brown squirrel.

But a fresh fall of acorns turns him back to his meditation on death in Nigeria, where the innocent (or 'indifferent') are being massacred. Unlike him at the moment, they are not strangers, for they are in their own land. Even had they been strangers, the Moslem greeting of peace, 'salaam aleikun', if truly meant, would have preserved them, for it is a Moslem precept to protect the stranger.

It is evident, I think, that Soyinka, at least at this time, gave greater weight to the element of religious persecution in the Igbo massacres than most commentators have done subsequently. The earlier reference to acorns as 'favoured food of hogs' is now explained, for the Moslems, inspired by their priests, are said to treat Igbos as fodder for the loathed unclean animal, the pig.

With phrases borrowed from the ending of T. S. Eliot's *The Waste Land*, Soyinka closes the poem. In this alien land, with broken shards of acorn around him symbolizing the destruction that arises from 'pride of race', he tries to come to terms with the horror that threatens to invade his mind, horror that he has tried unsuccessfully to escape from by recourse to the movement of mind represented in the poem.[16]

'Civilian and Soldier' tells of an incident that Soyinka had experienced back in Nigeria during the overthrow of Ironsi and the installation of Gowon, the 29 July 1966 counter-coup. It picks up not only the sardonic tone from the end of 'Ikeja' but also the image of lead and bread as alternative ways of life. The poem, in its scene and its mode of narration, bears some resemblance to Wilfred Owen's 'Strange Meeting', though Soyinka's poem is unrhymed. It is one of the simplest of all the poems in this volume, a straightforward narrative, except for Soyinka's thought when facing death: 'nor is Your quarrel of this world'. This is a reference perhaps to the unreality of the world of war or to the involvement of the deities in the war. If the latter, the idea might seem to be in opposition to the line in 'Ikeja' about 'Unbidden offering on the lie of altars'. The two positions can, however, be reconciled by reference to the myth in 'Idanre', where Ogun is only very reluctantly persuaded to engage in war, but having done so he runs amok.

'For Fajuyi' is a kind of praise-song to Lieutenant-Colonel Francis Adekule Fajuyi, Military Governor of the Western Region. He was appointed after the January coup, and his honourable and effective attempts to govern justly and to punish corruption greatly impressed Soyinka. Soyinka did, indeed, undertake a tour of the North in order to report on the situation to Fajuyi. He was the most active and innovative of the military governors and came to be regarded as a radical by General Aguiyi-Ironsi.[17] At the end of July, Aguiyi-Ironsi was a house-guest of Fajuyi. On 29 July agents of the Northern-inspired counter-coup asked Fajuyi to surrender Ironsi to them, but in honour, hospitality and duty he would not hand over a house-guest who was his military and governmental superior. As a result, both were seized and later killed. Soyinka's praise-song, though understandably guarded and obscure, nevertheless expresses the greatest admiration for Fajuyi, unqualified by the sense of personal withdrawal that he expressed in the earlier praise-song, 'Fado Singer'.

Fajuyi is praised in a series of noble images: flame, steel, kernel, 'a miracle of boughs', the sun and flowers. By contrast, the nation, now he is dead, is characterized by the repeated imagery of paths choked by weeds, cold kilns in the factories, and mines (presided over by Ogun) blocked. The bridge imagery first refers to the mass returns of Nigerians (especially Igbos) to their homeland regions at this time. The returning feet are unaware of the importance of bridges, doubly in the realm of Ogun, for they are part of a road and they are made of *asen*-like 'iron spines'. There is nothing left for 'pilgrim feet' but journeys to the sacred places of local deities; they will come in contact with spirits, but they will perform no 'lonely feat' like that of Fajuyi. Yet the bridges remain (though not, in fact, historically for very long, as many communities destroyed their means of contact with the rest of the nation and other bridges were blown up by retreating soldiers). In the last stanza, Soyinka injects a note of hope, the injunction to 'Tread the span of bridges' rather than grieve for the dead, an injunction to seek once more to have communication with the rest of the nation.

This praise-song is followed by 'Malediction', a series of solemn curses on a woman who rejoiced at the death of clan 'enemies' in the disturbances. It is a commination of specific vile curses that extend even to 'your children and your children's children'.

By this stage all the myth-making elements have been assembled for an extended, comprehensive narrative treatment of myth, which Soyinka attempts in the seven scenes of 'Idanre'—seven being a number sacred to Ogun 'of seven paths', as 'In Memory of Segun Awolowo' reminded us. He is able to use a great deal of material from other poems, so that the individual poems and 'Idanre' seem to be constantly conducting a dialogue with each other, mutually illuminating and adding meaning. When, for instance, Soyinka says in 'Idanre', 'A human feast Is indifferent morsel to a god' (p. 76) one can think back to a use of 'indifferent' in 'Massacre, October '66':

> A host of acorns fell, silent
> As they are silenced all, whose laughter
> Rose from such indifferent paths . . . (p. 52)

Paths are, of course, the province of Ogun, who is indifferent to deaths occurring on them. In 'Massacre, October '66', then, not only are the paths in Tegel indifferent to the fall of the acorns, not only were the 'strangers' laughingly going about their business outside their own homeland indifferent to the resentment gathering around them, but also Ogun himself is indifferent to the plight of wayfarers, at any rate while they are still alive.[18] The additional meaning is reflected back, as it were, into 'Massacre' from 'Idanre'.

While a great deal can be gained by such cross-referencing, it will not always work. Immediately after the passage I referred to in 'Idanre' comes the line 'A lethal arc' (p. 77), referring to the sweep of Ogun's sword as he slays his own men. In 'To One, in Labour', Soyinka had used the same combination of adjective and noun:

> In solitude
> Of catacombs the lethal arc contracts . . . (p. 38)

referring, I take it, to the lessening of the killing of sperm and eggs in the womb as pregnancy grows. Here there is very little connexion between the applications of the words in the two poems: they do not illuminate each other.

'Idanre' is a very long poem, in places difficult, and with some parts that seem not to cohere closely. The sources are the Yoruba myths of creation, Soyinka's own dedication to and appraisal of Ogun, and a certain amount of the spirit, energy and narrative power of Blake's treatment of emanation and division in his prophetic books. Soyinka's comments in the Preface and the Notes about the personal origin of the poem are somewhat distracting, for not all the details he relates find their way into the poem, and where they do, as in the personal relation to a girl killed in a road crash, they can be seen as unnecessary and intrusive.

Most of the poem is concerned with a myth about the philosophical question of union and fragmentation or the one and the many. It is conveyed in a cosmogonical myth, but it is also reduced to personal terms by being applied to the question of how far one person can enter the life of another or, in rather more general terms, how far one can accompany a god without destruction. These are matters that have concerned almost all the preceding poems. 'Dawn' was about the reception of a god, 'Death in the Dawn' about identification of oneself with suffering and dead humanity, 'The Hunchback of Dugbe' about the acquisition of understanding by being an individual on whom the world seems to turn, 'Abiku' about the succession of fugitive children who are all one, 'Bringer of Peace' and 'Fado Singer' about the degree of intersection of a male and female life, 'Massacre, October '66' about national vs. clan unity. This is by no means a complete list of the poems that can be related to the central theme of 'Idanre', merely a representative sample.

'Idanre' conveys the question of unity and fragmentation in a set of myths and symbols. In sections I and II, there are several references to the creative union of Ogun and Sango. In I the rain of Ogun is accompanied by the lightning flashes of Sango, 'the axe-headed one'. The 'spiked symbol' of Ogun is used as a lightning conductor:

> He catches Sango in his three-fingered hand
> And runs him down to earth, (p. 61)

the result being safety for Soyinka as he watches the storm from his house. The wine-girl who is encountered in II by the poet 'At pilgrims' rest beneath Idanre Hill' (p. 62) is clearly a votary of Ogun, and it is quite clear from p. 67 that we are to equate her with Oya, the wife of Ogun. Oya subsequently, of course, became the wife of Sango, but this second marriage, though referred to in the Notes, does not find its way into the poem. Indeed, the wine-girl, because she also has to do duty as a friend of Soyinka's who was killed on the road ('a dark sheath freed From Ogun's sword'), can only with difficulty carry the burden of representing Sango's wife. When she returns to the poem in VII, she still seems to be the votary of Ogun, frozen in the moment of the charity she has extended to the climbers when offering them wine. It is, indeed, in this dual capacity, of offering love both to Ogun and to the group of travellers, that she best contributes to the investigation of the meaning of the one and the many.

The chief image of the union of Ogun and Sango is the scene in II where the high-tension wires of Ogun carry the electricity of Sango:

> One speeds his captive bolts on filaments
> Spun of another's forge. (p. 64)

In the storm, the union is celebrated with a spectacular dance of wires and flames:

> Through aeons of darkness rode the stone
> Of whirling incandescence, and cables danced
> In writhing ecstasies, point to point, wart to wart
> Of electric coils (p. 64)

Soyinka takes care to remind us that union is always accompanied by fragmentation or atomization, which leads in turn to new unions:

> The unit kernel atomised, presaging new cohesions
> Forms at metagenesis. (p. 64)

('Metagenesis' is here used not in its normal biological sense but in one of its etymologically correct senses of sharing or pursuing or changing genesis.) Soyinka's comment in the Notes—a crucial one—applies the notion to human relationships: 'This is the ideal fusion—to preserve the original uniqueness and yet absorb another essence' (p. 86).

Unity and fragmentation as part of the creative process are also explored through the myth of Atunda, 'First revolutionary Grand iconoclast at genesis' (p. 83). Rolled by him 'down the hill of the Beginning' (p. 68), the 'First Boulder' (p. 68) 'Shred the kernel to a million lights' (p. 68), that is, it fragmented the original godhead or unity.[19] Though at first spoken of as the act of a traitor, for Atunda was the slave of the godhead, this creative/divisive act is celebrated in section VI, and Atunda is raised to sainthood:

> Rather, may we celebrate the stray electron, defiant
> Of patterns, celebrate the splitting of the gods
> Canonisation of the strong hand of a slave who set
> The rock in revolution . . . (p. 82)

The iconoclastic nature of the act relates Atunda to Ajantala, the fully adult child of Yoruba myth who opposes his mother and his clan. He appears very briefly in the poem (section II, p. 67) as a 'Monster child, wrestling pachyderms of myth'. This is in some ways an unnecessary or needlessly confusing entry, though it serves to remind us of Soyinka's resemblance to Ajantala; he too is an iconoclast, questioning the wisdom of the tribe and nation, but wrestling with the myths to make something new and apposite to his society. Perhaps he goes even further than Ajantala in so far as his scepticism extends to the gods—even Ogun has to be treated with wariness, detachment and even condemnation at times.

In the partial reconstruction that followed Atunda's act, the individual gods were gradually formed (p. 69), and

> a mere plague of finite chaos
> Stood between the gods and man (p. 70)

But this chasm could not be bridged by Orisa-nla, Orunmila, Esu or Ifa; that is, overlordship, wisdom, chance and magical order were inadequate to make the connexion. What was needed was the special practical and communicative powers of Ogun. As god of the forge and the 'primal mechanic' he made a road of red clay between the gods and mankind. The redness of the clay proved ominously symbolic, for when he would modestly have retired to his godhead on the hill of Idanre the men of Ire, using the honeyed words of diplomacy, persuaded him to

remain and be their king. From this special immanence to man has
flowed both good and evil, creativity and destruction. His beneficence
is seen in the progress of science and technology and (though this would
perhaps have occurred had he remained transcendent) in rain and
harvest. His malevolence is seen in his capacity as the God of War and
in his ambiguous (mostly indifferent) guardianship of the Road.

While the men of Ire would have engaged in war without Ogun's
help, the destruction would have been far less. They were foolish to
seek his aid, for

> We do not burn the woods to trap
> A squirrel; we do not ask the mountain's
> Aid, to crack a walnut (p. 73)

and

> To bring a god to supper is devout, yet
> A wise host keeps his distance till
> The Spirit One has dined his fill. (p. 76)

As it is, Ogun, drunk with wine and maddened by blood, turns in
carnage on his own men, and they respond by beginning to vilify him.
This is section V, in some ways the high point of climax both of the
poem and the book. It is not merely that the epic event, a god berserk,
is brilliantly described; the interpretation following the event bears
directly on the philosophical question of union and fragmentation,
especially on the kind of union where men, for their own benefit, seek
alliance with the gods. The men of Ire found

> that a god
> Is still a god to men, and men are one
> When knowledge comes, of death.
>
> And they were cast adrift, without
> Direction for new prayers, their cry
> For partial succour brought a total hand
> That smothered life on crimson plains
> With too much answering (p. 78)

But there is, in fact, a union between men and gods, for they share grief
and remorse at what has happened. Their attempt at united action has
resulted in the destruction of many supplicants and the mourning of
those remaining; the god has, 'With too much answering', behaved
according to his own unique character, which neither he nor the men of
Ire made allowance for; the result is that the abused god is now a 'Divine
outcast', only too well aware of his own nature and its results.

Section VI, 'Recessional', extrapolates from the Yoruba myths of the
original undivided god, Atunda's action of generation through fragmentation, and the bloody act of Ogun to the poet's outlook and func-

tion. Death will come soon enough to bring undifferentiated union with the divine; in the meantime the poet must 'remain in knowledge' of his own diverse self, must 'celebrate the splitting of the gods', and must also proclaim the acts of his chosen god.

At the end of this section, Soyinka uses two other symbols for his analysis of unity and diversity, one, 'the creation snake Spawned tail in mouth' (p. 65), that he has fleetingly referred to before, the other a new one, the ' "Möbius Strip" '.[20] The creation snake is a symbol of continuing creation by rearrangement of existing matter. It is a theory that Soyinka seems to apply not only to men but also to gods, for he asserts that the gods of the various religions follow each other in snake-like fashion. As he says in the Notes, the tail-devouring snake is sometimes hung by Ogun around his neck as a symbol of 'the doom of repetition' (p. 88). The Möbius Strip is a more subtle form of the same symbol. It is a rectangular strip with the ends joined together after one end has been twisted 180°: a loop with a kink in it. The figure thus formed has only one side and one edge (whereas, of course, the original unjoined rectangular strip had two sides and two edges and, for that matter, two ends). It is, in fact, the simplest possible one-sided surface. One of its other interesting properties, which obviously appealed to Soyinka, is that if split down the middle it remains a single loop, though now with a further kink and two sides and two edges again. If split again down the middle it forms two linked loops, each with a kink. This is 'the interlock of re-creative rings' Soyinka speaks about, the diversity in unity that fascinates him.

For Soyinka, Ogun is quintessentially the god of diversity in unity and of repetition. Each seed-time and harvest is different, yet the same; each road is different, yet the same. The self-devouring snake is recreative yet repetitive. The Möbius Strip remains the same but takes a variety of forms. The recognition of the unity is important, but so is the expression of one's own individuality.

Ogun is 'my god' for Soyinka. This is no slavish worship; that would be union without individuality or diversity. It is exposition and prophecy about the state of the world by explication of the nature of Ogun. Soyinka is, above all, a myth-making and prophetic poet.

His second volume of poetry, *A Shuttle in the Crypt*,[21] represents both a self-contained *livre composé* and a continuation and extension of the concerns of *Idanre and Other Poems*. Its first poem, 'O Roots!', takes up one of the assertions of the crucial section V of 'Idanre':

> Who has no root
> In earth
> Flee the shelter
> Of a god possessed (p. 79)

Roots in 'Idanre' might preserve one from a god. In *A Shuttle in the Crypt*, a volume in no way dominated by Ogun, they may provide a harmonious link between the poet and the natural world, enabling him to resist the evil of his tormentors and the threat of mental chaos.

This is, as Soyinka points out in the Preface, a volume almost entirely written or drafted in gaol, during the twenty-five-and-a-half months he was detained by Yakubu Gowon's Government in the course of the Biafran War. It is a volume where, in a sense, Soyinka has provided his own commentary, in *The Man Died: Prison Notes*. That commentary tells the story, albeit in a fragmentary way with many lacunae and time-shifts, of Soyinka's political life between 1965 and 1969. The poems create a complex symbol of the prison and its life that dominated Soyinka's existence in those years. Where the prose work presents dynamic, pulsating, jagged, raw experience, the poems are a distillation of that experience, presented less as myth than as static symbol. Ogun, God of the Road, is, of course, almost absent from poems about confinement. This is a complex symbol centred on the prison house itself, especially the Crypt of the title, the solitary confinement cells where Soyinka's mind shuttled incessantly in the weaving of symbolic threads.[22]

A Shuttle in the Crypt is a book that begins with disappointed hopes for a cleansing of Nigeria, the thwarting of which results in Soyinka's imprisonment. The middle of the book ('Chimes of Silence' and 'Prisonettes') is confined within the prison. The last two sections open a window on the outside world, following Soyinka's release and the ending of the Biafran War.

It is a book with a good deal of bitterness and a certain amount of hate, but also much love (though not forgiveness and certainly not forgetfulness). Soyinka portrays himself as

> a cursing martyr I,
> No saint—are saints not moved beyond
> Event, their passive valour tuned to time's
> Slow unfolding? A time of evils cries
> Renunciation of the saintly vision
> Summons instant hands of truth to tear
> All painted masks ... ('Joseph', p. 21)

'Truth' and 'justice', following the breakdown of 'trust' and 'purpose', are to be key words in the volume, as they are in *The Man Died*.

Why Soyinka found himself in prison, first in Lagos (mostly in Kiri-kiri Prison), then in Kaduna in the North, is explained at the beginning of Chapter 2 of *The Man Died*:

> My arrest and my framing were two entirely different affairs. The one was prompted by the following activities: my denunciation of the war in the Nigerian papers, my visit to the East, my attempt to recruit the country's intellectuals within and outside the country for a pressure group which would work for a total ban on the supply of arms to all parts of Nigeria; creating a third force which would utilize the ensuing military stalemate to repudiate

and end both the secession of Biafra, and the genocide-consolidated dictatorship of the Army which made both secession and war inevitable.

I was framed for my activities in gaol. I was framed and nearly successfully liquidated because of my activities inside prison. From Kiri-kiri I wrote and smuggled out a letter setting out the latest proof of the genocidal policies of the government of Gowon. It was betrayed to the guilty men; they sought to compound their treason by a murderous conspiracy.

Soyinka was arrested in August 1967, a month after hostilities had broken out between Federal Nigeria and the newly declared secessionist Biafra. During that period, Soyinka had been in Enugu, the capital of Biafra, trying to avert full-scale war. There he had seen Christopher Okigbo, who told him:

> 'You know, I learnt to use a gun right in the field. I had never fired even an air-rifle in my life. I swear it, you know I'm not a violent man, I'm not like you. But this thing, I am going to stay with it till the end.' (Chapter 22)

He also saw Victor Banjo, a brigadier in the Biafran forces, who was appointed, unexpectedly, to lead the Biafran invasion of the Mid-West Region. He was subsequently accused of plotting to engineer a Federal victory and the removal of Colonel Ojukwu (the Biafran Head of State), was tried by court-martial, and shot. Banjo was seen by Soyinka as

> the military leader of the Third Movement which tried to break away from the secessionist principle and at the same time repudiate the Central Government in Lagos which was, whether you liked it or not, founded on a certain genocidal event ... this Third Movement got caught between the two because it set out to repudiate the two aspects. While it accepted the moral justification of Biafran secession, it felt that this was the wrong political action, but at the same time it could not accept or condone the moral basis, that is, the non-moral basis or the non-ideological basis of the government in Lagos.[23]

Even without these overt acts, it is clear that the military government would have been anxious to keep Soyinka out of circulation, if only to prevent further scornful satiric sketches such as *The New Republican* and *Before the Blackout* which Soyinka's Orisun Theatre Company had been performing to packed houses.

A Shuttle in the Crypt bears comparison with *The Waste Land* and the *Cantos*, for it represents, like the work of Eliot and Pound, an exploration of the poet's own being as it comes close to madness and dissolution. Soyinka's mind often inhabits the grey twilight world of those who have recently died. In the first poem, 'O Roots!', he prays to Roots:

Press these palms, that they shall join in talk,
In memories, sights, to blindfold passing ones
Borne to the eternal banquet on wine-tidal runs ... (p. 3)

Later in the same poem he speaks of

A grey plunge in pools of silence, peace
Of bygone voyagers, to the close transforming pass. (p. 4)

In 'When Seasons Change', the spirits are said to whisper 'Old truths
upheld in mirrors of the hour' (p. 15). In 'Purgatory' the poet's mind
communes briefly with 'Epileptics, seers and visionaries' (p. 38), recognizing that some have retreated from such a life to the 'comfort of a
gelded sanity'. Then, in the pivotal poem of the book, 'Vault Centre',
as twilight comes, he speaks of himself as if a cloaked worshipper or
devotee, 'a shawl of grey repose', concerned to 'gather dusks in me'
(p. 41).

The next poem, 'Procession', is set on 'Hanging day' in the prison.
Part II contains a number of dreams or visions derived from childhood
memory (each introduced by the word 'Passage'). Among them is the
scene of white-washed stones, representing ghosts, where old women

Through intertwine
Of owlish fingers on the loom, [they] gave
And wove a spell against this hour
And kept a vigil upon dearth and death. (p. 44)

One of the other (though related) functions of the weaving is 'To wind
the effigy of changing seasons' in an elusive design, as the women
remember and recreate folk history. He recalls their story that you
could 'trap a sky-soul bird' by stepping on its shadow, causing it to fall
like rain. Now he thinks of a similar action to engage himself with those
executed 'By a hermit's footfall on the wings'. In thus capturing them
he becomes one of them—'Mine the bedraggled wings'—but again he
disengages himself into the poet walking by Lake Tegel, 'Floating on
lakes to cries of drowning' (p. 46).

Death, memory, the loom and the momentary crossing of the threads
of one's life with those of others thus form a cluster of images. They are
not all used together in a single passage, but they are clearly imagined
by the poet to go together in 'Procession' and in 'Seed' (pp. 56–7).

The Crypt in which the shuttle of Soyinka's mind spends a good deal
of its time was the punishment cells of Kaduna Prison, turned into
accommodation for political prisoners. They are described in some
detail in *The Man Died*, ch. 31, though, oddly enough, there is a slight
discrepancy between the 'sparse twenty-three paces by seventeen' of
the prose description and the

Sixteen paces
By twenty-three

of 'Live Burial' (p. 60).

This central image of the crypt expands into a whole series of Christian images of communion and other rites. They are mostly expressive of injustice, inhumanity and corruption. It may be that Soyinka selected these images as a form of ironic invective against Yakubu Gowon. Gowon was the son of a Church Missionary Society evangelist, and he continues to make a point of his Christian belief in *Who's Who* entries.

In 'Conversation at Night with a Cockroach' there is an ironic song about the infectious corrupting spirit of Nigeria conveyed in images of 'man, ghoul, Cockroach/Jackal and brood of vile cross-breedings' (p. 10), 'the new abiding' as Soyinka calls them, sitting down to a 'love-feast' (the Christian *agape*) in which the bread and wine will be 'our pulsing hearts'. In 'Wailing Wall' images of 'stained-glass', 'tattered surplice', 'collection plates', 'white collar', 'Choirmaster', 'verger' and 'prayers' are applied to 'altars of evil', where not bread but the 'Word' is broken and where 'evil feeds/Upon the wounds and tears of piety' (p. 34). Soyinka's distress about the untruthfulness of his society's leaders is manifest once again; they will break not only their own word but also, through their hypocrisy, the Word of God.

In 'Hunt of the Stone', the priests are the priests of Sango, who are also said to be 'full of evil rites', seeking the 'Homage of clay hearts' (p. 52). Soyinka, though he has been asked to be part of this corrupt privileged society, has remained a chronicler of the evil not a participant. 'This hermit', as he calls himself, is 'Waiting, peaceful in passage of the looms'.

Even when his own incarceration and the war are both over, he has a feeling of separateness. He cannot participate in the fragile, probably hollow communion of national reunification:

> And so with bread and wine
> I lack the sharing with defeat and dearth
> I passed them on my way. (p. 85)

His own experience has been more searing, and he feels as if the 'love and welcome' extended to him are somehow alien, as if offered by 'Usurpers'. 'Flowers for My Land' again represents the poet as being outside communion, this time the false comradeship offered to him in the wheeling and dealing before the start of the war.

But the 'Chimes of Silence' section uses Christian imagery for more favourable meanings. In 'Recession', imagery of the Christian church (bells, baptismal fonts, carillons, communion bells) is used, perhaps rather confusingly, both for life in wartime and for the individual death that releases the spirit. In 'Vault Centre' II, at the end of the day and in a moment of spiritual peace, Soyinka participates in nature's communion, with the 'choir of egrets, servers at the day's/Recessional' (p. 40). With his 'eye on chapel ruins', he, like an oriel window jutting out to catch the available light, gathers in the dusk. In 'Last Turning', a quite unmournful elegy on the death of the last of the five prisoners executed at Kaduna, he speaks of him as a lenten pilgrim, who has travelled

> Where the peaks' fine needles have embossed
> Missals on the heart (p. 47)

Soyinka chooses imagery of the daring pilgrim rather than more conventional heroic imagery. For him enemies of the military government are martyrs rather than warrior heroes.

'Conversation at Night with a Cockroach' is a poem dealing at some length with events of this period. The 'year's crucible' he speaks of is presumably the year up to the second outbreak of systematic killing of the Igbos on 29 September 1966. Over that period Soyinka had been heavily involved in Western Region politics, opposing the corruption of Chief Akintola; in Ibadan the Orisun Theatre Company had been offering satiric comment on the situation and promulgating the need for cleansing. With the October massacres the possibility of campaigning successfully must have seemed hopeless: reforming zeal ('The first fire-arc of regenerate eyes') had cooled; the political manipulators had won again. As Cockroach says in one of his speeches,

> We knew the tread and heard
> The gathering heartbeat of the cyclone heart
> And quick our hands to forge coalitions new
> Of tried corruptions, East to West, North to South. (p. 7)

And, as Soyinka says sarcastically in the final song,

> All was well. All was even
> As it was in the beginning. (p. 13)

It is in this poem that Soyinka introduces the symbol of the Visitation (pp. 6-7), which he takes up again in 'Hunt of the Stone' (p. 52). The details are vague and flexible. In 'Conversation at Night', the Visitation seems akin to the plagues of Egypt, except that they have been visited on the captive nation and not on the oppressors: 'Our firstborn It was that died' (p. 9). In 'Hunt of the Stone' it is the disaster of being visited by a meteor, with the misfortunes it brings. In both cases, the original intent of religious myth is reversed: the oppressors escape punishment in one, the priests of Sango profit in the other.

In 'Seed', both the resurrection of Lazarus and hopeful divination about the new-lit hearth (using palm-kernels, salt, oil, yams, camwood, chalk and antimony), end in despair: 'Dirge, loom, emptiness of passage'. The hopeful presages of rain, wind, ashes and tendrils have been aborted. Once again, the traditional meanings and hopes have been reversed.

Even rain can be shifted from its fructifying association with Ogun to represent something evil or at least dubious: 'Ulysses' speaks of 'the rain of nails' (p. 27); 'Procession' II of a bird dropping from the sky 'as rain' (p. 45); and both 'Hunt of the Stone' and 'Space' speak of present troubles as 'the deluge'. In *The Man Died*, Chapter 31, Soyinka describes the punishment of flooding a cell with a naked prisoner in it and explains that he was incarcerated in one such special cell at Kaduna. The deluge may here have a highly personal connotation. The immediate point is, however, that once again Soyinka has reversed the usual significance of the traditional image he uses.

By contrast, the imagery of flying, natural imagery for a caged poet, is imbued with entirely favourable connotations in such poems as 'When Seasons Change', 'Vault Centre', 'Procession', 'Recession' and 'Space'. In 'When Seasons Change', Soyinka is the dove-like peacemaker; in 'Vault Centre' he is at the focus of the wood-pigeons' gyrations and the egrets' flight; in 'Recession' the soul about to pass into death is 'egret-breasted'; and in 'Space' the bird sent from the ark (an image of Soyinka soaring mentally beyond the prison) is apparently not a dove now but a weaverbird, a common symbol for a poet, and especially appropriate in this volume where woven patterns figure so prominently.

In the second section of the volume, Soyinka finds 'Four Archetypes' against which he can measure himself. Like Joseph he is falsely accused, but unlike Joseph he is not meek. 'Hamlet' is mainly a negative archetype, where fear of error, excessive thought and insufficient submission to duty, justice and passion atrophy action till it is too late. Gulliver, who finds himself among Lilliputians, seeks to help them by prompt action, but is castigated for breaching taboos. He slides back into favour, works for the state, then enrages the politicians by advocating compassion and reason in the war with the enemy Blefuscoons, to whom they are related—Soyinka significantly alters the name from Swift's 'Blefuscudians'. Here is an allegory of Soyinka's attempts to be a servant of the state. The sentence is loss of sight, including such 'abnormalities' as 'foresight, insight, [and] Second sight' (p. 26). 'Ulysses' is full of Joycean puns ('matriseas', 'a sea of faeces', for instance) and touches on several of the episodes in Joyce's novel: the 'Circe' episode in 'Swine-scented' and the 'Symplegades' incident in 'Vaginal rocks', for example. It even asks the literary question, as if in a seminar, of how worthwhile all the labour of exegesis on this difficult novel is: 'How golden finally is the recovered fleece?' Here, then, is Soyinka as witty teacher, but more importantly as Odyssean quester:

> It turns on quest cycles, to track a skein
> Of self through eyeless veils ... (p. 28)

All four archetypes are of 'lone wanderers', all with a strong sense of duty, all unjustly treated by the world.

By contrast, the military leadership, and the general spirit of corruption are treated in terms of cockroaches, ants, lizards and beetles. Soyinka's most savage invective is reserved for General Gowon.[24] In 'Background and Friezes' he describes him as 'a mud reptilian', puns on his name as 'Jacques d'Odan' ('Jack' Gowon, of Dodan Barracks), accuses him of hypocrisy, vanity, falsehood, obsession with pomp (such as having the roads cleared hours before he was due to drive along them) and window-dressing for international observers (the last of these prisonette stanzas occurring with a prose exposition of the circumstances in Appendix C of *The Man Died*). In 'Relief' he tells the story (amplified in *The Man Died*, ch. 30) of Gowon's wedding, including the displacement of relief supplies by festive supplies for the celebration.

Gowon released Soyinka in October 1969, following the amnesty for political detainees declared on the first of that month. Soyinka took up the position he had been appointed to before imprisonment, as head of the Department of Theatre Arts at the University of Ibadan. He resigned after a few months, however, to devote himself to writing and to renew contact with the international literary world. He could not return to Nigeria after the publication of some of the anti-Gowon poems in *Transition* in 1971, at least not until the fall of Gowon in 1975.

In an interview in the same journal, Soyinka described himself as believing 'what goes under the broad umbrella of socialist ideology' but as being not an ' "orthodox Marxist" '.[25] He went on to say:

> There is no political leadership in Nigeria at present, and there are only three political leaders worthy of the name on the continent. Nigerian leadership is *not* one of them. Continental politics have become inevitable. It is easier today than it was some years ago to declare that one is less a Nigerian (or Congolese or Sierra Leonean) than a black African. (p. 64)

This Pan-Africanism was to be more fully developed by Soyinka in the First Full Congress of the African Writers Union in Dakar, 4–6 February 1976, in the Constitution of The Union of Writers of the African Peoples (largely written by Soyinka and accepted at the Congress), and in his third volume of poetry, *Ogun Abibimañ*.[26] At this point, however, one should merely note that Julius Nyerere is clearly one of the three African leaders Soyinka admires. 'Ujamaa' is dedicated to him.

In *A Shuttle in the Crypt* Soyinka speaks much more plainly and directly than in *Idanre and Other Poems*, but with no diminution of his image-making and pattern-making facility. From the beginning of the volume his poetic skill is evident. 'O Roots!', for instance, consists of three parts, the outside ones full of doubt and fear, the middle one more serene. Accordingly, Soyinka has used full rhyme in the middle section, para-rhyme in the outer ones. In 'Conversation at Night with a Cockroach', the poet speaks in loose four-stress lines, the Cockroach in three-stress lines (with some hints of rhyme, especially in the song on pp. 7–8). Puns are possible for Soyinka even in these depressing conditions, and the poems often lightly touch on lines from English poets, ranging from Lovelace's

> I could not love thee (Dear) so much
> Lov'd I not honour more

in 'And What If Thus He Died' to the Vietnam War-period song 'Where have all the flowers gone?' in 'Flowers for My Land', and even such faint echoes as the shape of Yeats's 'His mind moves upon silence' in the phrase 'Their hands are closed on emptiness', used in 'Procession' and repeated with small changes in 'Hunt of the Stone'.

Centred on the image of the four-walled Kaduna Prison, this volume is as carefully contrived as *Idanre and Other Poems*. But it is more static. Despite the dramatic narrative of 'Purgatory' and 'Procession', meditation is the prevailing mode. The cosmological sweep of myth-making found in *Idanre and Other Poems* was temporarily in abeyance while Soyinka coped with his own situation and that of Nigeria.

The large-scale myth-making facility returns to prominence in *Ogun Abibimañ*. It is a song in three parts. The first and last are songs on the eve of battle (or at least expressions of the necessity for such songs), the battle to sweep the whites out of South Africa. The middle section is a confessional song by the great amaZulu king, Shaka, with choruses and shouts of praise by his listeners. Shaka is there because he discovers his nature as an avatar of Ogun. 'I feel, and know your tread As mine' (p. 10) he says. He realizes himself in the being of another, while preserving, indeed, seeking to develop, his own individuality. As Soyinka had said in the Notes to 'Idanre', 'This is the ideal fusion: to preserve the original uniqueness and yet absorb another essence.' Shaka was, of course, the inventor of the *panga* or assegai, the short stabbing spear originally fashioned for him by the greatest blacksmith of his day, and far superior as a weapon to the javelins in use before. He resembled Ogun in other ways, too, for he was not only a great leader in battle but also, towards the end of his life, one who turned against his own men. In this poem (p. 14), he is given the opportunity, like Ogun, to admit his error and to seek forgiveness.

The central section of the book is then a celebration of the union of Ogun, Shaka and Abibimañ, the Akan word, as Soyinka points out in the Glossary, for the whole of the Black World, land, peoples and concerns. This union, as the Induction makes clear, is in 'A Cause that moves at last to resolution' (p. 4), the reclaiming of the white-dominated south. That Cause is so absorbing and all embracing that 'Time and space [are] negated' (p. 4): all epochs fuse with the present, all parts of Africa are one, peace and greenness are swallowed up in the iron and blood of a just war. For this Cause, the Act of Atunda, the original fragmenter, is reversed, as Ogun in his role of Craftsman causes the world to be

> Swayed
> To chimes of re-creation, recalled
> To an Origin, a oneness ... (p. 4)

In such an all-embracing unity, the individuality, the personality as an ordinary human being, might seem to be incorporated in the Black World or to be, at any rate, negligible. Such a notion would, however, be foreign to Soyinka's way of thinking. It may produce some inconsistency in the poem, but Soyinka obviously feels it necessary that Shaka should, in an acknowledged digression on p. 14, confess a yearning for being an individual man as distinct from the embodiment of all his people.

This is the most declamatory and rhetorical of Soyinka's poems, despite the fact that it celebrates silence and action rather than dialogue and indolence. It is disingenuous of him to say in part III, 'Preach who must, I listen and take note' (p. 19), for, though a song, it is a song that teaches, interprets and preaches not only through the myth but directly as well. It preaches against the cant, hypocrisy and subterfuge of whites, with their talk of dialogue, protest or sanctions as appropriate weapons to secure justice. Symbolically, Ogun taps the strength of the white deities (who presided over the profanation of Africa) for transfusion to the black god of Abibimañ:

> Ogun goes to let ambrosia from profaning gods,
> From skins of curd and sea-blue veins
> To stir that claimed divinity of mind and limb
> Whose prostrate planet is Abibimañ . . . (p. 5)

The whites had, of course, come to Zululand in the time of Shaka, who received them graciously, but found them termites who

> gnawed
> The houseposts of the kraals even while
> We made the stranger welcome. (p. 12)

Later, his fellow kings and successors had to wage war upon the whites, but the task is still unfinished. His pride, his tap-roots, his seeds, his manhood (all images familiar from Soyinka's earlier poetry) need to be restored. False 'claimants to the sandals' of Shaka, such as Amin with his 'mock-heroics, laying waste to ant-hills' (p. 15) or his pompously stage-managed Summit Meeting of Heads of State of the Organization of African Unity in Kampala in 1975 (referred to in 'The world is called . . .', p. 15),[27] offer no substitute for the heroic warfare waged by Shaka himself, no substitute for the eradication of 'the life-usurpers' fortress To the South' (p. 15).

As the poem comes to an end, there are reminders of outrages against humanity, white as well as black: Guernica during the Spanish Civil War; Lidice in Czechoslovakia, the mining village completely destroyed by the Germans in 1942; and above all the Sharpeville massacre of 1960.[28] They are to be remembered, lest dreams go sour. The action of Ogun to redress these wrongs will result not in vengeance, hate or unawareness of accompanying human loss. It will result in the 'Cessation of a long despair' (p. 21), as

> We celebrate the end of that compliant
> Innocence of our millennial trees. (p. 21)

The first line of the whole poem had been 'No longer are the forests green' (p. 1). Literally they were, of course, among the things destroyed by the white invaders in their rapacious search for quick wealth; symbolically their treatment represented the treatment meted out also to the people of Africa by

> Midwives of fireraze, heartburn, soulsear,
> Of rooting out, of rack and mindscrew . . . (p. 3)

And this despite the frequency in white explorers' memoirs of comments about the peace, greenness and beauty of the landscape. Now, of course, the greenness symbolic of fruitfulness and peace must be set aside by the devotees of Ogun Abibimañ as they gather to sing and dance before the battle that will take them south along the roads and railways that lead to Johannesburg and the Cape.

Ogun Abibimañ is the simplest of Soyinka's long poems. Despite the play of intelligence and the concern for human values, it is perhaps oversimplified. Its concern for unity is so powerful that it almost blots out Soyinka's earlier concern for diversity and individuality.[29] As a result, there are inconsistencies, even in individual images. (The execrated white midwives on p. 3, for instance, interfere with the image of black midwives who revive the study of black history in p. 21.) Nothing has failed in the patterning; any failure as poetry lies in the extremity with which passionately held political beliefs are announced. There is, in a sense, too much preaching to the converted and not enough analysis of the problems. But, of course, Soyinka is saying that the time for dialogue has passed. As with the circumstances that gave rise to *A Shuttle in the Crypt*, events shoulder reflection aside.

Notes to Chapter 7

1. See Bernth Lindfors's two articles, 'The Early Writings of Wole Soyinka', *Journal of African Studies* 2, No. 2 (Spring 1975), 64–86, and 'Ladies and Gentlemen at Ibadan', *Ba Shiru* 8, No. 2 (1977), 33–6. Publication details of most of the early poems can be found in *Africa South of the Sahara: Index to Periodical Literature, 1900–1970*, compiled by the African Section, Reference Department, Library of Congress, vol. 4, pp. 713–14 (Boston: Hall, 1971) and its *First Supplement* (Boston: Hall, 1973), p. 424, and in *A Bibliography of Literary Contributions to Nigerian Periodicals 1946–1972*, compiled by Bernth Lindfors (Ibadan University Press, 1975), items 1735–59.
2. *Idanre and Other Poems* (London: Methuen, 1967). All subsequent page references are to this edition.
3. The first three appeared together in *Black Orpheus* No. 5 (1959), 9–13, the second having appeared a little earlier by itself under the title 'Insulation' in *Ibadan* No. 5 (1959), 24. 'Telephone Conversation' appeared in *Ibadan* No. 10 (1960), 34, and later in *TLS*, 10 August 1962, p. 569; it is reprinted in *A Book of African Verse*, ed. J. Reed and C. Wake (London:

Heinemann Educational Books, 1964), pp. 81–2. 'Requiem' was first published in *Modern Poetry from Africa*, ed. Gerald Moore and Ulli Beier (Harmondsworth: Penguin, 1963), pp. 113–15 (but omitted from the second edition, 1968); this volume also contains 'Telephone Conversation' (pp. 111–12).

4. In a 1962 broadcast interview, Soyinka referred to 'the "Immigrant" poems which I hate now and which I want to forget, but which I'm not allowed to forget!' See *African Writers Talking: A Collection of Interviews*, ed. Dennis Duerden and Cosmo Pieterse (London: Heinemann Educational Books, 1972), pp. 174–5.

5. See *West African Verse: An Anthology*, ed. Donatus Ibe Nwoga (London: Longman, 1967), p. 196.

6. See 'Oriki Ogun', *Black Orpheus* 2, No. 3 (1968), 'Yoruba Poetry' supplement, pp. 21–2.

7. London: Rex Collings, p. 148. The chapter goes on to introduce two other characteristic images of Soyinka, the madman and the healer (here combined in the one person). Then follows a description of the road and an accident.

8. *Myth, Literature and the African World* (Cambridge: Cambridge University Press, 1976), p. 27.

9. Chief Awolowo, founder of the Action Group party and former Premier of the Western Region, was charged with treasonable felony in 1962 after intervention in the Region by the Federal Government. It was while he was on trial that his son was killed. In 1963 he was found guilty and sentenced to ten years' imprisonment. In protest at the injustice of the whole sordid political manœuvre, Soyinka resigned from his position at the University of Ife.

10. In chapter 9 *Season of Anomy*, there are repeated references to the climbing of a tree by a character named Zaccheus. His purpose is to spy out the church of the refugees.

11. This interpretation broadly follows that of Eldred Jones in *The Writing of Wole Soyinka* (London: Heinemann Educational Books, 1973), pp. 109–10. Jones expresses some insecurity about the interpretation, but no other seems to me to account so adequately for all the details.

12. *Black Orpheus* 2, No. 3 (1968), 'Yoruba Poetry' supplement, p. 22.

13. For a helpful discussion of the lore associated with *abiku* see Christie C. Achebe, 'Literary Insights into the *Ogbanje* Phenomenon', *Journal of African Studies* 7, No. 1 (Spring 1980), 31–8.

14. The military government of Nigeria had, unexpectedly, nominated him as an official representative for a month-long cultural programme in Berlin. His account of the difficulty he had to fly out of Nigeria, of what he learnt of the government's plans against the Igbos while in Berlin, and of his walk by Lake Tegel is contained in *The Man Died: Prison Notes* (London: Rex Collings, 1972; Harmondsworth: Penguin, 1975), chs. 20 and 24.

15. Gerald Moore, in his *Wole Soyinka* (London: Evans, 1978), p. 92, has him swimming in the lake, but this is clearly a misreading.

16. A number of commentators have seen a reference to Nazi racialism in 'pride of race' and have linked it with Hitler's genocide against the Jews. The analogy is, however, in part reversed because the Jews, who also abhor pork, were the victims not the perpetrators. I feel that the Nazi

reference is confusing and unnecessary and that 'pride of race' can be applied solely to the racial clashes in Nigeria.

17. The details of the close relationship between Fajuyi and Soyinka for several months of 1966 are contained in Soyinka's *The Man Died*, ch. 22.

18. Ogun is also 'godfather of all souls who by road Made the voyage home', that is, of wandering spirits.

19. In his article, 'The Fourth Stage (Through the Mysteries of Ogun to the Origin of Yoruba Tragedy)', originally published in *The Morals of Art*, ed. D. W. Jefferson (London: Routledge & Kegan Paul, 1969), pp. 119–33, then reprinted in Soyinka's *Myth, Literature and the African World*, pp. 140–60, he speaks of Orisa-nla as 'the first deity' (pp. 144, 152). The whole essay is illuminating for Soyinka's ideas about the gods.

20. It is not entirely new, however, if one considers earlier references to Ogun in the poem, such as 'His path one loop of time, one iron coil' (p. 68).

21. London: Rex Collings/Eyre Methuen, 1972.

22. *The Man Died*, ch. 33, is a meditation on the symbols of shuttle and Crypt.

23. Karen L. Morell, ed., *In Person: Achebe, Awoonor, and Soyinka at the University of Washington* (Seattle: University of Washington Institute for Comparative and Foreign Area Studies, African Studies Program, 1975), pp. 111–12.

24. He was promoted—perhaps the verb should be active and reflexive—to Major-General in 1967 and full General in 1971. *A Shuttle in the Crypt* was first published a year later.

25. Interview by Biodun Jeyifous, *Transition* No. 42 (vol. 8, no. v, 1973), 62–4 (p. 62).

26. London: Rex Collings; Ibadan: Opon Ifa, 1977.

27. Soyinka was involved in a number of denunciations of Amin, including resolution passed at the First Meeting of The Union of Writers of the African Peoples, Accra, Ghana, 7–8 June 1975 (a meeting which also sought to have the coming Summit Meeting of the OAU moved from Uganda); resolutions at the First Full Congress of the African Writers Union, Dakar, Senegal, 4–6 February 1976 (when Soyinka was elected General Secretary); and items in *Transition* 49 and *Ch'Indaba* 1 and 2 (which he edited). The 1975 meeting is conveniently summarized in *Africa Currents* No. 2 (Summer 1975), 19–24; the 1976 one in Bahadur Tejani's report, 'African World Alternatives', *Ch'Indaba* No. 2 (July/December 1976), 33–7 (reprinted from *MOKO*, the Newsletter of the Canadian Association for Commonwealth Literature and Language Studies, 1, No. 7 (March 1976), 24–9).

28. The events of May to December 1976 in which hundreds of rioters were shot by police in Soweto and elsewhere—events to which the book is dedicated—seem to have occurred after the poem was written.

29. Soyinka's explanation of the apparent contradiction might be in the terms he applies in 'The Fourth Stage' to Ogun's bridge-building to man, involving

> a disintegrating process within the matrix of cosmic creativity, whence the Will performs the final reassemblage. The weightiest burden of severance is that of each from self, not of godhead from mankind, and the most perilous aspect of the god's journey is that in which the deity must truly undergo the experience of transition. It is a look into the very heart of the phenomena. To fashion a bridge across it was not only Ogun's task

but his very nature, and he had first to experience, to surrender his individuation once again (the first time, as a part of the original Orisa-nla Oneness) to the fragmenting process; to be reabsorbed within universal Oneness, the Unconscious, the deep black whirlpool of mythopoeic forces, to immerse himself thoroughly within it, understand its nature and yet by the combative value of the will to rescue and re-assemble himself and emerge wiser, powerful from the draught of cosmic secrets, organising the mystic and the technical forces of earth and cosmos to forge a bridge for his companions to follow. (*Myth, Literature and the African World*, pp. 153–4).

This account seems not uninfluenced by the Jungianism of G. Wilson Knight, Soyinka's tutor at Leeds. It appeared originally in Wilson Knight's Festschrift.

8 Gabriel Okara

▼▼▼▼▼▼▼▼▼▼▼▼▼▼▼▼▼▼▼▼▼▼▼▼▼▼▼▼▼

Whereas Kofi Awoonor began with the translation of African oral poetry and gradually moved to a personal synthesis of African and European elements in his work, Gabriel Okara began as an imitator of English Romanticism but gradually emancipated himself from the in-fluence of foreign diction and phraseology to become a characteristically African poet. His career spans some forty years. In the course of it he became first one of the earliest 'modern' African poets and later one of the first truly African poets in English.

When he began to write, in the early 1940s, there were few outlets for African poetry written in English. In the late 1940s and early 1950s, however, West African poets found that local newspapers such as the *West African Pilot* (Lagos), founded and originally edited by Nnamdi Azikiwe, and the quarterly journal *African Affairs* (London), published by the Royal African Society, were prepared to print their work. For the first time there seemed to be a substantial body of West African poets using English. It is true that in the 1930s local newspapers had carried some poetry, and Gladys Casely-Hayford from the Gold Coast had published in *The Atlantic Monthly* as early as 1927, but sporadic publication of this kind had given no hint that there might be a con-siderable number of poets writing in English. In the late 1940s and early 1950s, however, poets such as Michael Dei-Anang, R. E. G. Armattoe, and Chief Dennis Osadebay showed what could be done to express a strong commitment to the past and the future of Africa in tones borrowed from Scott, Keats, Tennyson, Kipling, Rupert Brooke, and the early Yeats. Adeboye Babalola showed what might be done in the translation and adaptation of traditional song.

For the most part, this kind of work seemed like a local adaptation of the emotional attachment to the spirit of nature and the patriotic fervour to be found in the English poems of the school readers. It was often not much more than versified sentiment or gesture. The application of individual sensibility to African material and experimentation with, rather than mere imitation of, style came in the first half of the 1950s. The 'pioneer' or 'pilot' poetry (the terms are sometimes used more or less interchangeably, sometimes to represent a difference between Ghana and Nigeria, sometimes to represent a sequence between the 1930s and the 1940s) was supplemented by identifiably 'modern' poetry from Abioseh Nicol, Gabriel Okara, and, a few years later, Christopher Okigbo, John Pepper Clark, Wole Soyinka and Lenrie Peters.

Okara recalls that he began to write poetry 'probably when I was twenty, after I had left secondary school'. He told an interviewer that:

I felt the urge to write. I began with poetry because I had read the poem 'Spring' by William Wordsworth, and I was very touched by it because it recalled my childhood experiences in my home village, where we used to go beneath the trees with bamboo bows and arrows and wait for birds to come and perch, and then start shooting. One day there was a very, very beautiful bird and I was fascinated by it; my companions wanted to shoot it but I made some noise and the bird flew away. And so when I read 'Spring', by William Wordsworth, talking about birds and so forth, it really touched me and just set things going. I didn't write a poem about that particular experience, but it sort of opened the lid of other emotional conflicts.[1]

Despite his long and prolific career, only one slim volume has been published, *The Fisherman's Invocation*.[2] In the Introduction, Theo Vincent refers to the 'thousands of poems now lost to history' (p. ix) that Okara must have written. During the Nigerian Civil War, when he was Director of the Cultural Affairs Division of the Ministry of Information for Biafra, he began to put his manuscripts together. The early ones had not been kept but he assembled the later ones, only to lose them in the period immediately after fighting stopped.

The earliest extant poem is thus 'The Call of the River Nun', which won for Okara in the Nigerian Festival of Arts of 1953 the prize for the best work of literature. Wordsworth's 'Lines written in Early Spring' and 'Valedictory Sonnet to the River Duddon' lie behind the work, as does Tennyson's 'Crossing the Bar', and, but for the title and the 'canoe', it might easily be mistaken for a work by a British poet in the first two or three decades of this century. To say that is to characterize the style, not to judge the poem. It is, in fact, a work of originality and interest. It was written not in Okara's homeland, the Ijaw country of the Niger Delta, but in Enugu. Okara had been working as a bookbinder for the Government Press in Lagos, but was sent in 1950 to help begin a new branch in Enugu. He obviously found the Udi Hills surrounding the city rather oppressive, and his imagination took him back to the River Nun, near where he had been born.

The poem expresses a good deal of the Romantic sense of religious interaction between the human soul and the soul of nature that he recalled much later in the interview already quoted. Like many Romantic poems it falls into two parts, the first depicting the poet in nature (here in desire only), the second applying the experience to his sense of himself in relation to the eternal. The opening strophe applies equally well to both parts.

The image of life as a river flowing to the sea is in no way original. Okara's 'found'ring canoe', eventually upturned and splitting to release the poet's soul, is, however, both original and memorable, and it provides, as well, an identification with the Delta country. Through the poem runs the word 'call', except in the second strophe where the poet is in imagination actually in or beside the river. In the other strophes he is called by the river or, in the second half of the poem, by life and death. In the second last strophe, the 'call' becomes quite insistent: it occurs three times, and on the last occurrence is 'the final call' of death or rather, as the last strophe in taking up this phrase makes clear, a call home to God. The strategic placement of the word and the quickening of urgency in the second last strophe recall some of the effects of Keats, a poet whom Okara greatly admired.

'The Call of the River Nun' was not published until 1957, when it appeared with 'Spirit of the Wind' and 'Were I to Choose' in the first issue of *Black Orpheus* (pp. 36–8). In the volume *The Fisherman's Invocation*, all the poems up to 'To Paveba' were written between the time of 'The Call of the River Nun' and early 1962 at the latest. In 'Were I to Choose', for instance, he speaks of himself as having lived to 'the close of one and thirty', suggesting that he was about to turn 32 and thus indicating that the poem was written in 1953. The last of this group is the so-called ' "Franvenkirche" ', dated 1963 by Okara, and then there is a gap of five years before the next poems available.

The poems of this ten-to-twelve-year period, Okara's first extant poems, represent, of course, the second decade or so of his poetry writing, the period when he was aged about thirty to his early forties. Many of them express a sense of getting old. 'Once Upon a Time', addressed to his son, speaks of having learnt through experience the unattractive face of the world. 'Piano and Drums' refers to the sound of the jungle drums as rejuvenating: his blood 'topples the years'. 'Were I to Choose' suggests that life is oppressive: it is a cry that he uses to 'thread the years', and he wishes that his 'tired head' might be 'free'. 'New Year's Eve Midnight' contains a sense of the directionless, purposeless quality of life, for among the key words are 'tolling', 'dead', 'mute', 'ghosts', 'dream', 'dying', 'fading', 'shrouded', and 'dimly'. 'The Snowflakes Sail Gently Down' has a similar air of weariness and meaninglessness, ending with 'the earth lying inscrutable like the face of a god in a shrine'. Finally, in 'To Paveba', 'the dead weight of years' seems momentarily to roll 'crashing to the ground', but in the end the 'creaking years' have dampened the renewed fire of love.

Associated with this feeling there is often a sense of preference and nostalgia for an earlier world, particularly the world of childhood. In 'Once Upon a Time' he wishes he could relearn the artlessness and innocence of childhood. In 'Piano and Drums' the jungle drums are interpreted as 'speaking of primal youth and the beginning'.

Here, of course, we have passed beyond individual personal nostalgia for childhood to a symbolization of the primal youth of Africa before white invasion. In this poem and a few others Okara comes close to the symbolic celebration of traditional Africa as a child, youth, maiden, or mother that is found in both the Négritude and the pioneer poets. 'Spirit of the Wind' perhaps rather self-consciously fuses the whiteness of the storks with the blackness of the poet, as Léopold Sédar Senghor might fuse the sun with the bright blackness of skin. And, like 'Piano and Drums', 'You Laughed and Laughed and Laughed' creates contrasting images for Africa and the West, but unlike 'Piano and Drums', thoroughly rejects the Western image. In this poem the images convey very forcefully the poet's balance of sympathies, for Africa is represented by fire and 'the living warmth of the earth', whereas the West is represented by a motorcar (admittedly a smoothly running one) and ice-blocks. Furthermore, the West misunderstands and misrepresents Africa, interpreting the poet's (or Africa's) song in its own thoroughly inappropriate frame of reference as a 'motor car misfiring stopping with a choking cough'; but Africa has no interest in knowing the cars or the ice-blocks of the West.

Sometimes Okara sacrifices the vigour of this thoroughgoing rejection of the West in favour of a more accurate historical view in which the West succeeds in penetrating African life and consciousness. In 'Piano and Drums' he appreciates both the speaking drums and the 'wailing' piano, though he writes more passionately and at greater length about the drums than about the ambiguous, complex, even menacing piano, the phrase of which ends 'at daggerpoint'. The drums on the other hand represent a simple unworried life (again a Négritude concept) that is in sympathy with nature and has human warmth and purpose. The ending of the 'Drums' section almost repeats, in fact, the ending of the more thoroughly Négritude poem, 'You Laughed and Laughed and Laughed': Okara speaks in one of 'the naked warmth of hurrying feet' (p. 20) and in the other of 'the living warmth of the earth through our naked feet' (p. 25).

In 'The Snowflakes Sail Gently Down' he again brings Africa and the West together for comparison, this time a very complex comparison indeed. The poem was written during a visit to the United States when he saw snow for the first time.[3] Seen from inside a heated room, the landscape is weary, disconsolate, and suggestive of death. Seen again at the end after a visionary dream, the same landscape is enlivened, though not made more intelligible, by having superimposed on it an African scene, of 'white robed Moslems salaaming at evening prayer'. The death and destructiveness of the West interpreted in its own terms has been transmuted into the ritual of daily purposeful life by Africa.

In between these two views of the same scene is a prophetic dream, induced by the warmth of the room. The black birds of Western depredation (the image is similar to that of the 'fleet of eagles' in Okigbo's 'Limits' VIII and X, and to J. P. Clark's kites from the west in 'Ivbie' V) seek untold wealth from Africa. But the traditional culture is rooted too strongly and dents 'the uprooters' spades'. Then Africa generously offers some of her wealth to the West, but the West, not recognizing its value in the indigenuous tradition, is churlish and disgruntled because it is not as valuable as gold.

In both the dream and the renewed natural landscape, Africa has contributed to the West, partly perhaps in a material way, but more

importantly in a spiritual way. The West, however, is uncomprehending and ungrateful.

The sense of understanding coming from deep psychic forces within
the poet either through dream or through communion with nature is
pervasive in Okara's poetry. In 'Spirit of the Wind' the poet sees the
storks returning after the rainy season. They are 'Spirits of the wind',
guided by 'instinct' and not governed by any 'god'. By contrast the poet
is earthbound, 'sitting on this rock'—the contrast with the wind is
dramatic—and 'willed by the gods'. But the concentrated observation
of the storks stirs within the poet something akin to the wind, 'the spirit
urging within', the call of instinct, something that he can call 'my stork'.
In a reversal of Négritude pride, he seems to identify this communion
with European Romanticism, for he asks why he should not heed 'this
prayer bell-call' although he is an African: 'my stork is caged in Singed
Hair and Dark Skin'.

The use of the gods in this poem points to the fact that Okara, unlike
Achebe, Okigbo or Soyinka, always seems to think of the gods as quite
external to man, even slightly alien; they never dwell within man, never
allow man to become incorporated with them; their urge is to rule man.
They are as separate and different from man as the Graeco-Roman
pantheon, and it is not the gods but a Romantic notion of the spirit of
nature that man seeks to be identified with. In this quest man is often
the originator, sometimes not even needing an external stimulus. He
has within him, or at any rate the poet as a special kind of man has
within him, the power not only to unite with nature but sometimes
actually to affect, woo, and charm nature.

In 'New Year's Eve Midnight' he has a vision as the bells of New
Year's Eve 'toll' for the old year and 'chime' for the new. The language
is highly Yeatsian,

> and ghosts hover round
> dream beyond dream (p. 23)

being reminiscent of Yeats's 'flames begotten of flame' and 'Spirit after
spirit' in 'Byzantium'. The final vision is, however, thoroughly indigenous: the poet sees the spirits of the departed walking along paths to
a river. It is similar to the riverside ending of 'Piano and Drums' and as
in that poem and a number of others the mood is one of uncertainty,
dimness, mistiness, of being gathered instinctively into nature rather
than exercising individual rationality. In 'New Year's Eve Midnight',
of course, the psychic forces are stimulated by a man-made event, the
bells, rather than a natural one, but the final image is of near-identifi-
cation with natural forces.

In 'The Mystic Drum' no outside stimulus is needed. 'The mystic
drum' is beaten by the poet 'in my inside'. This drum can bring him
into communion with human beings, whether alive or dead, making
them 'dance and sing'. It can also bring him into communion with
nature, not merely making it respond as in the first strophe, but actually

breaking the barriers between man and nature so that, after due invocation, the drum has the effect that

> the trees began to dance,
> the fishes turned men
> and men turned fishes
> and things stopped to grow (p. 26)

Time is suspended in this dance of all life, as it is by the laughter in
'You Laughed . . .' But this time the object of his desire, the sky woman
behind the tree, is unmoved: for the third time in this increasingly
mystic drumming 'she only smiled with a shake of her head'. Such a
person can hardly be human, and indeed when the drumming stops the
woman turns into a tree, and a rather demonic one at that. It is a symbol
of the unyielding woman, the ungratified desire, perhaps even of some
deficiency or suppressed desire in himself that might be linked with the
desire to be an asexual 'stone' in 'Were I to Choose'.

'One Night at Victoria Beach' is another poem that seeks through
vision to pierce beyond the veil of the visible world. The members of
the Aladura sect shout out their prayers to 'what only hearts can see'.
The phrase is used three times, becoming most explicit at the end,
where they are said to

> pray
> to what only hearts can see behind
> the curling waves and the sea, the stars
> and the subduing unanimity of the sky
> and their white bones beneath the sand. (p. 29)

This vision is stimulated then by the elemental forces, but the poet is
an observer, not a participant. At the end he is caught up in the fervour
of the Aladuras, so much more impressive than the highlife music or
the couples haggling about the price of sex, or even than the fishermen
having their fortune told by Babalawo. The poet, almost unaware of
what he is doing, finds that he has knelt on the sand and is about to
shout out with the Aladuras 'but the rushing wind killed the budding
words'. Perhaps the suggestion is that the elemental force of the wind
is telling him that this is not the right way to seek communion with the
spirit of life and death. In any case it is another uncertain, dim ending.

'Adhiambo' is a poem of desire frustrated by rejection like 'The
Mystic Drum', and it uses again the frustrated aspiration for magical
power that gives 'One Night at Victoria Beach' its character. The poet
(rather like Okolo in Okara's novel, *The Voice*) does not know whether
he is madman or medicine man (the uncertainty is a feature of Okara's
work) but in his visionary blending of man and nature he finds that the
figure of a woman supervenes. She is, however, unresponsive to his
attempt at invocation, and like the woman in 'The Mystic Drum' she
signals rejection.

In his love poems Okara uses the fusion of man with nature as a symbol of sexual desire. This is so not only in 'The Mystic Drum' and 'Adhiambo' but also in 'To Paveba', where, in imagery similar to that of the other poems, the onset of desire causes the poet to say:

> ... I laugh and shout to the eye
> of the sky on the back of a fish
> and I stand on the wayside
> smiling the smile of budding trees (p. 33)

This time, however, he is not rejected by a woman but censors 'the fire' in himself, in accordance with a 'vow' he has made.

Okara's longest poem from this period, 'The Fisherman's Invocation', has been widely regarded as a failure.[4] It was written before Nigeria's Independence, which it analyses and celebrates, but not published until 1963 (in *Black Orpheus* 13, pp. 34–43). Two superimposed images govern the poem: one is of two fishermen discussing philosophical matters in their canoe; the other is the ritual and celebration surrounding the birth of a child. The first fisherman is more optimistic, patient, and wise than the second, who readily lapses into despondency verging on nihilism. The first fisherman persuades his companion that he is capable of giving birth to a new life, and section 2 details the birth pangs, but even then the second fisherman is doubtful of the value of the child and for the first part of section 3 wants to throw it into the river. But the first fisherman in a long homily persuades him not to reject the child, which has yet to grow and justify itself, but instead to land and celebrate the birth. Section 4 is a responsorial dancing song with the first fisherman singing the stanzas and the second, now thoroughly caught up in the celebration, responding with a chorus. Section 5, the only part normally anthologized, is a retrospective view of the celebrations and the child's prospects for growth.

Okara chose the superimposed images of fishing and parturition because he needed a narrative framework to incorporate, as central symbols, translations of two Ijaw concepts, the Back and the Front. The Back is the reflection of 'past moons past suns past nights and past gods' (p. 3), that is, it is the communal past, history up to 'Today', particularly the traditional past symbolized by the gods that is 'trying to slip through the Meshes like a fish'. At the instigation of the first fisherman, however, the two men hold the Back in their net. It is his belief that (in another superimposed, perhaps slightly confusing, image):

> The Front grows from the Back
> like buds from a tree stump (p. 4)

The Front, yet to be born as a child, is, of course, the future, and specifically here the future of Independent Nigeria. The first fisherman believes that water comes from a womb 'at the back of your Back' to provide life for the birth of the Child-Front. But the second fisherman has lost his traditional past: he cannot now remember the shape of his 'first little paddle' (p. 5). In these circumstances, representing gloom and inertia about the future of Nigeria, the first fisherman needs to take on the role of invoking the Back and the gods, of singing power into them. This he does in section 2 so that, after hard labour soothed to some extent by 'midwife moon', the Child-Front is born. Yet even so the action is not ended. The second fisherman, still sceptical about the worth of the child, has to be told that he was born—and this is, of course, a propitious event in Nigerian belief—'without teeth' (p. 10). The past will exercise a nurturing influence till the child can talk for itself; the fishermen must be patient until

> the sun ends his play
> the Back its moulding dance
> the mermaids their water song
> and midwifemoon her rise (p. 11)

After the celebration of section 4, the meditation of section 5 acknowledges that the festivities must end: hearts must return from dancing feet to chests, palmwine settle into stomachs, bodies turn cold. But now the child-Front will begin to sing 'green lullabys which tingle our heads', that is, new but puzzling problems will have to be faced. They will be approached by 'half familiar half strange songs' and 'half familiar half strange rhythms fashioned in dreams'; in other words the coming way of life will be partly traditional, partly new.

This rather banal conclusion is one reason why 'The Fisherman's Invocation' has been only tepidly praised. A great deal of excitement has been generated in the poem, yet this is the disappointing outcome. The excitement, the musicality, and some of the debate are, however, vigorously achieved and one ought not to undervalue them. Another reason for critical coolness is perhaps the surrealistic superimposition of images: fishermen catching the past in a net; new buds growing from old stumps; water to reinvigorate a desert flowing from the back of a womb; one fisherman giving birth to a child with the moon as midwife. This is a surreal set of archetypal images imposed on fairly literally described myth. The fishermen in the boat seem solid enough, despite the mythical nature of their quest; they need, indeed, to be fairly solid in order to discuss Independence. But there is some incongruity about these two carefully delineated figures becoming involved in the clash of surreal imagery. A dramatic dialogue such as this runs into some of the same intractable problems as, say, the symbolic plays of Yeats.

' "Frauenkirche" ' (the false form 'Franvenkirche' must be due to the misreading of handwriting) is an occasional poem set in Munich, as the poet contemplates the curious twin towers of the late-medieval cathedral. This poem of 1963 marks the last for some five years, until the thirteen poems in *The Fisherman's Invocation* concerned with the experiences of the Biafran War, some written during it, the last written at Christmas 1971.

These poems of war and peace include graphic description in 'Suddenly the Air Cracks' and 'Cross on the Moon'; moving rhetorical appeals about the suffering of civilians in the dramatic monologues 'Expendable Name' and 'Come, Come and Listen'; poems growing out of a single image as in the brief imagist pieces, 'Moon in the Bucket' and 'Cancerous Growth', and the somewhat longer, more meditative ones, 'Freedom Day', 'Rural Path', 'Silent Girl', 'Rain Lullaby', and 'The Dead a Spirit Demands'; and poems of double or more complex images, like 'The Glowering Rat' and 'Christmas 1971'. Many of Okara's characteristic images recur from the earlier period: water, wind, trees and budding, pathways, song, dreams, and most pervasively, the moon. Unexpectedly, bones and rock do not, and fire imagery occurs only in 'Come, Come and Listen'.

Okara's control of rhetorical form in most of these poems is of a very high order indeed. 'Moon in the Bucket' uses the imperative 'Look!' five times. The first is to gain attention; the second directs attention to the first part of the image, the 'rusty bucket with water unclean'; the third directs attention to the second part, the moon, floating like a 'luminous plate'; the fourth addresses and characterizes the audience, the hate-filled partisans of the war; and the fifth brings the two parts of the image, the audience, and the meaning all together, ending with the highly suggestive description, 'this bucket war'. These last words set the mind off on a reassessment of the whole war: the nation is a rusty bucket, the war filthy, the whole thing unnecessary, like a storm in a teacup.

'Suddenly the Air Cracks' has an eightfold structure based on a repeated threefold sequence of events with the third element of the third sequence missing. There is first the air raid, with the diving jets mirrored by the bodies 'diving under beds'; then the silence; followed by the babble of voices; then a repetition of this threefold sequence in three more scenes; then, the third time round, a street scene that resembles a raid because children, reflecting the assumed nonchalance of their elders, play at being aeroplanes; and lastly the final silence of the day, accompanied by the ultimate silence of 'mangled bodies stacked in the morgue'. The third element of the threefold sequence, the renewed babble of voices, is missing this last time. There is no one, save the unobtrusive poet, to memorialize the day. It is too like other days to be worth remembering by the townspeople. All that remains is the black smoke of rubble; hearts that are 'sadless' because, presumably, they are too involved in their own survival to be able to mourn; and the bodies 'stacked' unceremoniously and without respect to individuality in the morgue.

'Cross on the Moon' is the other poem describing a war fought largely, at least from a Biafran civilian's point of view, in the air. (One should remember, of course, that Okara had wanted to be a pilot in the Second World War.) In this poem he repeats an image from 'Suddenly the Air Cracks', the image of a plane superimposed on the moon. In 'Suddenly the Air Cracks' the moon, a symbol of peace, albeit temporary, rises 'where the jets were'. In 'Cross on the Moon' the order is reversed. The moon is there first, the aircraft, a friendly one with supplies seeking a path to Uli airfield—the last remaining to Biafra when this poem was written—crosses and recrosses it until it seems caught as 'a cross on the moon', a double image of peace and succour.

Okara's earlier tendency to fade out on a soft image of doubt and vagueness has been stiffened by the nature of his subject matter. 'Expendable Name', a poem of powerful but unbitter reproach to the comfortable warmongers, ends with the gesture of a weak, starving mother, an 'expendable name' in the statistics of the war, but the gesture, though physically weak, is a joyous acceptance of death. 'Come, Come and Listen', the other poem addressed to warmongers, ends with 'questions I cannot now answer', but they represent a determined rejection of the politics of war and a determined seeking of another way.

'Rain Lullaby' is an unsentimental poem condemning the war, which was conducted largely by day, and celebrating the mercy flights to Biafra, which of necessity were conducted at night. Its final image of mother birds feeding their young is in no way a 'fade-out' of Okara's earlier type.

The same contrast between the activities of day and night is made in 'Rural Path'. Day is 'harsh' and 'whimsical', containing an 'idiom of war and death'. But night, suffused by moonlight, is a 'Tunnel of dreams', a 'rural path' of 'soft sands and night sounds'. That image is dominant in the poem, but Okara realistically recognizes at the end that 'this abbreviated peace in dreaming' will be 'effaced' by the new day.

Even 'Silent Girl', which has an image of a girl reminiscent of a favourite Négritude image (just as the 'Come sit with me awhile' rhetoric of 'Come, Come and Listen' may be derived from the same tradition), is realistic about the war. Though the final condition is to share a silent dream away from the pressing horror of the war, the inescapable existence of the war and the recognition of the temporary nature of any respite run through the poem. The last words are indeed 'away from the hot sneering days'. And 'The Glowering Rat', written a few months after the end of the war (in Port Harcourt, where Okara lost his manuscripts), ends with water imagery that in earlier poems would have suggested soporific softness but here is 'turbulent' as it receives the 'grumbling days' of waiting for rehabilitation that have succeeded the 'unrecorded' days of war. The water imagery at the end of the last of this group of poems, 'Christmas 1971', redeems what might otherwise have seemed merely the pious hope that 'love and peace will surely sprout skywards like a sapling straight and strong'. Okara asserts this, without any demonstration of its likelihood, but he does so while recognizing the sanctimonious disavowal of responsibility for war to be found on all sides: the whole land is, in his sardonic phrase, 'dripping with water from Pilate's hands'.

Although these poems show evidence of being written from the Biafran side, they are much less partisan than John Pepper Clark's 'Casualties' sequence. They are also much less based on personal or public events of the war, but are instead songs deploring the hatred, suffering, and loss of war without being maudlin. Perhaps the difference is that Okara was much closer to the front line (where mutual respect is more common than in the corridors of power) than Clark and did not feel the need or lacked the political opportunity to justify his side, which, after all, lost the war.

Okara told Bernth Lindfors in 1972 that 'since the end of the war I haven't been able to write a line of poetry . . .' (*Dem-say*, p. 46). Obviously this was not strictly true, but there was a gap of some years between 'Christmas 1971' and the remaining poems in *The Fisherman's Invocation*. They are mostly occasional pieces, not greatly different from those Okara wrote early in his career. The familiar images of water, wind, rock, bells, song, and dreams recur. 'Flying Over the Sahara', 'Dispensing Morning Balm', 'To a Star' (which breaks the 'vow' he had taken not to yield to sexual love), and 'Celestial Song' all end with some degree of soft vagueness, though it is sometimes modified, as in the wartime poems, by a recognition of the harshness of day. What is perhaps more reminiscent of the early poems is the expression of ageing in the two love poems, 'To a Star' and 'Celestial Song'. Now however the ageing has progressed almost to decrepitude, and it applies equally to the body and to the song that comes from it. The poet speaks of himself as 'enfeebled by layers of falling years' (p. 55) and as walking on 'trembly feet' (p. 57).

The last poem is an unfinished pageant, 'The Revolt of the Gods', begun during the Biafran War. In this dramatic poem, gods and men separately discuss the nature of the gods and the balance of power between them and men. Three of the gods (who are not individualized by their attitudes or styles; they all speak in unrhymed four-beat lines) recognize that men and the gods began together and that they alternate in owning the world depending on whether man believes in the gods or asserts his own supremacy and kills them. As the Old God says, and the sentiment is reminiscent of the ending of many of Okara's poems:

> It's death not sudden or final
> as you know. But as always it's suspension
> in mists of suffocating doubts
> which swing us high up to the heavens
> and down to the very dust he tramples on. (p. 58)

The hot-headed Young God, however, will not tamely accept this cycle. He wants to control and guide man by an assertion of power, despite the other gods' assertion that power is useless without man's co-operation.

The scene changes to a discussion between four men, who are much more individualized than the gods. They represent a range of attitudes from sybaritic humanism, through orthodox Christianity, to prophetic cries of doom, with the 3rd Man wavering from one to another. The conventional wisdom of the old gods is vindicated: the Young God's voice begins to fade as the men dismiss the gods.

As it stands, 'The Revolt of the Gods' falls between antique fustian and heavy-footed attempts at levity. It is difficult to see how Okara could redeem it or even develop it. His strength is in rhetorical and lyrical not dramatic verse.

The non-dramatic parts of *The Fisherman's Invocation* indicate that Okara, using a limited range of images and making little use of specific historical or personal material, has created a body of powerful lyrics. They are singable, chantable poems that do not rely on the idiosyncrasies of a particular performer or on theatrically effective atmosphere to make them work. (In this respect they are different from the rhetorical verses of some African writers which are wonderfully effective in their performance but sit very coldly on the page.) His poems are explicit and direct, but almost never predictable or stereotyped. Imagery repeated from one poem to another is never taken for granted: it is given a fresh meaning in each work. And all the time Okara manages to depict, to sing, to declaim, and to construct his meaning in memorable artefacts.

Notes to Chapter 8

1. *Dem-Say: Interviews with Eight Nigerian Writers*, ed. Bernth Lindfors (Austin: Occasional Publications, African and Afro-American Studies and Research Center, The University of Texas at Austin, 1974), interview with Okara, pp. 41–7 (p. 41).
2. London: Heinemann Educational Books, 1978.
3. He was at Northwestern University, Evanston, Illinois, in the winter of 1959 when he wrote this poem: see the interview in *Dem-Say*, p. 42.
4. See, for instance, John Pepper Clark, 'Themes of African Poetry of English Expression' in his *The Example of Shakespeare* (London: Longman, 1970), p. 55: ' "The Fisherman's Invocation" ... like most other attempts by poets to erect fitting mansions to their names, appears to me a real disaster; and K. E. Senanu and T. Vincent, eds., *A Selection of African Poetry* (London: Longman, 1976), p. 48: '*The Fisherman's Invocation* in its entirety is in many ways also Okara's worst poem, of embarrassingly uneven quality, with only short spurts of brilliance until this last section.'

9 Okot p'Bitek

▼▼▼▼▼▼▼▼▼▼▼▼▼▼▼▼▼▼▼▼▼▼▼▼▼▼▼▼▼▼▼▼▼▼

As a poet Okot p'Bitek has several claims to importance. He was the first major East African poet in English; he has influenced a number of other poets; and he is a maker of abiding satiric myths. *Song of Lawino* (1966) not only showed that East African poetry could achieve more than the nonchalantly slight lyrics or brief graphic situation poems that had earlier appeared in periodicals and anthologies; it established that there was a readership for volumes of poetry in English by a single author, and so made possible the publication of such works as Okello Oculi's *Orphan* (1968), Joseph Buruga's *The Abandoned Hut* (1969)—two volumes heavily influenced by *Song of Lawino*—, John Mbiti's *Poems of Nature and Faith* (1969), Jared Angira's *Juices* (1970), Taban lo Liyong's *Frantz Fanon's Uneven Ribs* (1971) and Richard Ntiru's *Tensions* (1971). The East African literary desert for works in English that Taban lo Liyong had polemically described in 1965[1] clearly no longer existed; if, indeed, it ever had in Liyong's terms.

Okot p'Bitek has been reticent and even off-handed when questioned about his literary antecedents. Unlike a large number of African poets in English, he did not read English as a university subject and, though he has taught literature at school and university, he seems to have a mild contempt for the formal questions raised by its more earnest practitioners. That, together with his mischievous sense of fun, means that such statements as this comment on *Song of Lawino* and *Song of Ocol* cannot be taken too literally:

> I don't think they are very much influenced by the African oral tradition; they cannot be sung, for instance. Possibly they are influenced by *The Song of Hiawatha* by H. W. Longfellow and also by *Song of Solomon*. These books I enjoyed very much when I was a student and I consider *Song of Solomon* the greatest love song ever.[2]

Hiawatha seems at first an improbable suggestion, but Okot may have been referring to its discursive, repetitive mode of story-telling; its athletic hero ('Swift of foot was Hiawatha'); his love of music and story; and his requirements in a wife ('Feet that run on willing errands'). He may also have remembered its short unrhymed lines, though their trochaic tetrameter measure bears little resemblance to Okot's standard free-verse two- and three-beat lines. *Song of Solomon* is more plausible, for Okot is an expansive, even extravagant, love poet.[3]

The dismissal of orally composed and recited poetry as an influence must be considered playful. *Song of Lawino* was written in Acoli and translated into English. The two Acoli versions (composed in 1956 and 1969[4]) not only draw directly on many Acoli songs, but could themselves be sung. In the English translation, as Okot says in the preliminary matter to the poem, he has 'murdered rhythm and rhyme'; or at least has dispensed with rhyme and settled for a very free rhythm. Even so, one can readily appreciate something of the traditional Acoli songs quoted by Lawino and can appreciate how similar they are to the surrounding context of Lawino's own 'Song' or 'Lament'. So, for instance, the love song of the Acoli man imploring his father to 'Gather the bridewealth'[5] is the first part of the traditional song, *Wora kel lim*, translated in *The Horn of My Love* as 'Father, bring the bridewealth'.[6] Or, in section 8, when Lawino sings the dirge 'Fate has brought troubles' (pp. 130–31), she is quoting part of the traditional dirge, *Woko okelo ayela* (*The Horn of My Love*, p. 133). Or again, just before the end of the poem, when Lawino sings 'She has taken the road to Nimule' (p. 215), she is quoting from *Okwanyo ger Lumule*, the song about the 'Chief of all women, Alyeka, the brown one' (*The Horn of My Love*, p. 42).

It is not, however, only in direct quotation that Okot is indebted to the Acoli oral tradition. When, for instance, Lawino says

> My husband's tongue
> Is bitter like the roots of the *lyonno* lily (p. 16)

she is quoting an Acoli proverb referring to the bitterness of a wild lily, the tubers of which are eaten only when nothing else is available. When she ends section 2 with

> The pumpkin in the old homestead
> Must not be uprooted! (p. 30)

she is quoting a proverb much used by old men to make the point that old customs, like the wild pumpkins that grow over abandoned settlements, do no harm and may even be useful.[7]

The point is too obvious to need labouring. *Song of Lawino* is clearly related, in content, tone, and style, to Acoli songs. Its basic three-beat line, with frequent variations, is as close as one could expect to get in English to the pattern of the Acoli line. It is also very similar to the kind of line being written in English at this time by such East African poets as Taban lo Liyong, John Mbiti, Joseph Mutiga, John Ruganda, Edwin Waiyaki or Walter Bgoya.

What is new is the sustained rhetoric of the complaint, the organized characterization and satire of the dramatic monologue, and the use of translation as a subject to make polemical and satiric points. Of Okot's four major poems, this is the one that lies closest to his own education in traditional culture, for which he was largely indebted to his mother, Lacwaa Cerina, 'who first taught me to sing', as he says in the dedication to *Song of Ocol. Song of Lawino* is, indeed, named after her, for Lawino (meaning born with the umbilical cord wrapped round the neck) was one of his mother's names; and, like the fictional Lawino, his mother had been 'chief of girls'. It is also the poem closest to his academic studies in anthropology and religion; it contains a dramatic summary of some of the main positions taken up in his later study, *African Religions in Western Scholarship* (1971). It has the most detailed characterization of any of his works and, in that Lawino is very much a woman who has been brought up in an identifiably Acoli culture, the narrowest frame of cultural reference. Lawino is, of course, also representative of the values of village life anywhere in Africa, as contrasted with those of European colonialism. She represents, too, the values of the African woman (or at least of a certain kind of African woman) faced with rivalry in love. But her quarrel with Ocol is more personal and more specific than one finds in Okot's later works. They spread out into cultural and political comment on the whole of black Africa in a way that would be quite foreign to the mind of the village-raised Lawino.

The beginning of the poem and the last section are addressed to her husband, Ocol, meaning Son of Black, or Blackman, as Taban lo Liyong points out.[8] Once, says Lawino, he

> . . . was still a Black man
> The son of the Bull
> The son of Agik (p. 200)

but now—and there is hence a good deal of irony implicit here—

> My husband pours scorn
> On Black People (p. 16)

These two passages, like all the poem between the opening and section 13 (except for a brief passage in section 12), are part of the diatribe addressed to her clansmen as a complaint against her husband.

It is a proud complaint, however, for she was chief of girls and so has a 'Bull name' (p. 129), a title or nickname given to an outstanding person. This, like so many key concepts, is a literal translation from the Acoli, for in this poem, though not in others, Okot finds the strategy of literal translation a fruitful source of ironic comment. In this instance, however—and it is a fairly rare one—any amusement is immediately neutralized by an explanation of why such names are called 'Bull names' and how they come to be bestowed. Lawino says

> My Bull name is Eliya Alyeker
> I ate the name
> Of the Chief of Payira
> Eliya Aliker,
> Son of Awic. (p. 129)

The Payira, the most populous and most extensive in landholding of the Acoli chiefdoms, had as their chief in the 1940s Eliya Aliker, of whom Okot tells something in *The Horn of My Love* (p. 14). Lawino was given his name as a tribute to her leadership, but it was assimilated into the word *alyeker*, a term of affection. She is the daughter of a man with the title 'Lenga-moi' (p. 119), someone who has killed another man and is probably a respected leader in warfare. She knows that she is neither 'shy' nor 'easily browbeaten' (p. 142); that she is not 'a fool' and not 'cold' (p. 43). She is proud of her appearance, of her skin and her hair (p. 63), of her tattoos (pp. 34-5), her breasts and eyes (p. 35), and her singing, playing, and dancing. She knows that in fair competition she could hold Ocol's love by her appearance and by her housekeeping (p. 28).

Ocol, too, has reason to be proud of the place he holds in his own clan, for he is a 'Prince Of an ancient chiefdom' (p. 205), one whose grandfather and father were great men (p. 206). But he has been so seduced by European ways that he 'abuses all things Acoli' (p. 200), even threatening to cut down the *Okango*, the small sacred tree at his father's shrine (pp. 158, 214).

His change of heart is symbolized in his supplanting of Lawino by Clementine, 'a modern girl . . . Who speaks English' (p. 21). Lawino at first professes herself not jealous (p. 24), but then admits 'We all suffer from a little jealousy'. Her own common sense tells her, however, that it is impossible to prevent men from wanting women (p. 27) and her pride that 'I do not fear to compete with her' (p. 29).

Section 1 is a summary of the insults and arguments her husband has used against her; sections 2 to 5 contrast the ways of the rival, Clementine, with Acoli ways; sections 6 to 12 leave Clementine in order to concentrate on Ocol's other prejudices, all of which are contrasted with Acoli beliefs and customs; section 13 is a final appeal to Ocol. All of this would, of course, be mere raillery if Lawino had no desire or hope of drawing Ocol back. Despite his insults, she is still in love with him, deeply hurt that he treats her 'As if I am no longer a person' (p. 15). She is concerned that he will be ridiculed by the clan (p. 14); she recalls his infatuated courtship of her (p. 45); she imagines herself taunting him with his putative flabbiness (p. 49) and with her accomplished boyfriend who plays the *nanga* (p. 63); and she ends by asking him to let her dance before him and sing his praises. Her main argument, however, always implicit and sometimes explicit, is that Acoli ways, though not necessarily better than European ways, are the right ones for an Acoli; that he should be true to his lineage, should cease behaving like a woman (p. 200) and behave like the Acoli prince he is, having due respect for his ancestors. The ancestral shrine, the *otole* war dance praising past leaders of the clan, the Stool of the chieftain, the images of prowess with spear and shield in warfare are the outward emblems of large-scale argument in favour of Acoli ways.

Lawino's moderation, exemplified in her admission that talcum powder is 'good on pink skin' (p. 23), that white woman's hair 'Is soft like silk' (p. 53), that Ocol is free to eat 'White men's foods' if he enjoys them (p. 80), is intersected by passages of bitter raillery, not just at

Clementine and Ocol for foolishly aping white ways, but also at some of the white ways themselves. The coprologous description of a modern dance-hall in section 3; the description of white man's food as tasteless or repulsive (a fried egg as being 'slimy like mucus', p. 70); or the exposition of the idiocies and inconsistencies of Christian catechetical instruction in sections 8 and 9 not only are very funny in themselves, but they also serve to characterize Lawino as passionately biased and sometimes deficient in understanding or judgment.

She is, for instance, a believer in talismans or charms, saying that Ocol once beat her

> For wearing the toe of the edible rat
> And the horn of the rhinoceros
> And the jaw-bone of the alligator. (p. 155)

As she points out, though, the nuns of the Catholic faith to which her husband adheres seem to use the crucifix for similar purposes. In section 7 she says that Ocol is angry because

> I cannot keep time
> And I do not know
> How to count the years. (p. 85)

Her explanation that the Western system of time-keeping is unnecessary is rhetorically effective as far as it goes. In a rural environment, all events of the day, the year, and the lifetime can be satisfactorily timed by the sun, the cock, the stomach, the climate, the moon, the crops, and unusual events.[9] The notion of a continuum of time ticking away whether anyone notices or needs it, a single linear framework for relating all events to, even to the point where it dictates those events, is a scientific one. It was found necessary in Egypt, Babylon, China, and India originally, it would seem, as a basis for astronomical and astrological calculations. Even thoroughly rural communities have, of course, found some need for a calendar, if only to calculate regular market days. To that extent, Lawino's argument is a bit extreme. But then it is part of her character: she is prone to hyperbole. And to stubborn, almost incorrigible ignorance. She cannot tell the time and seems to refuse to learn; she uses the electric stove, but detests it and refuses to master the controls (section 6); she cannot or will not tune the radio (p. 47).

Ali Mazrui has criticized the poem for making Lawino

> a little too simple. A mind that exaggerates so much and in such an obvious way is not simply *culturally* distinct from the modernity which enchants Ocol; it is also a mind too naïve to stand a chance of saving Ocol from that enchantment.[10]

Similarly, in a review of the published Acoli version, *Wer pa Lawino* (1969), Okumo pa'Lukobo objects that Lawino is impossibly backward as a representative of a present-day rural Acoli woman: 'I know of no place in Acoli today where the village girls can't dance at least a sort of rumba'.[11]

This is no doubt true if we assume that the setting of the verse-novel is the 1960s, as the elections of section 11 and the availability of several sophisticated Western articles clearly indicate. But while this is so for the surface of the novel, the clash of culture-values has to be seen as placed a couple of decades earlier, contemporary, say, with Ngugi's *Weep Not, Child* or even *The River Between*. The gap between the date of the superficial life and the date of the work's more deeply felt cultural life should worry no one who is prepared to see the whole poem as a myth. Okot needed to sharpen the contrast between the traditional village and the Westernized town, even to exaggerate the two sets of *mores* by idealization and caricature. So Lawino is more stubbornly opposed to Western ways despite her assertions of tolerance, and Ocol more intransigent and fervent in his new faith and culture than would be literally credible in the 1960s. Such distortions and anachronisms are inevitable in myth from *Gilgamesh*, the *Mahabharata*, or the *Iliad* on. It is Mazrui's failure to understand that representativeness invariably implies some distortion of individuality in character that vitiates his criticisms of the poem.

The poem does, of course, contain discrepancies, but they can, I think, all be attributed to Lawino's blinding sense of outrage and the hyperbole or distortion that stem from it. When, for instance, in the section on time, she says that among the Acoli

> A person's age
> Is shown by what he or she does
> It depends on what he or she is,
> And on what kind of person
> He or she is (p. 105)

she has forgotten that earlier she implied a different system (one that her clansmen must have known very well) in the wonderfully vindictive jibe at Clementine as 'this age-mate of my mother' (p. 26) and in her reporting of Ocol as using the expression 'age-mate of my grandfather' (p. 27). While these are very broad categories of age-mateship, it is clear, as Taban lo Liyong points out (*The Last Word*, pp. 150–51), that the Acoli do in fact use a much narrower age-mate system, rather than relying on categorization 'by what he or she does'. The conclusion to be drawn, though, is simply that Lawino is inconsistent and that this is part of her vehement desire to make as bold a case as she can. To say that she is aware of putting on an act[12] is perhaps going beyond the literary evidence, but certainly Lawino is a performer and has always enjoyed being one.

Okot poured a great many of his own interests into the poem. Traditional dancing and singing, rites and ceremonies, education, religion, and other matters of cultural and anthropological interest; the role of the Christian church; and the two-party system of politics that operated early in Uganda's independence are all incorporated into the poem. His treatment of the church runs parallel to the more extended treatment he gives in his academic works. At the heart of his approach is the belief that in trying to relate their own religion to Acoli religion by translation, Christian missionaries misunderstood Acoli religion and distorted their own. They began with the assumption that the Acoli, clearly a poly-theistic people, must believe in a Supreme Being or High God. Okot considers this a gross error not just about the Acoli but about all the peoples of the Upper Nile, that is, the Nilotes. Their attitude to a *jok* or god he describes thus:

> When the Nilotes encounter *jok*, it is with a specific and named or easily definable *jok*, and not some vague 'power' that they com-municate with. The proper name identifies the *jok*, placing it in a specific category and social context, for action. There is no occasion when the Nilotes think of all the *jogi* (pl. of *jok*) simultaneously. And there is no evidence to show that they regard the named *jogi* as refractions or manifestations, or hypostases of a so-called High God. Each category of *jok* is independent of other *jogi*, although some are used against others. For the Nilotes there are many deities. Not one.[13]

The Christian idea of God as omnipotent and as creator, which Okot considers to be a Greek philosophical one applied to Jewish religious experience, thus could not be conveyed in Acoli. But according to Okot the Italian Catholic priests insisted on finding the appropriate words:

> In 1911, Italian Catholic priests put before a group of Acoli elders the question 'Who created you?'; and because the Luo language does not have an independent concept of *create* or *creation*, the question was rendered to mean, 'Who moulded you?'. But this was still meaningless, because human beings are born of their mothers. The elders told the visitors that they did not know. But, we are told that this reply was unsatisfactory, and the missionaries insisted that a satisfactory answer must be given. One of the elders remem-bered that, although a person may be born normally, when he is afflicted with tuberculosis of the spine, then he loses his normal figure, he gets 'moulded'. So he said '*Rubanga* is the one who moulds people'. This is the name of the hostile spirit which the Acoli believe causes the hunch or hump on the back. (p. 62)

And so 'The name of the Christian God in Lwo is *Rubanga*', as Okot notes on p. 157 of *Lawino*, and throughout sections 8 to 10 of the poem he insists on translating the Christian *Rubanga* as 'the Hunchback', making the unstated assumption that the Acoli *jok* responsible for spinal deformation in human beings is himself deformed. Similarly, the Acoli word for the Christian heaven is retranslated literally as 'Skyland', the Holy Ghost is 'the Clean Ghost', angels are 'the beautiful men With birds' wings', the Apostles' Creed is 'the Faith of the Messengers', the Holy Bible 'the Clean Book', and the gospel 'the good word'. None of the amusement of these literal retranslations could of course exist in the Acoli version, for the language has assimilated these meanings and lost the original incongruities. It is a little disingenuous of Okot to ignore the fact that words in any language change their denotations and con- notations over a period of time and that even at the one time a single word may have a wide range of connotations, the intended one being indicated by context and purpose. It is, nevertheless, all good fun in English, and serves the wider aim of showing the disparity between the two sets of value-systems. It is not a method used elsewhere in his work.

If Okot is right in believing that the Acoli could not accommodate the Graeco-Christian notion of God, it is difficult to see what he ex- pected proselytizing missionaries to do, except give up and go home. Even if their labour was ultimately vain, it seems a little harsh to blame them for trying, albeit misguidedly. The important point remains, though, that in Okot's view no accommodation was possible between two such dissimilar religions.[14] It serves to strengthen Lawino's view that the two cultural systems—religious, educational, artistic, aesthetic, medical, culinary, sartorial, architectural, political, and linguistic— should be kept separate alongside each other. Her attitude is

> I do not understand
> The ways of foreigners
> But I do not despise their customs.
> Why should you despise yours? (p. 29)

She is prepared for Ocol to adopt an eclectic attitude to the two cultures, provided he ceases despising his traditional one. But syncretism between the two cultures seems beyond her conceptualization, and is perhaps alien to Okot p'Bitek's own beliefs. She is prepared, though, to admit that her own culture changes, for she takes umbrage at being grouped by Ocol with her grandmother:

> He says there is no difference
> Between me and my grandmother
> Who covers herself with animal skins. (p. 27)

While the Western-educated reader may find goliardic verse, or Skel- tonics, or Elizabethan complaints, or Swiftian satire appropriate com- parisons for the tone of *Song of Lawino*, there is no need to go beyond what Okot himself says of Acoli oral literature, whether satirical attacks in short stories, or 'songs of bitter laughter', including dirges that include attacks on the living:

> these poems do not cause social strife among the clansmen. On the contrary, they provide a channel through which members of this close-knit group pour out their grievances and jealousies against one another, in public. These attacks, with all the abuse, ridicule

and cruel insults, act as a cleansing activity. (*The Horn of My Love*, p. 155)

Lawino herself represents her society as a competitive one: 'when a girl knocks you You strike back' (p. 33); a society where all she asks is the chance to compete openly for her husband's favours, eating 'in the open Not in the bed room' (p. 28). It is a lusty, vigorous community, where absence of noise is characteristic of wizards. If she seems overemphatic and raucous at times, she can also modulate her tone to blandishment and appeal, though she never becomes servile.

In this characterization of her society she is borne out by her husband's retort, *Song of Ocol*, which appeared four years later. He begins by drawing attention to the monotony and stridency of Lawino's song, and it is noticeable that his own is much more flexible and varied, its basic two-beat line (in contrast to *Song of Lawino*'s three beats) creating a general effect less of ululation than of curt bitter vilification. It is not a self-confident assertion of one set of values, as Lawino's song is; on the contrary, it mourns the passing of Lawino's values and their replacement by a dubious and, indeed, already collapsing set of values. It is an ironic lament for what has been lost, interspersed with the hollow face-saving formulae appropriate to an intelligent and self-critical member of the new Westernized élite. It hints constantly at an unstated self-disgust. It can also be seen to contain the seeds of Okot's two later *Songs*.

The tone of *Song of Ocol* has not, I think, been well grasped by most critics. It is not, except in superficial ways that the author intends us to recognize as such and reject, a defence of Westernization. It is certainly not an answer to Lawino. Indeed, except for section 1, it is not addressed to her.[15] It lacks the specific, dramatic setting of Lawino's monologue. Instead, it is addressed, more in Ocol's thinking than in actuality, to various groups of people, not just Acoli, but groups from all over East Africa. For the richly varied tone there are traditional African precedents, but not, I think, for the wide range of (mostly imagined) addressees. Here the analogy might be with some of Léopold Sédar Senghor's or Walt Whitman's poems, particularly those that combine rhetorical address with symbolic visions. Or, as a dramatic monologue, one might relate it to the fantasizing and the imaginary situations of *The Love-Song of J. Alfred Prufrock* rather than to the solidly dramatized situations of Browning; it is largely interior monologue rather than spoken monologue.

Its battery of imagery is not, as one would have expected had it been a reply to Lawino, drawn mainly from Western technology, economics, and social philosophy. It is true that in the first section Ocol refers to the boot of his car and to having the house painted by a professional; in section 5 to putting 'the Maasai in trousers' (p. 49); in section 6 to the modern party system and his own (probably imaginary) town house, farm, and Mercedes; in section 7 to grandiose engineering works; and in section 9 to Westernized Africans in various professions. Many of these references are, however, ironic, filled with a tone of self-loathing and disgust. But even so they are outweighed by the traditional African images, many of them, it is true, offered in a tone of denigration or repulsion, but others offered with affection or nostalgia. The balance of imagery is, in other words, at least as much in favour of traditional imagery as in *Song of Lawino*.

The extended image of the exiled monarch in section 1 represents not merely Lawino in her irreparable separation from Ocol, but more importantly—for this is a more widely symbolic and less localized poem than *Song of Lawino*—Ocol, the Blackman, irreparably exiled from his kingdom, the inheritance of his traditional society. Ocol, the character in the poem, is sympathizing with Lawino's plight, bemoaning his own separation from the clan, and then rising beyond these personal concerns into symbolic mourning for the African's separation from his roots. Even in section 1, the most specifically dramatic part of the poem, the wider symbolic framework is introduced.

It might be objected that he cannot be mourning for acts that he accepts responsibility for. He does, after all, say 'We will plough up ... We will uproot ... We will obliterate ...' (pp. 16–17). In fact, however, this responsibility for one's own destruction, this plucking up of one's own roots, is what makes the whole process so tragic. Ocol, as a character and as the symbolic African, is deeply divided. He knows he is destroying himself but he does not seem able to help it. He despoils his own culture but he loathes himself for doing so. The futile 'Song of the woman' (p. 13) is not merely the woman Lawino's lament; it is the representative case Lawino has put up for the preservation of African culture. It is a doomed case, represented by the symbol of an already defeated General. The symbol is taken up again at the very end of the poem:

> As for Shaka
> The Zulu General,
> How can we praise him
> When he was utterly defeated
> And killed by his own brothers? (p. 86)

It is not the mere defeat that is bitter and desolate: it is the fact that, after the defeat of the African dream, Africans themselves abrogated their leader and killed him.

Similarly, with the images that follow that of the General in section 1, the emphasis is on something once good that has been neglected or abused and allowed to decay: the song of Lawino is 'rotting buffalo', 'sour sweet', 'pork gone rancid', 'sour milk', 'rotting Pumpkin'. In section 2, affection and ridicule are mingled in a lyrical interior monologue that draws on Négritude images for affection and on white caricatures of Africa ('white teeth in bright pink gum') for ridicule.

The mood of section 3 is more violent as Ocol rouses himself to threats of root-and-branch destruction of African ways. This is much more hysterical than anything in Lawino's song, much nearer neurosis. 'All the village poets Musicians and tribal dancers' (p. 29) are to be put in detention, all the 'schools of African studies' (p. 30) closed down. Ocol expresses frenzied hatred for anything reminding him that he is black.

Section 4 changes from this vituperative tone to one of nostalgia, though not uncritical nostalgia, as Ocol recalls a scene of the blind *nanga* player Adok Too or Omal Lakana[16] singing while an Acoli woman returns from the well. Ocol adjures her and her sisters from elsewhere in East Africa to release themselves from their slavery, ignorance, and unhygienic ways, to revolt against a system that makes them chattels. Lawino had nothing of the feminist in her: she wanted her man to adopt the traditional male rôle while she entertained him and cooked for him; she even used the bridewealth system, which she obviously accepted, as an argument against the plausibility of the Christian story of the birth of Jesus. Ocol here professes concern at the subjection inherent in such a view of wifehood.

The review of traditional ways continues in section 5, though it is now applied to the more masculine pursuits of the peoples of East Africa and it ranges over various historical periods. The nostalgic roll-call of these people is then succeeded by further vicious threats to eliminate such practices and to turn these rural people into urban dwellers. The tone has, in other words, fluctuated between nostalgia and frenetic ideology.

Section 6 is a long piece of self-justification by Ocol addressed to a village man, a constituent who, it appears, has never seen his local-member of parliament before. It can be taken literally, but such is the extravagance of the tone that it seems best to take it as a daydream: Ocol imagining himself to be a member of parliament with a town house, a Mercedes and a farm, and imagining how he would deal with a constituent. If taken literally, then this is not the Ocol of *Song of Lawino*, section 11; it is a wealthier Ocol some years later and he has not got rid of Lawino in the intervening years. It seems better to interpret it as a dream of Ocol projected into the future when he has been elected to parliament and has begun to reap the rewards of his Party loyalty.

In section 7 there is another change of mood. Self-doubt is given expression in the prophetic vision attributed to a crippled beggar. Ocol is abusive to the frightened beggar, but quotes the whole of his song. It is about the cynicism and frustration following Uhuru, then their re-placement by anger, which results in a purifying explosion or revolution. The beggar's song reflects Ocol's own fear, but he sublimates his fear into vituperation, ending with the absurd hyperbole of the projected schemes to blow up Mount Kilimanjaro, fill in the Rift Valley, and turn the waters of the Nile into the Indian Ocean. Ocol's divided nature and his tenuous hold on reality are again in evidence.

Section 8 similarly balances nostalgia for tradition and brutal abolition of it. It has some lovely reminiscences of a woman once loved—not Lawino as a character, for this is a prophetic vision of the final destruction of traditional Africa, of the absorption of the country into the city.

The visionary strain continues in section 9, as Ocol surveys the roles of the modern intelligentsia. His cynicism has now taken a very sombre hue. The voice of 'United Africa' (p. 84) has been drowned out by guns, Marxism has been assimilated and distorted to make it seem peculiarly African, even though it is expressed in such widely dissimilar modes as Senghor's rhetoric and Nyerere's Arusha Declaration. The fever of Ocol's address reaches the madness it has always been threatening to embrace with the diatribe on

> the founders
> Of modern Africa
> Leopold II of Belgium
> Bismarck . . . (p. 85)

and ends with the sorrowful, tragic plaint:

> What proud poem
> Can we write
> For the vanquished? (p. 86)

Okot p'Bitek had of course written a proud poem for the people he now believes to be vanquished: *Song of Lawino*. *Song of Ocol* is, by contrast, a poem of despair for the lost culture of the vanquished. It is a poem much more varied in tone, without the long unrelieved stridency of Lawino's complaint. The variety and the deeply troubled subtlety of Ocol's mind have, regrettably, not always been appreciated by readers and critics.

Song of Prisoner arises generally out of the image of corrupt self-justification attributed to successful politicians in *Song of Ocol*, and specifically out of the following passage from section 6:

> Trespassers must be jailed
> For life,
> Thieves and robbers
> Must be hanged,
> Disloyal elements
> Must be detained without trial . . . (p. 63)

The anger and madness of Ocol are now transferred to one of the victims of such a policy of repression, a poor man who is delirious after (and while) being beaten up by sadistic warders in gaol. As Ocol lamented to his mother that he was born black (end of section 2), so Prisoner curses his father (section 4) and his mother (section 6) for his genes. Prisoner puts into words what was implicit in *Song of Ocol*: that 'the cancer of Uhuru' is 'Far worse than The yaws of Colonialism' (p. 50). In *Song of Ocol*, 'The lamb Uhuru' was a rotting carcase with deceptively open eyes (p. 67). In *Song of Prisoner*, the remains of the lamb's carcase are fought over by 'Old hyenas' (p. 31). Uhuru is also a 'fierce wild fire' (p. 15) that has burnt out the Prisoner, and a 'whirlwind' (p. 118). Its effects, in the hands of those who pervert and direct it for their own ends, are like a 'shark' devouring its own children (p. 65), a 'Rhino' prodding its brothers in the back (p. 85), or an 'arrow' bringing down an eagle (p. 94).

Song of Prisoner has evoked a good deal of puzzlement and specula-tion about the dramatic situation in the poem, much of it generated by Edward Blishen's unfortunate remarks in his Introduction to the New York edition about a multiple persona rather than a single characterized speaker. Apart from one or two very minor inconsistencies,[17] the poem makes sense as the more or less delirious dramatic monologue of a poor man who is being held and beaten up in gaol after he has assassinated an important political leader. The poem was begun immediately after Okot heard the news of the assassination in Nairobi on 5 July 1969 of Tom Mboya, the cabinet minister widely regarded as the most promis-ing candidate to succeed Jomo Kenyatta as President. According to Okot,

> The killer of Tom Mboya is the prisoner in *Song of Prisoner*. He hadn't been captured yet. I captured him first, in this poem.[18]

In section 11 he overhears another prisoner, a disgraced Minister for Police and Justice, being beaten up, and he intersperses his own com-ments. Section 12 is an interior monologue in the mind of the Minister; or, if one insisted on absolute singleness in the point of view, in the mind of the poor Prisoner as he imagines the Minister's thoughts or even overhears them (for the Minister is aware that 'the very air Has ears' (p. 90)).

It is not, I think, impossible to work this out from the poem itself, particularly from the clues given at the beginning of section 11, when the Prisoner hears and shushes the 'millipede'. If external support were needed, however, it comes from Margaret Marshment, who said of section 11:

> Okot tells me that this is the voice of a man in the next cell, whom the Prisoner overhears. This was not clear to me, and we could wish it were clearer because it is important . . . But we can guess at one reason why he might be in prison: that he was the assassin's employer.[19]

It is a plausible guess, for the Prisoner at one stage has no doubt that the machinery of the Law will soon set him free (p. 59), an appropriate theory if his hirer had been the Minister in charge of 'Law and Order' (p. 83), and if this was the same man he had been bodyguard to, political organizer for, and procurer of girls for (p. 117). But it seems as if the hirer-Minister-employer is unable to protect his assassin-bodyguard-Prisoner, for he himself has been thrown into gaol and beaten up in the wake of the assassination. In gaol, one of his desires is 'to sleep With experienced prostitutes' (p. 92), presumably the type lined up for him previously by the Prisoner.

Filling in further details of the dramatic situation, we can say that the Prisoner has apparently been arrested while sleeping in the 'City Park' (p. 15); that he has been before a magistrate for a preliminary hearing, charged with vagrancy (p. 16) and asked whether he pleads guilty or not guilty (a recurring refrain); that the police have beaten him up several times, perhaps sadistically asking him as they do so whether he pleads guilty or not guilty to other offences including the assassination (pp. 13–17, 30, 42, and 68); that he believes the man he killed was a gross political criminal (pp. 67–9) who had wrongfully imprisoned many citizens (p. 69); that he is so poor that his family is short of food and his children will never go to school (pp. 22–3, 60–1, 101); and that during his imprisonment, perhaps in the early stages, he has had visions or hallucinations of being treated as a national hero for his bold action (pp. 66–9, 74, 76–9). The height of his euphoria (p. 79) is succeeded by the Minister's monologue, and this is a highly dramatic and ironic interruption, for his dreams of adulation could presumably only be realized if his employer, the Minister, stood by him and acknowledged him as his instrument. But the Minister himself is disgraced. He too has hopes of quick release; he too is beaten; he too has thoughts of his children, though they go to school and should prosper (p. 86), and of his parents, though unlike the Prisoner's they are comfortably supported (p. 87); he too has hallucinations of wild pleasure (section 12) to contrast against the brutal realities of the cell.

The main bulk of the Prisoner's dreams of pleasure follow the return of the monologue from the Minister to him in section 13. His pleasures are to be first with his wife, family, and clan, not among the city prostitutes like the Minister's. Then, in sections 14 and 15 his mind takes him beyond his clan, beyond East Africa, to a world survey of music, song, and dancing. It is a visionary expansion comparable to what happens at the end of *Song of Ocol*. There is madness about it all, as there was in *Song of Ocol*. Prisoner has been tortured, he has admitted that his mind is on fire and that he is mad (pp. 13, 24–5). In his delirium, then, conventional moral attitudes are thrown away, and he can 'want to try the dances Of neo-colonialists and ex-Nazis' (p. 107). Margaret Marshment saw this as an indication of the Prisoner's unreliability as a moral guide, of his reprehensible denial of responsibility for his own act or, indeed, for anybody's acts. It could, of course, also be seen as evidence of delirium brought about by his action, his imprisonment, the brutal treatment he has received, his fears for himself and his family, and his hunger. Or we may recognize that at the end of the poem (as in *Song of Ocol*) the clear outlines of the human protagonist are being expanded and blurred as he is apotheosized into a symbol of the political detainee or political criminal anywhere in the world. Like many such people accused of acts against governments, he sees himself as a world

citizen, justified by the euphoric internationalism of his act and condition. But the balance of sympathy still lies, I think, on the side of the
Prisoner, whose exposé of the hypocrisy of the independent régime of
which he is a citizen has been all too convincing.[20]

In section 15, the examples of international brotherhood narrow
down to Africa, and the dancing images are now mingled with images
of war, famine, and bloodshed. The last word in the poem is 'Uhuru',
and the whole poem has to be seen as a bitter and sorrowful myth of
what can happen after so-called Independence, an indictment of African governments and nations as no better than anyone else at establishing a just society. More generally, *Song of Prisoner* can be seen as a
myth of the oppressed citizen, deprived of freedom and dignity in the
unjust state. Once again Okot p'Bitek has created a memorable myth
centred on a representative type. Once again he has begun with a
character and turned the character into a symbol.

The myth of *Song of Malaya* concerns African attitudes to sex in
contrast to missionary-advocated exclusivity and repression. Once
again, the seeds of this poem can be found in the earlier ones. Lawino,
accepting that she should share her husband with Clementine, asked

> Who has ever prevented men
> From wanting women? (p. 27)

At the end of *Song of Malaya*, the prostitute (*malaya* in kiSwahili, but
used in East Africa even by non-Swahili speakers) asks

> Who can command
> The sun
> Not to rise in the morning? (p. 184)

This is a poem celebrating sex as joyful, good, and liberating. The
malaya says *karibu* ('come near' in kiSwahili) to all: sailors, soldiers,
Sikhs, Hindus, whites, schoolboys, teachers, chiefs, drivers, factory
workers, shop assistants, political organizers, doctors, municipal
officers, Kaffirs, farmers, policemen, even perhaps the detested 'advi-
sors The experts and mercenaries', the 'one pest' of Africa (p. 140).

There are, however, detractors and enemies to be combated. The
chief who complains of contracting venereal disease is reminded in
section 2 of his visit a few nights earlier, when his virility was impaired
by drunkenness. But the section ends with some practical advice on
sexual manners: the Kaffir is advised to get circumcised and to bring
'Gum boots' or contraceptives next time; and her Sister Prostitutes are
similarly advised to have 'boxing gloves' in their handbags. The out-
raged wife is met in section 3 with the argument that her husband is
made happier and more amenable by his visits to the prostitute; and
there is also advice to do something about bad breath. The moralizing
black bishop in section 4 is reminded that he is himself a bastard and
that both chastity and monogamy are alien to nature. It is in this section
that the poem (like *Song of Ocol* and *Song of Prisoner*) moves outward
in time and space, drawing analogies from Eve, Hagar, the daughters of

Sodom and Gomorrah, Rahab, Esther, Delilah (all Old Testament examples, by no means all normally considered as prostitutes), Magdalena, Theodora, and St Augustine's whore (examples from the New Testament, Byzantium, and the Church Fathers). The analogies are continued into section 5 with the illegitimacy of Jesus, used as a comforting example by the prostitute to her son who has been taunted at school by a teacher, himself indiscriminately licentious. The moral disapproval of her own brother is met by the prostitute in section 6 with evidence of his own reliance on prostitutes, his wife's unfaithfulness, and his own illegitimacy. There is also here a diatribe against wives as 'slaves Of the world', 'Married whores', 'Penned like goats To unwilling pegs'. After the harshness of her criticism she demurely offers to help her brother find a suitable partner, but he apparently storms out in affected disgust while she is speaking. Section 7 begins with her arrest by a police sergeant. She reminds him that he had visited her in another capacity only the previous night and then, echoing the words of the Prisoner, she asks

> But how can you now
> Call me
> A vagrant? (p. 182)

Then follows a malediction, summarizing her proud defiant argument in the whole of the poem. She defies all her enemies and detractors to do their worst and consign her to hell,

> But
> Who can command
> The sun
> Not to rise in the morning? (p. 184)

This is a less serious, less gloomy, and less political poem than *Song of Ocol* or *Song of Prisoner*. Its joyous celebration and its relatively unvaried rhetorical tone are more reminiscent of *Song of Lawino*. But like all the other poems it expresses ideas important to Okot p'Bitek through the monologue of a character who rises into symbolism. The *malaya*, however, remains very much an individual to the end: her representative character has been conveyed by the repeated addresses of her song to her sister prostitutes of the world.

Okot's uncollected poems are few in number, and can easily be related to his four major works. 'Return the Bridewealth', [21] for instance, fits easily into the world of *Song of Lawino*. The village man wants to marry a second time. Apparently improvident, he shamelessly asks his father for bridewealth, but is ignored. He thinks of borrowing money in the town, but is rejected, apparently as a bad risk. He then has the effrontery to ask his first wife (whose father he says he cannot trace) to return her own bridewealth. And, with a taunt, she does—by cheque. 'Harvest' and 'Order of the Black Cross'[22] are political pieces of a slightly sibylline kind, the second marking the end of the war in Biafra. They can be

accommodated within the world of *Song of Ocol* and *Song of Prisoner*.
They can also be seen as pointing forward to Okot's fifth major poem,
which he discussed with Bernth Lindfors in 1976:

> I am now working on *Song of a Soldier*, which examines the
> destructive role of the military in Africa. It raises the question of
> just how are we going to get rid of them? The central character is
> a particular soldier, this great thief, parading all over Africa. I wish
> he was only a thief! He's much worse than that! He is the one
> speaking in most of the poem, but the book will have a slightly
> different structure from most of the others because there is also a
> narrator who comes in every now and then saying things like, 'He
> came soon after midnight and sneezed.' Then the soldier will
> speak, and the narrator will return later. So it's a two-sided sort of
> thing, the kind of structure you saw in *Song of Prisoner*. Even the
> corpses, the victims of the soldier, will speak and interact with
> their murderer, and then the narrator will push the story on to the
> next phase. It's a very painful thing I'm writing. It's been going on
> for some time because it's a very tearful thing to do ... But it is a
> very terrible book because I lost quite a lot of relatives in the
> Uganda coup, a lot of friends too, and after I write a few lines, I
> drop it because it causes a lot of tears. (*WLWE* interview, p. 292)

This dramatic monologue will, then, present the horrific corruption
and corrupting influence of the individual agent of destruction. The
humorous idiom has now turned very sour indeed, and Okot has moved
a long way from the celebratory ebullience of *Song of Lawino* and *Song
of Malaya*. The new poem confirms the fact, however, that his strength
lies in the extended poem. In his four major published pieces he has
created memorable symbols of African culture, the perversion of Westernization, the corruption of independent régimes, and African sexuality. The fifth will bring the cultural analysis even closer to the present
time.

Notes to Chapter 9

1. 'East Africa, O East Africa, I Lament Thy Literary Barrenness', *Transi-
   tion* 19 (1965), 11; reprinted in *Transition* 50 (1975/6), 43. Much expanded
   as 'Can We Correct Literary Barrenness in East Africa?' in *East Africa
   Journal* 2 No. 8 (December 1965), 5–13, an article which gave rise to 'The
   Literary Drought: A Roundtable Discussion' by Ezekiel Mphahlele, Gerald Moore, Okot p'Bitek and Rajat Neojy in *East Africa Journal* 2 No. 10
   (March 1966), 11–15. The expanded article is reprinted in Liyong's *The
   Last Word: Cultural Synthesism* (Nairobi: East African Publishing House,
   1969), pp. 23–42.
2. Interview, *Kunapipi* (Aarhus, Denmark), 1, No. 1 (1979), 89–93 (p. 89).
3. He quotes from *The Song of Solomon* as an epigraph to 'The Love Song'
   section of *The Horn of My Love* (London: Heinemann Educational Books,
   1974), p. 39.

4. See G. A. Heron, *The Poetry of Okot p'Bitek* (London: Heinemann Educational Books; New York: Africana, 1976), ch. 3, for details of these versions. The whole book offers a great many aids to the understanding of p'Bitek's work.

5. *Song of Lawino: A Lament* (Nairobi: East African Publishing House, 1966), pp. 122–3. All quotations and references relate to this edition. The other editions of Okot's work referred to in this chapter are *Song of Ocol* (Nairobi: East African Publishing House, 1970) and *Two Songs: Song of Prisoner; Song of Malaya* (Nairobi: East African Publishing House, 1971).

6. Pp. 48–9. The whole book is a useful source of commentary on *Song of Lawino* and, to some extent, Okot's other major poems.

7. See Heron's references to Okot's Oxford B.Litt. thesis (1964), 'Oral Literature and Its Social Background Among the Acoli and Lang'o', in *The Poetry of Okot p'Bitek*, pp. 38–9.

8. 'Lawino is Unedu' in his *Last Word*, pp. 135–56 (p. 142).

9. For a good treatment of time in African literature see Gerald Moore, 'Time and Experience in African Poetry', *Transition* 26 (1966), 18–22.

10. 'The Patriot as An Artist', *Black Orpheus* 2, No. 3 (1968), 14–23 (p. 20); reprinted in G. D. Killam, ed., *African Writers on African Writing* (London: Heinemann Educational Books, 1973), 73–90 (p. 85).

11. *Nanga* (National Teachers' College, Kyambogo) 2, No. 3 (May 1970). Quoted extensively by G. A. Heron, pp. 67–73 (p. 72).

12. As H. O. Anyumba does in '*Song of Lawino*: A Creative Audacity—An Appreciation', *East Africa Journal* 4, No. 6 [ii] (October 1967), 31–6.

13. Okot p'Bitek, *African Religions in Western Scholarship* (Nairobi: East African Publishing House, 1971), p. 71. (Also published Totowa, N.J.: Rowman and Littlefield, 1972.)

14. He himself professes atheism:

> I admit I am neither a Christian nor a pagan. I do not believe in gods or spirits. I do not believe in witchcraft or supernatural forces. Heaven and hell do not make sense to me; and for me metaphysical statements are nonsense.

('Reflect, Reject, Recreate: A Reply to Professors B. A. Ogot, Ali Mazrui and Peter Rigby', *East Africa Journal*, 9, No. 4 (April 1972), 28–31 (p. 31).)

15. I think it is tendentious to consider that p. 80 is an address to her, as G. A. Heron does in *The Poetry of Okot p'Bitek*, p. 64. She has, I think, vanished from the poem by this stage, as Ocol's mind roams among mostly imagined or symbolic audiences. The woman addressed here is, I think, merely a Lawino-type, not his own wife; this is a vision, not everyday reality.

16. A real person; Okot p'Bitek describes how he came to be known as Adok Too in *The Horn of My Love*, pp. 12–13, and quotes some of his newer poems in 'The Poet in Politics', *Black Orpheus* 2, No. 3 (1968), 29–33.

17. Such as where the Prisoner first met his wife, a matter about which pp. 58 and 102 give different versions, as G. A. Heron points out (p. 82). In contrast to the interpretation given here, Heron sees three speaking characters in the poem, for he interprets the 'vagrant' as being separate from the 'assassin'.

18. Bernth Lindfors, 'An Interview with Okot p'Bitek', *WLWE* (World Literature Written in English) 16, No. 2 (November 1977), 281–99 (p. 290).

19. 'Song of Prisoner: A Reply to Atieno-Odhiambo', *Busara* 4, No. 1 (1972), 62–70 (pp. 68–9); reprinted in Chris L. Wanjala, ed., *Standpoints on African Literature* (Nairobi: East African Publishing House, 1973), pp. 124–38 (pp. 134–5).

20. The American edition is dedicated to 'lumumba mondale kimathi mboya tshombe balewa', a judicious and neutral assemblage of independence leaders, heads of state, ministers, secessionists and freedom fighters against the existing state.

21. *Transition* 24 (1966), 52–3; most readily available in *Poems from East Africa*, ed. David Cook and David Rubadiri (London: Heinemann Educational Books, 1971), pp. 124–9.

22. Originally printed in *East Africa Journal* 6, No. 1 (January 1969), 7, and *Journal of the New African Literature and the Arts* 9 and 10 (Winter and Spring 1971), 73–4, respectively.

10 Mazisi Kunene

▼▼▼▼▼▼▼▼▼▼▼▼▼▼▼▼▼▼▼▼▼▼▼▼▼▼▼▼▼▼

By a paradox of contemporary publishing opportunities, Mazisi Kunene, who writes in Zulu and then translates some of his poetry into English, has had much more of his work appear in translation than in the original. Born in Durban in 1930, he began writing as a boy, and by the age of ten or eleven was submitting poems to newspapers and magazines. A small collection of poems in Zulu, *Idlozi Elingenantethelelo*, won an award in the Bantu Literary Competition in 1956, and poems were published in *Ilanga laseNatal* and the *African Teachers' Journal*. But it was not until after he came to England in 1959, initially to study the Zulu literary tradition but interrupting his studies to become an official of the African National Congress, that English versions of his Zulu poems began to appear.

If Dennis Brutus is the most Westernized of all the poets considered in this volume, Mazisi Kunene is the most thoroughly African. His chief influences have been Magolwane, the court-poet of the great Zulu king, Shaka, and Dr B.W. Vilakazi, the twentieth-century poet, scholar, and teacher. The world of discourse of his poems is a Zulu one, with the philosophy, the imagery, and the rhetoric relying heavily on the oral tradition of Zulu poetry from the eighteenth century to the present day. Translation into English inevitably sacrifices a great deal: the sound-pattern (an important feature of Zulu poetry), the flexible construction of one part of speech from another, the repetition and parallelism, the multiple concrete and mythological meanings of words, and the rhythm (though this is perhaps a less important feature of the Zulu poetic tradition than of the English). Kunene's English versions, often representing a rather truncated version of the original, are nevertheless important poems in their own right, just as Okot p'Bitek's *Song of Lawino* or Kofi Awoonor's 'I Heard a Bird Cry' are.

The major works so far published by Kunene are two epics which he worked on from the early 1960s. Both have been published only in English versions. The first was *Emperor Shaka the Great: A Zulu Epic* (London: Heinemann Educational Books, 1979). It is a poem of some 17,000 lines dealing with the rise of the Zulu empire under Shaka: it is a national epic, based on the life of a man of great political and military vision. Kunene told Alex la Guma in 1966 that he intended through the national theme to 'express the general experience of mankind, and that general experience I think in turn, must emphasize the oneness and the unity of man'.[1] The other epic, he said,

deals with the creation, the origin of life, the concept of the origin

of life held by an indigenous African community. And since this is
a discussion, basically, about a philosophy of life (which I think is
what any religion is), the social expression of the philosophy of life
of a particular community; the epic then deals with this philosophy,
the beliefs in the organization of society, the beliefs in the ultimate
destinies of man, and the belief in the actual history of the community itself. (p. 88)

All that was published for a long time was an extract of 218 lines in
an English version. It appeared as 'Anthem of Decades' at the end
of Kunene's first volume in English, *Zulu Poems* (London:
André Deutsch, 1970), pp. 89–95. When the entire work was
published in 1981 as *Anthem of the Decades: A Zulu Epic* (London:
Heinemann Educational Books) this section appeared, with slight
changes, as Book One.

It is often asserted that African poetry, by contrast with European,
is spoken not by an individual but by the representative of a community,
that its scale of values is community-centred, that it gives symbolic
expression to the community, and that it assumes and manifests a
continuity of tradition from the past, through the present, to the future.
These bold generalizations, when applied to much contemporary
poetry, can seem matters of faith rather than of demonstration, but in
regard to Kunene's work they are demonstrably true. It is perhaps not
unduly fanciful to see in the very titles, *Zulu Poems* and . . . *A Zulu Epic*,
a self-effacing suppression of individuality in favour of an assertion of
collective identity. As much of his first volume consists of poems concerned with life, mortality, the Ancestors, exile, revolution, and rebirth,
'Anthem of Decades' can provide a solid introduction, for it traverses
many of the subjects raised in the shorter poems.

Unlike Gabriel Okara's 'The Revolt of the Gods', this celestial debate
occurs before the creation of man and is, indeed, about whether such a
creation is desirable. The earth, moon, and stars exist in a dark, silent
universe. Into the silence comes Sodume, the spirit of deep-voiced,
male thunder, which acts as 'the Intelligence of Heaven' to bring fructification to the earth. He splits open the earth, releasing all the animals
that people it. So ferocity and fear are released, as one beast preys on
another in 'general carnage'. Fertility, then, must be accompanied by
destruction; 'good things must feed the ruthlessness of appetites'
(p. 90) and Sodume, the spirit of fertility, is also responsible for
destructive earthquakes.

The debate about the creation of man is conducted between Nomkhubulwane, 'the princess of life', the daughter of the Creator, and
Somazwi, a god critical of the proposed creative activities. Nomkhubulwane argues that

'We have fulfilled the other tasks of creation
But they are not complete without man,

He who will bind all things of existence,
A great shepherd who excels with wisdom.' (p. 91)

The more militant Sodume had earlier argued that man would be
'Proud and defiant before all things' (p. 90), so it would seem that man's
unification of 'all things of existence' will be by virtue of his superior
understanding, self-esteem, and power.

The contrary argument presented by Somazwi begins with a similar
assumption, that man will have 'a new power That will supervise all
things with knowledge' (p. 91). He argues that this position inter-
mediate between the beasts and the creative forces will be unsatisfactory. Unlike the beasts, man will not be content with the joys of
existence. His mind will range over the past and the future, doubting
the very value of existence, knowing too much for his own comfort.

Nomkhubulwane's answer is accompanied by the sun, now mentioned for the first time (p. 93) as being in the sky. She rejects the
conservative argument that creation ought to be considered finished. In
her view, creation is a continuous process inherent in life: 'creation
must always create. Its essence is its change' (p. 94). Man's superiority
will partake of this very nature of creation, for his struggle to attain
wisdom will be the source of his power. As Sodume later puts it, this
mental effort will represent 'the extension of life' (p. 95). This participation in the central creative, life-giving quality is, then, not only a
source of power, but also a participation in 'the oneness of which he
[man] is extension' (p. 94).

The equation of creativity with unsatisfied mental activity is a bold
and exciting one, probably the most radical metaphysical notion to be
found in the whole of African poetry. The argument of Okara's 'The
Revolt of the Gods' seems petty by comparison.

Many of Kunene's shorter poems seem like chips from the creation
epic. They take up some of the same concerns and use the same cosmic
imagery. 'From the Ravages of Life We Create' (p. 31), for instance,
focuses on the emergence of creation from destruction, the renewing
process of life, the interrelationship of grief with joy. Each of the images
says almost the same thing, but each defines the concept in some
particular way. Suns are 'torn from the cord of the skies', to mingle in
shame with fallen leaves, but the cord itself remains and the combination of winter suns and leaves offers a hint of the process of natural
decay that feeds the next generation of life. The 'wedding party' image
of fecundity is mingled with 'the moon disintegrating', a suggestion of
renewal only through decay, whether the decay is in inanimate nature
or a woman's monthly cycle. The power of man as it is found in the
searching intellectuality that can never rest is again asserted, and the
poem ends in a splendidly original image combining the notion of man's
power and his limitations, the good and the evil that he is capable of:
even a plague of locusts 'with broken wings' can shelter the earth from
the intense heat of the sun.

'In Praise of the Earth' (pp. 32-3), 'Wenishet-Jusmere' (pp. 33-4), 'Master of Days' (p. 34), and 'The Night' (pp. 34-5) all deal with one paradoxical aspect or another of the creation or life process: ugliness and beauty, decay and re-creation, time and continuity, grief and hope. They proceed mostly by a procession of cosmic or natural images, related to each other in tenor or meaning but often quite unrelated in vehicle or imagistic device.

'Man's Power Over Things' (p. 36) and 'Triumph of Thought' (p. 37) memorably assert the value of humanity over the value of 'things', including the fearful thoughts man can create. 'Cycle' (p. 40), 'Abundance' (p. 43), 'Isle of Man Christmas 1967' (p. 45), and 'Triumph of Man' (p. 79) concentrate on the endless cycle of death and renewal, 'Triumph of Man' going so far as to say that it is man himself who alone has created the notion of endlessness or eternity. 'The Valley of Rest' (p. 64) speculates on why man cannot possess certainty, and 'Realization' (p. 74) offers part of an answer in that it points to the status of man as only one part of created beings: 'we did not inhabit this earth alone'.

The blanket of the sky, the ribs of the earth, the children of stone that emerge from the ribs, the brutality and indifference of iron, the light of the stars and moon, and natural phenomena such as rain, sunlight, wind, and storms form the recurring imagery of these metaphysical poems. The grandeur of the universe, the wonder of creation, and the central power of man as a restlessly investigative and concept-making being are vividly conveyed. Kofi Awoonor has expressed considerable sympathy with them[2] and writes well about their indebtedness to Zulu cosmology, though he rather oddly sees an influence of Milton's *Paradise Lost* on 'Anthem of Decades'. Awoonor's own poetry makes similar use of rhetorical strings of traditional images to approach and define a single concept, though with less intellectual precision than Kunene.

Kunene draws on Zulu oral traditions not only in these poems on epic subjects but also in his elegies, which, as he points out in the 'Introduction' to *Zulu Poems* (pp. 24-5), use the traditional device of understatement. Understatement of the grief felt by the poet is achieved by adopting an almost light-hearted sense of grievance against the dead person. The magnitude of death may be scaled down to seem equivalent to the embarrassing absence of the guest of honour from a feast, for which the poet reproves the dead one. 'Elegy for My Friend E. Galo' (p. 42) chides the friend for dying 'without my knowing' while the poet was out collecting firewood, buying expensive cattle, and preparing stories for the celebration. At the end, however, there is a bitterer tone, as the poet turns from the imagery of the feast to that of predatory locusts and 'the discordant symphony of naked stars': what had been made to seem casual absence from a celebratory occasion is now recognized as part of the universal mortality of man and nature. 'An Elegy to the Unknown Man Nicknamed Donda' (p. 75) is addressed not to the dead man but to the poet himself, as he muses on what he should do in his grief. He decides to take the elephant's advice to follow Donda into death, 'the place of the setting sun'. Death is again understated: here it seems to be just an everyday journey where one might meet an uncomprehending traveller. The ending this time recognizes not the universality of death, but its personal quality: one man's grief is another man's idle curiosity. In both these poems, the feeling is personal. In 'Elegy for Msizi' (p. 55), however, the voice is largely a communal one, representing the grief of the Bhele clan. Msizi's fame and achievements are matched by the magnitude of grief felt for him, and the poet ends with a prophecy of the clan's future greatness.

'Elegy for Msizi' has the poet rhetorically addressing the dead man, describing and commenting on the funeral rites, speaking personally, speaking on behalf of the clan, and speaking as a prophet. The multitude of voices provides some resemblance to another traditional form, the pithy, often satirical conversation poem, represented in Kunene's work by poems such as 'For a Friend Who Was Killed in the War' (p. 37), 'Two Wise Men' (p. 54), and 'A Great Generation' (p. 65). The conversation poem is a form widespread in Africa; it exists, for instance, among the Yoruba, Igbo, Ijaw, and Ewe in West Africa, and is represented in English in the work of Soyinka, Okigbo, J. P. Clark, and Kofi Awoonor. Often it is used for a somewhat riddling children's poem, but Kunene's use is more solemn. He retains the responsorial form of a cantor and chorus, but uses it for utterances about death, the Zulu nation and its future, and major ethical values. His conversation poems thus resemble less the normal Zulu form than the elevated responsorial passages in some of the praise-songs, such as that of Zwide, king of the Ndwandwe.[3]

Three other categories of Kunene's poems, though not closely related to traditional Zulu forms, draw heavily on the same store of imagery. They are love poems, poems about creativity and the writing of poetry, and political poems. The love poems, 'Presence' (pp. 42–3), 'Restlessness and Experience' (p. 71), and 'Uneasy Love' (p. 87), all have the speaker separated from his beloved. In 'Presence' she appears fleetingly in a dream; in 'Restlessness and Experience' she has provided bitter experiences in the past but remains in the memory; and in 'Uneasy Love' their meeting is a remote symbolic one represented by washing in the same pool. These are romantic poems, creating the feeling of what it is like to be absorbed in hopeless love; there are no direct descriptions of the beloved, though the focus is at least as much on her as on the poet who experiences and expresses the emotion.

The poems about the creative act of composing poetry are also romantic in imagery, though it is more cosmic and less homely than in the love poems. 'The Power of Creativity' (p. 60), 'To the Watcher of the Gates' (pp. 60–1), 'The Sweet Voice' (p. 61), 'To the Reluctant Poetess: Alicia Medina' (p. 72), 'Conquest of Dawn' (p. 81), and 'Dedication to a Poet' (p. 88) present an elevated view of the poet's craft and function in imagery of the skies, the sun and moon, wind and waves, bird flight and song, caves and rivers, flowers and fruit, battle and wayfaring. Discouragement by others and doubts about oneself have to be struggled with and set aside; but in each poem the struggle is successful and the ending is confident. The sense of the poet's tradition, his communality not so much with his people in general as with his fellow-poets who have passed on the task of preserving and nurturing the poetic heritage, is strongly expressed in 'Dedication to a Poet', addressed to Magolwane, the great court-poet of Shaka.

The political poems range in mood through the thirst for vengeance of 'Thought on June 26' (p. 41),[4] the bitter invective of 'The Civilisation of Iron' (pp. 61–2) and 'Europe' (p. 76), the heroic hope for the future of 'The Spectacle of Youth' (p. 72), and the muted sense of the problems of political belief and action in 'Three Worlds' (p. 78) and 'The Political Prisoner' (p. 85). The more philosophical and elegiac poems offer a mood familiar elsewhere in Kunene's work.[5] The bold rhetoric of the more aggressive poems is unparalleled elsewhere in this volume; its closest analogues are with some of the more bellicose parts of his great epic, *Emperor Shaka the Great*, which is in part a political poem attesting to national greatness in the past and national liberation in the future.

To compose a national epic demands both historical skills and literary courage of a high order. Kunene's *Emperor Shaka the Great: A Zulu Epic* was a long time in gestation, not only in the sense that some of the materials used are over two centuries old but also in so far as Kunene's own composition spanned many years. In the 1966 interview with Alex la Guma already referred to he said that he was writing this work, in Zulu, partly because he considered Shaka 'a great political and military genius' and partly because he hoped, through a national epic, to 'express the general experience of mankind', emphasizing 'the oneness and the unity of man'. This second reason is, in fact, a belief that he attributes to Shaka himself many times in the epic, for he presents Shaka as wishing neighbouring peoples to live in peace (though under a strong unified leadership) and as respecting the customs (though not the acquisitiveness and ill manners) of white traders. A third reason lying behind Kunene's demanding and ambitious work is the respect he has for Shaka's court poet, Magolwane, 'one of the greatest of African poets, indeed I would say one of the greatest world poets'.[6] To Magolwane he ascribes a revolution in Zulu poetry, including the introduction of political and social analysis, penetration of character, philosophical ideas, and abundant imagery (notably of ferocious animals). A great deal of Magolwane's 'epic' or 'poem of excellence' about Shaka (other writers call it a 'praise-poem' or 'praise-song') is in fact incorporated in Kunene's work.

Emperor Shaka the Great concerns the rise of the Zulu empire under Shaka. Its historical scope begins with the period of Jama, Shaka's grandfather, whom he was supposed to resemble, but after a few hundred lines has arrived at Shaka's birth (in 1795 or, according to some historians, 1787). In Book Two, Shaka, growing up in exile, becomes a young man. By Book Four he is engaged in military and political training in the court of King Dingiswayo of the Mthethwas. At the beginning of Book Five he succeeds his father, Senzangakhona, as king of the Zulus (1816) and in the following book is welcomed by the Mthethwas as Dingiswayo's successor (1818). The remainder of the work details the extension of the Zulu empire, the death of Shaka's close friends and relatives, the seeds of dissent and jealousy, and his murder by his half-brothers, Dingane and Mhlangane, and his court councillor, Mbopha, in 1828. The last book, the seventeenth, is followed by a 'Dirge of the Palm Race', a lament for Shaka and the other heroes who have died, an exultation in Shaka's glory, and a declaration that the earth will be made 'free for the Palm Race' (p. 433).

This ambitious poem, written like most of Kunene's poetry, in Zulu (a version still unpublished) and then, with the excision of some scholarly historical material, translated into English, partakes of many of the commonest qualities of the oral epic, whether found in Greece, Scandinavia, Yugoslavia, Mali, or India. It is an exaltation of the history (whether actual or mythical) of a nation, interpreting and commenting on the events; it has, in part, a hieratic, elevated language, suitable for formal enunciation to a national gathering; there are repeated formulaic passages and a variety of praise-names given to the major characters; it presents a courtly society, in which the rôle of poet is honoured and in which the king himself sometimes composes poetry; the hero is of almost superhuman strength, ability, and insight, and plays the major part in consolidating and protecting his people; there is a sense of continuity between the human characters and an unseen world (in this case the Ancestors) which may commune with human characters in dreams or visions; it has single-combat fighting in the midst of large-scale warfare that is crucial to the welfare or survival of the nation; it has roll-calls of heroes, warriors, and nations; before and, more importantly, after successful battles there are celebrations involving dancing, the recital of praise-poems, feasting, and athletic games; there are inset poems from an older oral tradition (including, in this case, the praise-songs, or poems of excellence as Kunene prefers to call them, of the Shakan court poet, Magolwane); and there is a sense of irresistible fate dictating the undeserved downfall of the hero and casting its shadow before events.

Kunene's interpretation of Shaka draws on pre-Shakan literary methods, the revolutionary technique of Magolwane, and later scholarly and literary developments. A pre-Shakan poet would have emphasized Shaka's blackness, tallness, strength, beauty, bravery, and craftiness, as in the praise-poem of Dingiswayo quoted in Book Six, where the king is twice called 'Black one'[7] or in the praise-song of Senzangakhona (a part not quoted by Kunene) where the king is said to be

He whose body was beautiful even in the great famine:
Whose face had no fault,
Whose eyes had no flaw,
Whose mouth was perfect,
Whose hands were without defect;
A chest which had no blemish
Whose feet were faultless,
And whose limbs were perfect ...[8]

Kunene almost takes this pre-Shakan tradition for granted. He off-handedly says that Shaka 'grew tall in size and reputation' (p. 30) or that he was 'tall and proud and defiant' (p. 66). His descriptions of Shaka's appearance dwell on his sinuous strength and mobility as a dancer or on his adornments rather than on his body. 'He swayed his body as if he would beat the ground' (p. 66), 'His whole body was uplifted by his movements' (p. 66), or, near the end of his life, 'His whole physique trembled with movement' (p. 384); even in talking to his men his voice radiates the strength of his personality: 'Then his whole body would light up' (p. 360). On occasions of celebration or grief he puts on ceremonial dress:

Shaka caused many eyes to stare as he emerged,
Adorned for the festival in colours of triumph.
On his shoulders were epaulettes of the soft otter skin
And on his shoulders was the long feather of the loury bird
He carried a large white shield centred with a black spot.
The poet, inspired by this spectacle, declaimed:
'The glorious feather that bends over beyond the Nkandla forest,
Arching to devour the crowds of men!'
The majesty that was Shaka was embellished with white tails;
His arms were covered with ivory amulets.
As he stood facing the noonday sun his body glistened,
Radiating the secrets of mind and contentment. (p. 174)

For Kunene the body is a reflection of the mind, and is far less inter-esting in itself than for what it represents. He is, in fact, critical of pre-Shakan poets for their traditional descriptions of physical charac-teristics.[9] Though he occasionally calls Shaka or other kings 'Black One', on about half the occasions this is because he is quoting traditional poems. He has nothing of the extravagant pre-Shakan glorification of the body, which is represented even in Thomas Mofolo's *Chaka: An Historical Romance* in the passage:

in this quarter of the city Chaka used to walk naked with only a loincloth on at the request of his sisters, so that they might feast their eyes with gazing at his body, for Chaka was a man of extra-ordinary beauty. He was taller than any in his tribe, and to add to this he had breadth as well. He was not thin. From his head to his feet he was without blemish, a giant among men.

Even in war the last request of many of his men wounded to death was that they might gaze upon their chief naked for the last time and die in peace, and he used to comply with their request.[10]

Following the practice of Magolwane, Kunene tries to give motivation and character to Shaka and the other chief figures. Yet his extraordinary respect for Shaka prevents him making as convincing a character study as Thomas Mofolo. Mofolo wrote a novel that sees substantial weaknesses of character in Shaka: he is superstitious, impetuous, ruthless, jealous, and brutally cruel. His novel unfolds like a Shakespearian tragedy or history play on Bradley's interpretation, with faults of character (often the defects of virtues) interacting with inauspicious circumstance to bring about destruction. Kunene writes an heroic poem, in which what tragedy there is, for there is more celebration than tragedy, flows from the nature of fate and humankind, not from the hero's personal defects. Shaka is impetuous, irascible, changeable, and superstitious, but much more is made of his intelligence, careful planning and organization, military genius, inspiring leadership, generosity, capacity for friendship and comradeship, hatred of privilege, and concern for justice. Where Mofolo has Shaka murder his mother, Nandi, Kunene has him humour her wishes in her old age, provide her with every possible medicine, even that of the white man, and institute widespread and bitter mourning when she eventually dies. His own tragic downfall comes not as in Mofolo with a breakdown of his admirable qualities and his possession by jealous, vindictive, and cruel monomania, but by the emergence of 'internal enemies', inevitable as kingdoms grow, and emerging inevitably in this instance, in Book Eight, as Shaka is about to achieve the pinnacle of his exploits with the second battle against Zwide. In Shaka's case, they are the internal enemies he has always feared: his kin. The reason he had never acknowledged any children as legitimate, or allowed them to live, was that 'Generations divide' (p. 104), that sons are inevitably dangerous rivals to a powerful father, as Dingiswayo had been to his father. What he overlooks in his fraternal generosity is the danger posed by his brothers and aunt.

Mofolo commented that:

> I do not think that anyone's life was ever so involved in mystery as was Chaka's. Dingiswayo's life is obscure and hidden, but when the facts are known they can be easily understood. But with Chaka all is mysterious and incredible right up to this point in the story [1818]. (*Chaka*, ch. 15, p. 116)

Mofolo nevertheless felt an obligation to interpret Shaka as best he could. V. W. Vilakazi, the twentieth-century Zulu poet from whose work Kunene derived a good deal, was on the other hand content to leave an ultimate mystery at the heart of Shaka's character. At the end

of 'UShaka KaSenzangakhona' (Shaka, Son of Senzangakhona) he
wrote:

> Your name, reviled throughout the earth,
> Will live while men can speak and write
> And strive to solve your mystery!—
> Yet who, mighty Shaka, shall fathom your heart?[11]

Kunene, though having undertaken a scholarly investigation of the
historical sources, also preferred to leave a large element of mystery in
the central character. His historical investigations led him to the belief
that Shaka, rather than being illegitimate as he had said in his M.A.
dissertation ('an illegitimate son of the playboy chief Senzangakhona',
p. 103), was in fact born in wedlock (*Emperor Shaka the Great*, p. xvi)
as, indeed, Mofolo had believed. But his character he was content to
leave an insoluble mystery. His protector and mentor Dingiswayo says
'This boy is a riddle' (p. 63); the diviner Mqalane calls him 'you who
are a mystery, You the diviner above all diviners, the oracle above all
oracles' (p. 304). As his kin and associates die, his natural brooding
becomes intensified: 'Death itself seemed to fascinate him' (p. 259).
When the white traders discuss the relationship between kingship and
healing medicine, Kunene says

> The Strangers thought Shaka would say something in their support
> But he never commented, letting them talk uninterruptedly.
> His eyes were focused on their foreheads
> As if he saw a shadow that made him uncertain.
> What was in Shaka's mind at that moment? People have often
>   asked. (pp. 272-3)

Kunene has given up part of the fabulist's task and resorted to inscrutability and mystification. The effect might have been to make Shaka
supra-human and incredible. In fact, however, the mystification projected to the reader by the author is accompanied by increasing introspection on Shaka's part. It is not revealing introspection: its results
are not, of course, revealed to the reader, but they seem not to be
revealed to Shaka either, and he therefore becomes an object of greater
interest. He had often given long thought to a tactical problem (most
notably the problem of how to scale the Fortress of the Phephethas,
which took 'five days' (p. 197) to solve), but now he seemed often to
retreat into himself: 'His mind [was] absorbed in thoughts of things to
come' (p. 296); those who watch him 'claimed he saw the shadows of
the dead With whom he shared the thrill of such events' (p. 330);
'People heard him speak alone as if to commune with the Spirits'
(p. 378); he himself feels that 'I am obsessed with the voices of the
dead' (p. 380); he has a 'visitation' from his dead mother Nandi (p. 338);
he begins to fear that 'It seems whatever I treasure withers suddenly'
(p. 374); 'the terrors that obsessed the king' (p. 381) seem largely generated by the trauma of his mother's death and there is even a spiteful

rumour that he killed her (p. 393); the premonitory 'truthful dreams' (p. 402) to which he has always been subject seem to weigh heavily upon him; and, lastly, 'He sat in a far-distant spot, silent like a figure carved in stone' (p. 408), so awesome that the assassin sent by Mbopha retreats, saying ' "He is fearful!" ' (p. 410).

The inner life of Shaka remains a mystery to Kunene, though an increasingly interesting one. His interpretation of Shaka's external actions is however clearly delineated. Shaka was a military innovator, commissioning the short stabbing spear and instructing his men in hand-to-hand combat, discarding the customary sandals worn in battle as cumbersome, emphasizing the importance of speed of attack and pursuit, instituting boy-carriers to see to the supply of food and camping necessities, thinking out tactics either by himself or in dialogue with a trusted confidant, imagining the effect of tactics in his mind's eye, and conveying the results he wanted by metaphors such as 'A great fighter imitates the movements of the wind./A war is a dance' (p. 57) or a battle must be 'Like the approach of each giant wave to the seashore,/Like a succession of angry waves' (p. 366). He was also a social and political innovator, incorporating defeated states into the Zulu empire with equal privileges for all citizens and uniform laws, denying patronage to the royal family but bestowing it where merit dictated, abolishing initiation and circumcision as detracting from the preparedness of young men for war, and for the same reason forbidding warriors the distraction of marriage and children. A little more tendentiously, Kunene emphasizes Shaka's democratic spirit in his speeches dwelling on the credit and spoils being due to the whole army:

> ... It is not I who won against Phungashe
> But the concentrated power of all our heroes;
> And so it shall be in all our wars.
> I am rich with gifts from the king [Dingiswayo], yet these are not mine.
> We shall feast on them and pay tribute to our Forefathers.
> We shall honour the great past heroes of our nation.
> We shall compose poems of excellence to all our fighters.
> (pp. 59–60)

or

> Brave men of Zululand, my heart is filled with joy.
> I know now I do not rule this land alone
> But with all those whose visions have enriched our land (p. 217)

Again with half an eye on the present, he has Shaka condemn slavery, particularly as practised by the Boers (pp. 226–7), and oppression, particularly when it can lead to exile on 'the Island of Stones, Known otherwise as the Island of Robin' (p. 209). Shaka treats the white traders, representatives of 'the Pumpkin Race' (p. 206), with skin the colour of pumpkin porridge, as emissaries of King George, whom he imagines as an equal monarch with similar ideas on national unification. He is puzzled by their violence and acquisitiveness, their love of possessions and land; he is impressed by the power of the gun and cannon but considers the gun too slow in reloading and cannon too cumbersome in transport for them to displace the spear; and he tries to convert the whites 'to the Zulu religion of generous and selfless giving' (p. 214). He is, in other words, much more intellectual than previous writers had made him; a fuller character, certainly, but not entirely convincing. He is also far less bloodthirsty than in previous accounts, including Mofolo's. Kunene's account represents a considerable softening of manners from those in which he is represented as personally killing his favourite concubine and slitting open her womb to see how a baby lies in it, automatically killing all of his children and their mothers, and murdering Nandi, his own mother. This egomaniac rage, brutality, and madness is absent from *Emperor Shaka the Great*. When, for instance, it is discovered that Nandi has hidden the child of Shaka's favourite, Mbuzikazi, and is rearing him as a prospective heir, Kunene has the child killed, almost without any assent from Shaka, by Mbopha, the powerful and evil courtier. Nandi, grief-stricken, turns her frustration and bitterness upon him not upon Shaka, saying to her son:

> I fear Mbopha; I fear him as I fear a snake.
> Often I feel he shall bring great tears to our house.
> Even now our talks no longer have meaning
> Since, by his orders, he has killed the very child I loved. (p. 180)

In some ways it is the two principal women, Mkhabayi, the inscrutable, majestic aunt of Shaka, and Nandi, his quarrelsome, bitter, jealous, suspicious mother, who are the most credibly developed characters. It may be that the women characters in most Zulu literature are presented with greater individuality than the men, for they have the opportunity to play a greater range of rôles, not only the military ones of the men (like the warrior Queen Mantantisi of the baTlokwa, referred to on pp. 254-5) but influential and powerful political ones like that of Mkhabayi, whose private rhetoric is very persuasive and whose real feelings and motives are never revealed to Dingane and not always to the immensely more perceptive Shaka. They are plotters, using their sexual attractiveness, as well as their powers of inventiveness and language, to control or conquer men. After Shaka's brothers' plans for assassinating him have failed, Mkhabayi is wily and persuasive enough to subvert one of his concubines into making preparations to kill him. She 'waited and hid her sharpened weapon' (p. 414), but even while engaging in love-play Shaka becomes suspicious, and after sexual intercourse seeks out the weapon with his eyes. Perhaps he remembered that Dingiswayo had owed his death in large measure to the treachery of a woman. At any rate, he is ruthless in dealing with such dereliction. The punishment is banishment rather than death, for Kunene's Shaka is, as I have pointed out, much less bloodthirsty than other writers had made him.

Earlier in the epic, towards the end of Book Eight, both Nandi and Mkhabayi give advice to Shaka. Nandi's is querulous, complaining of his treatment of her, warning him of Mbopha, and longing for an end to war and a continuation of the family. Mkhabayi's is nationalistic and warlike, rousing a warm fellow-feeling in Shaka as she puts a plausible gloss over the machinations that she knows him to be surrounded by. The contrast between the two women is dramatic: Nandi has foresight and right on her side, but Mkhabayi has the greater sense of presence and presentation and is able to subvert Shaka's mind. Though there is no question of where his affections lie, he tends to be neglectful of Nandi and her good advice. He is not susceptible to sexual blandishment, but he can be manipulated by the scheming of his aunt, whose good faith he seems never to question. Nandi represents the sentimental and affectionate side of Shaka, which Kunene emphasizes, though without ever losing sight of his essential bellicosity.

The traditional poems of excellence or heroic poems incorporated in the epic represent Kunene's abridgment and rearrangement of these works. As he points out in his Introduction they serve the purpose not only of attributing praise to heroes and other worthies, but also incapsulating the social and ethical wisdom of the people. Thus heroes are praised for their approximation to the noblest tenets of the nation or criticized and satirized for falling short of the best or for exemplifying false values. Kunene places the traditional poems at strategic points of the narrative, typically before and after battles or at times of celebration, mourning, or diplomacy. Their public or social character is thus emphasized and their placement enhances the grandeur of the events. They are also used as rewards or honours for valour in battle, for this is one of the occasions when the king himself acts as poet. In Book Five, for instance, we learn of 'Poems of excellence given to Shaka by Dingiswayo' (p. 113), though in this instance the narrative continues with the court-poet pronouncing a large part of his own poem of excellence to Dingiswayo. It may be that Kunene is suggesting that this whole poem was later transferred to Shaka, in the same way as he inherited part of his father's and grandfather's praises. A clearer example is in Shaka's actions after victory against the Bhaca in Book Fifteen, when he moves among the troops, occasionally 'conferring a title of honour on a hero' (p. 360). Sometimes they are recited not by a poet but by the hero himself, as Zulu does in Book Ten (p. 224). Kunene selects these passages with scholarship and with deep appreciation of their dramatic effectiveness. They are normally inserted so unobtrusively that they seem entirely of a piece with Kunene's own composition. It is rare to find such an awkward self-consciousness about their place in the epic as in Book Nine, where Kunene says:

> Listen to the words of the great poet who was there,
> Who saw with his own eyes the celebration of the new era (p. 185)

Poems of excellence are thus not the private property of the poet. They become part of the naming and identity of a person not only in his or her own eyes but also in the eyes of the whole people. As such they will be recited by court-poets or praise-singers, or by the person they identify without concern for the originating creative poet. Any poet, indeed any person, will be expected to know the existing poems of excellence for the important members of his clan; a competent poet will select from and rearrange this traditional material to bear on a particular occasion, and an inventive poet, such as Magolwane, may not only transform the interpretation and form of the traditional material but also add a great amount of original material to it.

Almost all the poems of excellence quoted in *Emperor Shaka the Great* can be found in their Zulu originals in such standard works as *Izibongo: Zulu Praise Poems.* Kunene's own translations into English are, however, of far superior quality to those of Malcolm as edited by Cope. Where, for instance, in Magolwane's heroic poem of Shaka, *Izibongo* has

> Pursuer of a person and he pursues him unceasingly;
> I liked him when he pursued Zwide son of Langa,
> Taking him from where the sun rises
> And sending him to where it sets;
> As for Zwide, he folded his two little shoulders together,
> It was then the elder was startled by the younger.
> Fierce animal in the homes of people;
> Wild animal that was in charge at Dibandlela's. (p. 94)

Kunene translates the Zulu as

> 'The chaser of men who chases without stopping—
> How I loved him as he pursued Zwide, the son of Langa,
> Following him from the regions of the rising sun
> And making him seek sanctuary in the land of the setting sun.
> Zwide was the man whose little shoulders he broke in two,
> Like an old man surprised by a youth!
> Fierce one, whom they announce in terror
> As they flee from their homes.' (p. 172)

The *Izibongo* version seeks to keep close to the Zulu parts of speech and word order and to represent the very common characteristic of Zulu poetry of repeating the stem of a word but as a different part of speech. Kunene, while preserving these qualities as far as possible, is prepared to sacrifice them at times in the interests of making sense or achieving a more rolling oratorical rhythm. Where the *Izibongo* versions sometimes read like word-for-word cribs in which the meaning has to be elucidated by a footnote, Kunene's versions show the selective freedom and judgment exercised by someone thoroughly familiar with both languages, having a scholarly and imaginative insight into meaning and a poet's way with words.

The ritualistic placement of these excerpts is paralleled by the occasional use of original set passages, common in most long epic poems throughout the world, at such times as battle or the natural occurrences of the day, like morning or evening. When Shaka, newly appointed to the kingship of the Zulu, is about to wreak vengeance on those of his mother's Langa people who had humiliated him as a youth, Kunene writes:

> The great night swallowed the shadows of the regiments;
> Only the rhythms of their footfalls echoed in the river.
> Sometimes they walked on the anthills, leaving their imprints and
>   broken ants,
> They climbed the little hill, approaching abasemaLangeni,
> And there began to split, forming their strategic movements.
>
> Shaka sat waiting until he heard the last cock crowing.
> He raised his head and saw the large villages of the
> abasemaLangeni clan.
> The sun spread its light from the night into the earth.
> A crimson ribbon hung all around the horizon.
>
> The eagle, disturbed from its night of peace,
> Hovered high over the neighbouring mountains
> As though to spy out those who should fill the earth.
> The old dog flopped its ears near the cattle-fold,
> Casting its eyes and peering at the rising shadows.
> The Zulu army rose with the morning star.
> It was as though they awaited the butterflies of dawn,
> To see them fly in all directions and colours.
> The glimmering spears caught the light of the sun!
> Young men leaped like flashes of lightning from fence to fence.
> The sons of Sokhulu skirted their way to the dark side of the
>   village.
> There they combined with the forces of Gebhuza-of-the-side-
>   boards. (pp. 89–90)

Several elements from the equipment of the traditional Zulu poet are incorporated here: the anthills, the eagle, the butterflies, and the glinting spears, for instance. But Kunene has woven them seamlessly into a new fabric that emphasizes cosmic grandeur, repose, and tense activity about to be unleashed. The elevation of the narrative achieved by romantic suggestiveness is of the same order as that achieved at similar moments by the incorporation of traditional poems of excellence. It is a device used rarely and unrepetitively. When, for instance, in Book Thirteen Kunene unfolds another dawn scene (pp. 314–15), the immediate purpose and the effects used are entirely different: on this occasion he wants to contrast the idyllic early morning scene of Shaka bathing in a rocky pool with the destructiveness about to be unleashed among the Zulus by white infiltration and weaponry.

Emperor Shaka the Great has the unblinking, monumental quality of inevitability possessed by many great world epics. Its story cannot surprise us, for it is a known one, reassembled and interpreted many times before Kunene. Even if the events were unknown to the reader, Kunene takes care to remove any element of surprise through the announcement of future events, the clarification of Shaka's motivating policies, and the use of premonitory dreams and visions. Much of the action is foretold, though in an oracular fashion, at the beginning of the epic, when a diviner comes to the court of Jama, Shaka's grandfather, and pronounces a long prophecy (pp. 2-4). Shaka himself or old men in his retinue are visited by prophetic dreams that foretell his future greatness (p. 30), warn him of danger (pp. 37, 243-4, 247, 402), warn him of his mother's death (pp. 241, 273-4, 328), advise him of his future among the Ancestors (pp. 297-8, 380-1, 422), or give advice for necessary action (p. 338). There is thus an inevitability, an inescapable fatefulness, almost an impersonality or inscrutability about the whole work that makes causation and motivation virtually superfluous. If, however, the action cannot startle us, the author's presentation of it can delight us. This is, I believe, a great epic or at least one verging on greatness. Its language and tone are stately yet unaffected, decorous yet unassuming, imaginative yet unassertive. This is the language of the tribe, composed for the tribe by creativity of a high order. Its translation into English enables a wide readership both to appreciate the history and the culture of the Zulus and to speculate on the universally applicable human virtues.

The second of Kunene's epics to be published addresses itself to an even greater subject. It is a cosmological epic concerning itself with the reasons for the creation of mankind; his place in the universe; the nature of creation and creativity; the apparent contradictions of life, death, and eternity; and human social organization. It is a philosophical or theological epic, not a military one, being made up to a large extent by councils of the gods debating the nature and future of mankind. The Zulu myth of the origin of death as a change of mind by the Creator God, who sent the speedy salamander as his messenger of death to overtake the earlier messenger of eternal life, the dilatory chameleon, is expanded into a symbolic contrariety between the cosmic and the pragmatic sides of man. This symbolic tension, which is ultimately brought into balance, lasts from Book Five to the last book, Fifteen.

Kunene conducts *Anthem of the Decades* with a severely attenuated cast of characters. Though heaven, the earth, and the abode of the Ancestors, the three main scenes of the action, are heavily populated, very few personages come to the foreground. In heaven, the discussion is left to Sodume, who is the Intelligence of Heaven, the voice of male thunder, and the chief advocate of man's creation and preservation; his wife Nodume, the voice of female thunder; Somazwi, a god of some deviousness, sarcasm, and vindictiveness, who opposes the creation of man as misguided and self-indulgent and for a time seeks to destroy him; his wife, Nokufa, the Hunchbacked One, who becomes a spirit of implacably destructive urges as a result of her husband's sin; and Nomkhubulwane, the Princess of Heaven, the chief agent of fructification on the earth, or, as Kunene more abstractly describes her, 'the goddess of change and ultimate balance'. None of these gods possess full knowledge of the truth or complete understanding of goodness. They do indeed argue for a great deal of the epic about what policies are true and good:

> For even the gods do not know all the truths
> Nor do they possess the power to know absolutely what is
> good.
> Thus their efforts are not without blunders. (p. 75)

Nomkhubulwane, troubled by the disputes among the gods, seeks 'a symbol that shall reveal the truth' from her father, the Creator, Mvelinqangi. He, however, refuses the request, saying:

> Such knowledge would negate life itself.
> Creation must grow from ever newly fathomed truths.
> If you possess such omniscience your thinking would cease.
> Indeed, should someone discover you possessed such
> powers
> Then they themselves would stop creating and thinking.
> For whoever finds ready-made solutions loses
> It is better for all ceaselessly to search for the truth.
> In this way life goes on forever and ever. (p. 47)

Mvelinqangi himself thus makes few appearances among the councils of the gods. He is a kind of rarely used final arbiter, who expects that the powers of creation he has given to the gods will be used in accordance with their collective wisdom. Kunene tells us that:

> Mvelinqangi did not utter many words
> Since all truth and beauty and balance is in him. (p. 109)

One other god, Mthobi, has a major rôle. He is the great poet of heaven who devises the shapes of the human body and through his frequent recitals acts as a chorus or commentary on the action.

Between the gods and the land of the Ancestors is the Second World, containing the young man of the sun, that is, the powerful but somewhat timid force of the sun, and the Sun-Mother, who is full of plenitude and kindness but is blind. In Book Nine, Nsondo, the first Ancestor, comes to her and having, despite the machinations of Somazwi, fulfilled the Sun-Mother's desire for a herd of white heifers, enters into an alliance with the sun, who promises fruitfulness to the earth and an assurance of man's ever-renewing quality.

Nsondo is one of the few men to be named. The other major speaker on the earth is Mbili, a prophet, whose advice is frequently sought. The other earthly creatures with a major rôle are the chameleon and the salamander. In his Introduction (pp. xxvii–xxviii) Kunene includes among the concepts that they signify a distinction that in the Introduction to his later volume of shorter poems, *The Ancestors*, he calls the social or philosophic intellect (the chameleon) and the 'precision' intellect (the salamander). This is, however, not a strongly marked aspect of his presentation of the two creatures, though it is clear that they represent two fairly extreme kinds of human thinking and behaviour, in the same way as the 'dogs of heaven', the children of Somazwi, represent human fears and viciousness. There is also a creature who balances the qualities of chameleon and salamander, as man himself ultimately comes to do. This is the sacred snake, the Nyandezulu, who prefers the company of man to that of his own kind and is thus regarded as an agent of divination and prophecy. He encounters the chameleon searching for mankind, and at first considers that 'This creature is seized by madness' (p. 151), but later urges him to fulfil his mission at once.

For a poem of some 12,000 lines (longer, for instance, than *Paradise Lost*), this is quite a small *dramatis personae*. As with *Emperor Shaka the Great*, two women stand out as perhaps the strongest characters. One is the ugly hunchback, Nokufa, who appears in the councils with her face covered. She is visited with the punishment meted out by the gods to her husband, Somazwi. He had sinned by releasing, against the collective intention of the gods, the charm of life among mankind in a terrifying form. Somazwi, the most rational and logical of the gods, one who is not swayed by emotional attachment or grand dreams but has a strong sense of consistent policy and justice, is punished by having his wife willed by the gods to unleash a 'century of destruction' (p. 43), a blind, undeserved vindictiveness against man. He is driven to grief and fear for man and, as a fond husband, is hurt by his wife's mindless, unforgiving fury. It is the force of emotion behind that fury, however, that makes Nokufa, unsuccessful though she ultimately is, a memorable character. She delays the chameleon and speeds on the salamander, she argues vehemently for man's destruction in the councils of the gods, she berates her husband for his pusillanimity and ineffectiveness, and she would have been successful in defeating the young man of the sun but for the intervention of the Ancestors. She is loved by no one in her indomitable rage; even her children desert her when she fails (p. 307); and she has been an outsider and an object of fear or scorn rather than understanding from the beginning. It is perhaps not perverse to have admiration for her as much as for the superficially more attractive Sodume and Somazwi, who inevitably engage attention and admiration in their persuasive speeches to the gods and who are in the end reconciled to each other in public. It is a Zulu characteristic to express admiration for the qualities of an adversary (Somazwi does so in regard to both man and Sodume, for instance), and perhaps the reader may legitimately do so for Nokufa.

The second powerful woman character is Nomkhubulwane, daughter of the Creator. At first she seems almost as remote as her father, and 'it is known that Nomkhubulwane is rarely seen' (p. 23). Later, however, she loses this remoteness and regal aura of unapproachability and becomes more like the other powerful gods, though her interventions in their debates are always treated with great respect. She combines justice in advocating the punishment of Sodume and Nodume, her closest friends, with pity in turning away and weeping as she does so. She prevails in her faith in mankind even when Sodume, mankind's most vehement advocate, has doubts. She believes that the gods are 'weaker than man' (p. 53) because of man's intellect and his indomitable ability to continue with life despite ignorance of his destiny. In Book Thirteen she visits the Ancestors, first joining them in an exercise to uproot any preoccupation with the self-image (a fault she herself admits to) and later joining in feasting and dancing. Among the gods, she is often perplexed, but always honest; and her interventions in debates are wise and tolerant.

Anthem of the Decades is divided into three parts, each of five books. 'Age of the Gods', set mainly in heaven, covers the creation of man and a large part of the debate about whether he should be destroyed or given additional powers. Part II, 'Age of Fantasy', largely concerns the journeys of the chameleon and the salamander; it ends with war between the two races of mankind symbolized by these creatures and the vision of a future generation to unite all races and factions. Part III, 'Age of the Ancestors', concerns life among the Ancestors, the final debates in heaven about the future of man, the final attempt by Nokufa to destroy him, and a final hymn of praise to the Creator, creation, the gods, and the Ancestors. From Book Nine to Book Fourteen is perhaps the dullest part of the epic. Books Nine and Ten, though full of interesting material, are vitiated by a loss of narrative clarity. It is as if Kunene finds difficulty changing from the philosophical to the narrative mode, and so in the end the mythological exposition suffers. Books Eleven and Twelve have the Ancestors relating their life on earth to each other. Although the question of enslavement is raised in Book Eleven, these stories are not of great interest or significance: they read at times like reminiscent chat. In Books Thirteen and Fourteen the mythological significance is conveyed largely in terms of the chameleon and, as I shall argue later, both chameleon and salamander change too much and too unpredictably to be effective symbols.

In some ways, Kunene is most successful when he presents his ideas in the form of doctrine or adage rather than as symbol or myth. Certain ideas provide a philosophical substratum to the action and are illustrated by it. The most important cosmological idea is probably the continuing nature of creation, including the creation of thought. The gods' task is never finished; there are always new worlds (in the Third

World, as Kunene terms it, that is, outer space) to be created. For gods and man, thought is a form of creativity, the loss of which results in stultification, inertia, and drabness. In the process of creativity there will be disagreement and conflict, but the aim is to secure harmony and balance between contrary forces and between the equally important realms of physical being and the unseen or spiritual forces that affect it. 'We are ordered to make all things harmonious in life' (p. 49) are the 'sacred words' of Nomkhubulwane, and Sodume later acknowledges that:

> 'True wisdom is only of a woman,
> She alone holds the balance between the two opposites
> She nourishes the forces that bind day and night together.' (p. 66)

But other gods too seek balance. One of the 'followers of Somazwi' (probably Somazwi himself is meant) alleges that his policy strives to achieve 'a delicate balance between his [man's] earthly life and ours' (p. 70).

Balance implies a holding of entities in harmony, not an assimilation of them into a new synthetic entity. This is apparent in what the narrator says about the immanent and the transcendental scales of time:

> There are two cycles of time, each fitting into the other:
> One spins from the inner centre with people and the earth,
> Creating day and night, summer and winter, life and death.
> Another follows a wide orbit, forming an eternity.
> If the two cycles should meet,
> The great death would overtake all things.
> That is why the chameleon must move at its own pace,
> Following its cycles undeterred by success or failure.
> Only man suffers, only his life is drawn into the inner circle. (pp.
>   156–7)

In his Introduction, Kunene says that in the Zulu cosmos truth is relative, by which he means primarily that ethical and social standards can only be understood in the context of a community and that life is not arranged in a hierarchy of being with each sphere superior to all those below it. On the contrary, each sphere of life has its own peculiar excellences and standards. One exemplification of this is that man is the supreme being on the earth; the gods know little about the life of humanity—they do not 'possess the wisdom of the earth' (p. 263)—and though they seek to manipulate it they have to work through intermediaries. Another exemplification is that no god (except the Creator) is always wise or good. The gods make errors in exercising their creative powers and they act towards man for a variety of motives, some high-minded, some selfish. There is at times truth in Somazwi's argument that 'The creation of man is for the aggrandizement of the gods' (p. 29).

Kunene does, however, consistently support a set of moral standards that seem to apply equally to gods, man, and the Ancestors. These standards have as one central principle the primacy of thought to all life. Thought, in its restless, exploratory nature, is seen as akin to creativity. It is praised in both gods and men. The Ancestors, who enjoy a greater measure of rest, are nevertheless not freed from the necessity and obligation to think: they too have their councils. But thought must not be impetuous; even Nomkhubulwane can be chided by the Creator for this failing:

'Foolishness rushes at all things
Claiming what is, and what is not of creation
But creation is the substance of all things,
To wait for things to unfold is wisdom.
You have erred in letting your heart follow the winds.
Learn then from this lesson:
Do not rush to make judgement on things beautiful,
Observe creation and behold its multiple truths.' (p. 46)

Thought must also be collective rather than vagrantly individualistic. Creativity such as Mthobi's is individual, but its products have to be approved by communal discussion. One of the aspects of Somazwi's sin is that he 'dared act outside the assembly' in a way that negated 'the work of collective achievement' and violated the collective 'intentions of the gods' (p. 39). Much later Nomkhubulwane, in explaining to the Ancestors the need to take action to protect the sun and thus save the race of man, says that:

your vows must be made in concert,
For whoever invokes his own soul alone fails.
Your promises must be made in the name of all humankind.
(p. 273)

The concomitant of this attitude is to condemn individual vanity, 'self-image', fears, whims, and fantasies. The gods are condemned for exercising individual 'whims' in creation (e.g., pp. 53, 98); the chameleon comes in Book Ten to symbolize man's fears, which are full of dangerous 'whims'; fantasies are said to 'open no new provinces' (p. 82); and when the chameleon indulges in self-pity and self-adulation the narrotor says:

Thus he brooded over his fate
Building fantasies of welcoming crowds (p. 117)

Such idle speculation about the future is uncreative; it elevates the individual above his society and leads to moral and psychological decay. The search for an individual identity is, then, often condemned as self-indulgent and harmful.

Selfishness is another frequently condemned evil. The hateful race of gorillas and baboons, the Thusi, were once men who violated the code of sharing and so were thrust out of the human community to sink into degradation (pp. 12–13). Generosity, on the contrary, is praised. It

is one of Somazwi's admirable traits, for instance, that he praises Sodume (e.g., p. 59) and man (p. 71), with both of whom he is intellectually
at odds; it is to Nsondo's credit that he provides a valuable gift to the
Sun-Mother.

Submission to collective decisions does not, however, imply lack of
individual initiative and responsibility. That would, indeed, be foreign
to the creative nature of thought. The Creator expects the gods to work
out their own problems; the gods and the Ancestors expect man to
exercise resourcefulness, courage, and self-help before he deserves any
help. Man is praised for combating the dogs of heaven and returning
with the fire of heaven; the gods are, indeed, in some awe of man's
limitless ambition, courage, and adventurousness. From such initiative
and activity, associated with the pursuit of truth, comes joy. As Sodume
says to the council of the gods:

> For if this creature was created without its power
> And spent its time mourning its existence,
> Then it would have failed, as would also its creator.
>
> .   .   .   .
>
> Woe to the man who grows up dependent on the gods. (p. 79)

The same beliefs are reiterated by the Sun-Mother, when she says at
the end of Book Eleven:

> ... There is a joy that fills the mind with contentment,
> But it must not wither the will.
> People must not die from happiness.
> They must fertilize their lives through their own effort. (p. 246)

It is not only characters in the epic who unburden themselves of such
general statements. By contrast with the self-effacing posture of the
narrator in *Emperor Shaka the Great*, the narrator here confidently
offers aphorisms and comments about the nature of human personality
and society. Many of them are about the nature of power and about
behaviour in public gatherings. He says, for instance,

> For in truth such is the curse of the powerful:
> Secretly they are haunted by fears of their own little crimes. (p. 27)

When the council is judging the case of Sodume and Somazwi, he says:

> Someone who was always eager to speak stood up
> But before speaking he made his usual flamboyant gestures
> Preferring ostentation to depth of thought. (p. 38)

From such discussions the author sometimes almost despairs of a sensible outcome:

> It was as if nothing good would ever come from the gods.
> No one seemed to pursue truth beyond their own boundaries.
>   (p. 80)

And he is sceptical about any great wisdom coming from unguided crowds:

> But crowds do not initiate a new era
> They often follow whoever promises escape from misery. (p. 185)

On the other hand, he attributes to wise leaders effective rhetorical attitudes in such comments as

> For it is not uncommon among the wise
> Constantly to assume the posture of uncertainty. (p. 273)

Similar remarks are scattered through the epic. The narrator adopts the rôle of ethical teacher, a person with at least as much insight at any time as the current speaker, and often a good deal more.

The conduct of the argument through myth, as distinct from its conduct through direct statement, is sometimes a little less secure. In Books Two to Five, for instance, the position of Somazwi is either that man should be destroyed and a new start made on a creature who would fulfil the ideals of the gods or else, his later position, that existing man should have his power raised to appropriate levels, he should be given a greater or higher mind (pp. 71–2). This does not happen, for the gods apparently accept Sodume's counter-argument that if man were perfected

> his power would wither.
> He would move puppet-like, awaiting only our commands.
> Such a being would be no more than a slave to the gods,
> Like a child, solely dependent on its mother's cupped hands.
> (p. 73)

Yet why this should be the result is never explained. The gods would perhaps then be able to communicate directly with mankind, but it seems unlikely that man would be impressed by their divisions, whims, fantasies, and imperfect grasp of truth into making himself their slave. On the contrary, he might come to think himself superior to them.

This slight flaw in the myth would be easily remediable. A somewhat more puzzling one, however, is the ambivalent and variable nature and interpretation of the salamander and chameleon races of mankind. Although Part II ends with a vision of the proud union of chameleon and salamander characteristics in mankind, Sodume subsequently changes his support from the salamanders to the chameleons (on the ground that they alone possess 'the true love of life' (p. 29) and that the salamanders have been perverted to destructiveness by Nokufa) and Nomkhubulwane secures the permission of the gods to multiply the chameleon people to 'fill the earth' (p. 290).

One of the problems is that Kunene has not always incorporated in the text the intentions notified in the prose synopses. In the synopsis to Book Nine, for instance, he announces that 'Man also discovers that the salamander has bred many human-like children, rather half-salamander, half-human. They claim descent from the gods' (p. 181). Yet this activity is not to be found described in the poetic text. The same thing happens when in the synopsis of Book Three he says that the 'huge estate' of Nomkhubulwane on which Sodume's messengers trespass 'should not have been the sole possession of the princess in the first place. She later acknowledges this and agrees to forgive the crime' (p. 16). The poetic text fails to cover this sequence of events.

These are slight flaws that hardly affect the reader's enjoyment. They come to notice only because for the most part the epic is so clearly and unaffectedly expressed. Milton's elevated and convoluted style is very far from Kunene's limpidity. His subject invites comparison with that of *Paradise Lost*, but it is only occasionally in the debates in heaven or in the approach of Somazwi's cohorts to the council that any comparison in detail can be sustained. Kunene's lightly rainbowed and cobwebbed universe is far from Milton's physically over-stuffed one, and more credible as a result. His sense of joy and celebration, expressed in frequent anthems, such as 'Life shall not cease with each generation of man' (p. 162) or the more elaborate anthems of the last Book, is the equal of Milton's and, some readers might think, theologically sounder or more plausible. Certainly he does not suffer Milton's disability of needing to characterize and praise a Creator who is a paragon of virtue and wisdom as well as a warrior-king. If the punishment of Sodume's messengers for stealing fruit in Book Three—they are condemned to centuries of hunger—seems somewhat Dantesque or if the heavenly poet Mthobi speaking through the mouth of the ram at the council of animals in Book Five ('we have seen all, felt all, suffered all', p. 87) seems reminiscent to T. S. Eliot, such references outside the world of Zulu belief and tradition are slight and rare. By writing in Zulu and then translating, Kunene has, as with *Emperor Shaka the Great*, produced an epic that is thoroughly uniform, self-contained, and self-validating. If it seems a somewhat lesser achievement than *Emperor Shaka the Great* that is partly because it is more philosophical (and it is notoriously difficult to make poetry out of reasoning), partly because Kunene has had to weave together more separate pieces of traditional material and invent for them a coherent framework. With the Shaka material more of it was already available.

Kunene's shorter poems of the 1970s, many of them collected in his *The Ancestors & the Sacred Mountain* (London: Heinemann Educational Books, 1982), concentrate on three main subjects. One large group is concerned with the liberation by bloodshed of South Africa, another looks forward millennially to the time after liberation (and sometimes looks beyond South Africa to the world and, indeed, the universe), and a third concerns the ecstatic nature of poetry. In these poems and in the smaller groupings (such as the poems about individuals, the laments, the poems on motherhood, and the personal poems) the sense of the Ancestors, observing and encouraging, is always present. In addition, some poems are directly about the Ancestors or

Forefathers. They represent for Kunene the whole company of those 'who have made their contribution to human welfare and progress', as he says in the Introduction to *The Ancestors*. It is to them and not to inventors of material improvements that the Zulus look for standards, guidance, and inspiration in continuing social life, and they treat them as a collective repository of wisdom rather than as a group of individual heroes.

In 'A Heritage of Liberation' the Ancestors are said to have given to the present oppressed generation 'in all these thin seasons . . . the visions of life'. They will also guard and preserve for use by 'generations hereafter' the weapons of liberation forged by those now about to depart from this life. The contemporary generation has been hovered over menacingly by 'the eagle' and 'the vultures'; it will need to pursue them, to 'follow the trail of the killer-bird', so that the 'dream of the festival' may be fulfilled in 'the rays of the morning'. The imagery here is taken up again many times in these determined poems of liberation. The government and its agents are referred to in symbols, often of predatory birds, and those symbols are then applied, though with a transformed freshness and glory, to the liberators who have had to learn from the techniques of the oppressors. So, in 'The Rise of the Angry Generation', it is the young generation, 'the children of iron' representing 'the abiding anger of the Ancestral Forefathers', who are spoken of as a 'great eagle' and a 'mysterious young bird' with 'merciless talons'. They will unleash retribution, symbolized by the 'volcanic mountains' of this poem, the devouring sword of 'Sword Eulogising Itself After a Massacre', the 'fearful light' of 'The Master and the Victim', or the 'chameleon's way' of 'Mercy'.

For the most part, Kunene is buoyantly confident of success against the oppressors. In 'The Master and the Victim' he announces that:

> The day of reckoning is within us
> The child has chosen to avenge his parent
> The wails explode ceaselessly into the distant horizon! (p. 22)

In 'To a South African Policeman' he says 'They have no future'. Even when he does not overtly declare such a belief, he expresses an inner cumulation of the sense of wrong that implicitly must triumph. In the lament, 'Congregation of the Story-tellers at a Funeral of Soweto Children', he says that 'Whatever we failed to say is stored secretly in our minds' and 'We have received the power to command'. Very occasionally, however, he almost gives way to despair. In 'Bitter Thought in Exile' he suggests that confidence of early success is tantamount to 'oceans of fantasy' (always a pejorative word in his vocabulary), that the dream has 'opened' to reveal 'a long winding path'. Symbols of success such as the sun and the eagle have vanished, and even his song is under threat. But the poem ends with resolution as he recalls those who have died for the cause.

The second large group of poems looks forward to the millennium beyond the act of liberation. In them the recurring images are of celebration, circles, life, light, dawn, ecstasy, peace, water, fruitfulness, flowers, and bird-song. 'First Day After the War' has the setting of a wedding and a first-fruits festival; both it and 'Brave People' have circles of fecundity; 'Changes' and 'Awakening' repeat many of the symbols common to this group; 'Return of Peace' ends with an anthem. 'Return of the Golden Age' adds laughter to the common stock of images, and in some other poems, such as 'Dream of Planets' and 'Encounter with the Ancestors', Kunene uses it as an indication of a good society. 'Dream of Planets' and 'World Wisdom' look beyond Africa to a common peaceful humanity either in the rest of the world or beyond in other worlds as well. 'Anthem of Peacefulness' emphasizes the communion between humanity and nature: the shepherd-boy sings the song of the wind, the poet greets the afternoon, and 'the quiet earth' embraces us. The post-war period will be characterized by love and forgiveness, for 'great loves enrich the earth' ('Nourishments of Love'), 'those who are wise are generous' ('Brave People'), and

> May we forgive those who have caused us pain;
> For today only.
> So that we may begin a new era
> Riding high on the shoulders of the hill. ('Today's Wish', pp. 28–9)

Again in nearly all these poems there is a sense of the Ancestors presiding over the succession of generations and rejoicing in the new era of freedom.

Rejoicing of an ecstatic kind is the mood of a large group of poems concerned with a poet's celebration of freedom. 'Son of the Beautiful Ones—the Dancer' presents the representative of contemporary society, faithful to the heritage of the Forefathers, the Beautiful Ones, uniting in sexual ecstasy with Nomkhubulwane, goddess of rain and harvest, the Princess of Heaven of *Anthem of the Decades*. In 'Ecstasy of a Song', 'To Nomazwi—A Reluctant Poetess', and 'The Unhappy Composer', the singer is also able to assume and even command the characteristics of nature. 'Journey to the Sacred Mountains' presents the singer as led by natural forces to the land of the Ancestors or Holy Ones, where he listens to 'the great epics ... of the ancient poets'. 'A Vision of Zosukuma' similarly has the present generation learning from 'the poem that is old'. But the most astonishing power of song is not that it can seize the poet and give him control of the forces of nature or bring him into communion with the Ancestors, but that it can enable him to give a second birth to Shaka. In 'The Second Birth of the Great Shaka of the Zulus' the poet undergoes fortifying rites (using the circle, water, fire, and herbs) and 'Then whirlwinds began to move'. He is however able to conquer them and ride them 'like a horse', so that Shaka in lightning and rainbow is reborn to symbolize the new battle:

I watch him walking on his path
To seize the fierce rays of the sun,
To fight until we break open the night (p. 62).

In most of these poems, and in others such as 'Uncontrollable Feeling of Ecstasy', the poet is drawn towards song, ecstasy, or magic initially by understanding the beauty and force of nature. In two poems, however, 'My Swazi Boy or Song of the Frog' and 'To a Navaho Boy Playing a Flute', he is first captivated by the physical beauty of a boy and through that recognition is released into ecstatic union with the forces of nature, song, and eternity. In a number of other poems too he eulogizes particular people, though in the other instances the people are named and do not submerge their personality in their symbolic significance. 'To Nomazwi—A Reluctant Poetess' has already been mentioned. 'Tribute to Mshongweni' honours the greatest of the nineteenth-century Zulu poets after Magolwane; 'Myeza and His Musical Instrument' a great player of the *makhweyana* or musical bow; 'To Tu Fu, Beethoven, Va Dong, Magolwane and All the Great Poets of Humankind' poet-musicians of Africa, Europe, and the Far East. Other poems are praises of political heroes ('Phakeni's Farewell'), kinsmen ('To My Elder Kinsman (Polycarp Dlamini)'), or friends ('A Salute to My Friend Zo'), or else are imprecations like 'Nozizwe'. With these personal poems can be grouped a number of poems with an autobiographical quality such as 'The Second Birth of the Great Shaka of the Zulus' with its muted reference to his own epic; '252 or at the End of a Volume', which also refers to his own composition of epics; ' "Advice" to a Young Poet', a sardonic account of the acceptance and power of the poet in society; 'The Return of Inspiration' on the overmastering influence on Kunene of Magolwane; and 'On Leaving Norway, From a Mission, Without a Penny', concerning his political activities on behalf of South African black nationhood.

If some of the poems about individuals partake to some extent of the nature of Zulu praise-songs or poems of excellence, some of the more sombre poems partake of the nature of laments. 'To a Friend Whose Family was Killed or Ngenimpi (A Late Recruit)' swallows up sorrow in rejoicing that Ngenimpi has become a political activist and is thus worthy of the Ancestors. 'Death of the Miners or The Widows of the Earth' poignantly contrasts the hollow pomp of an official ceremony with the numbing information, simultaneously available, of the death of the miners from the town. 'His Night of Sadness' is a very cold, ambiguous lament, whereas 'After the Death of Mdabuli, Son of Mhawu' draws on the rich store of natural, cyclical, and cosmic imagery to relate the hero to the history of the clan, the life of the Ancestors, and the continuity of the generations.

Poems directly about the Ancestors such as 'Encounter With the Ancestors', 'Playing With My Kinsman', 'My Forefathers', and 'In Praise of the Ancestors' are conducted in terms of the Zulu myth of

creation, symbols of continuity such as the circle, and images of nature
and eternity. The Ancestors both listen to earthly song and unite their
voices with it; they lead the poet to contemplate the certainty of victory,
the oneness of humankind, and the immensity of the cosmos. It is
because of their ability to extend the visions of humanity that 'the deep
eye of the universe is in our chest', as 'In Praise of the Ancestors' puts
it.

For Kunene, then, the social and cultural history of the Zulus as
incorporated in the cult of the Ancestors, can provide guidance, inspiration, and vision on every moral and political matter. Personal grief,
insecurity, and even rage are swallowed up in a communal experience
capable of producing the most intense ecstasy. The poet is possessed by
a sexual and religious frenzy that authenticates and gives certitude to
his message. Yet unlike the possession of, say, the Romantic poets, this
is possession of a spokesman who has a social duty to announce truth to
the clan. In this respect, it is like the traditional possession of the singer
of an epic who ascribes the glory of the tale of the tribe to divine
inspiration.

These poems of the 1970s are much more sharply focused than the
earlier ones on the contemporary political situation in South Africa.
But though they are more militant, they are not more strident, as Dennis
Brutus's or Lenrie Peters's political poems became. Kunene has the
confidence of the poet who speaks on behalf of the clan rather than as
an individual agonized voice. His work thus stands in sharp contrast to
the sense of romantic isolation and alienation expressed by most African
poets writing in English.

More importantly, however, he has written the two most ambitious
poems to come out of modern Africa. With modest confidence in the
face of much discouragement, he has created from his Zulu inheritance
two epics (and others that have not been translated or published yet)
that are both thoroughly African and at the same time of international
significance. His achievement may mark the end of the period when
African poetry in English turned to Britain and America for its style
and allusions. It may even mark the beginning of a reverse process, for
his work is more substantial and inspired than that of other poets
currently writing in English.

Notes to Chapter 10

1. See *African Writers Talking: A Collection of Interviews*, edited by Dennis
   Duerden and Cosmo Pieterse (London: Heinemann Educational Books,
   1966), pp. 88–9 (p. 89).
2. See his *The Breast of the Earth: A Survey of the History, Culture, and
   Literature of Africa South of the Sahara* (Garden City, New York: Anchor
   Press/Doubleday, 1975), pp. 193–201.
3. See *Izibongo: Zulu Praise-Poems*, collected by James Stuart, translated by
   Daniel Malcolm, edited by Trevor Cope (Oxford Library of African
   Literature; Oxford: Clarendon Press, 1968), pp. 128–9.

4. The date is observed as a national day by many blacks, coloureds, and Indians in South Africa. In 1950 it was first observed as a day of mourning organized by the African National Congress and the Indian National Congress to commemorate eighteen of their people killed during the May Day demonstration of that year. In 1955 it was the day on which a United Congress adopted a Freedom Charter directed against apartheid. Kunene's poem was originally published with a title that distanced the author from the feelings expressed: 'Poisoned Mind', *Afro-Asian Writings* 1, Nos. 2-3 (Summer 1968), 87.

5. The elegiac mood is also represented in later political poems, such as 'To Africa', 'Dreams in Exile', 'Algerian Night—To the Martyrs', and 'For the Woman Who Lost Her Only Child' (*South African Voices*, ed. Bernth Lindfors (Austin: Occasional Publications, African and Afro-American Studies and Research Center, The University of Texas at Austin, 1975), pp. 22-4 or 'Death of the Miners or The Widows of the Earth' (first published in *Bananas* No. 22 (August 1980), 24).

6. 'Portrait of Magolwane—the Great Zulu Poet', supplement to *Cultural Events in Africa* (London: The Transcription Centre) 32 (July 1967), pp. I-IV (p. I). Virtually the same article is also available as 'Portrait of Magolwane, the Greatest Zulu Poet', *Afro-Asian Writings* 1, No. 4 (January 1970), 13-17.

7. Page 113, lines 12-38. A poorer translation of the same passage can be found in *Izibongo: Zulu Praise-Poems*, p. 126, lines 51-77; the original Zulu is on the facing page, p. 127.

8. *Izibongo*, p. 76, lines 17-25. The editor points out that the Zulu uses the same term, 'without fault', in each line; the elegant variation is the translator's.

9. See Raymond Kunene [as he was then known], 'An Analytical Survey of Zulu Poetry Both Traditional and Modern', MA dissertation, Department of Bantu Studies, University of Natal, Durban, 1961; and Mazisi Kunene, 'South African Oral Traditions' in *Aspects of South African Literature*, ed. Christopher Heywood (London: Heinemann Educational Books, 1976; New York: Africana, 1976), pp. 24-41.

10. Translated from the Sotho by F. H. Dutton, London: Oxford University Press for the International Institute of African Language & Cultures, 1931, ch. 17 (p. 134).

11. Benedict Wallet Vilakazi, *Zulu Horizons*, rendered into English verse by Florence Louie Friedman from the literal translation of D. McK. Malcolm and J. Mandlenkosi Shakana (Johannesburg: Witwatersrand University Press, 1973), p. 42.

Index